EXECUTIVE THINKING

WHAT THE GREATEST LEADER POSSES

EXECUTIVE THINKING

From Brightness to Brilliance

EXECUTIVE THINKING SPEAKS TO
LEADERS/EXECUTIVES WHO WANT TO UTILIZE
GREATER THINKING CAPACITY TO FIGURE THINGS
OUT AND STEP UP TO MORE BRILLIANT CAREERS.

**MORRIS A. GRAHAM, PHD
AND KEVIN BAIZE, OD**

Gotham Books

30 N Gould St.
Ste. 20820, Sheridan, WY 82801
https://gothambooksinc.com/

Phone: 1 (307) 464-7800

© 2024 *Morris A. Graham, PhD*. All rights reserved.

No part of this book may be reproduced, stored in a retrieval system, or transmitted by any means without the written permission of the author.

Published by Gotham Books (September 6, 2024)

ISBN: 979-8-3304-0156-7 (H)
ISBN: 979-8-3304-0154-3 (P)
ISBN: 979-8-3304-0155-0 (E)

Because of the dynamic nature of the Internet, any web addresses or links contained in this book may have changed since publication and may no longer be valid.

The views expressed in this work are solely those of the author and do not necessarily reflect the views of the publisher, and the publisher hereby disclaims any responsibility for them.

Contents

Acknowledgments vi

Preface: *Realizing Bright to the Fourth Power* viii

Introduction: A Journey from Bright to Brilliant through Visual-Spatial Thinking 1

Chapter 1: *Increasing Our Capacity to Think* 5

Chapter 2: Visual-Spatial Capacity *Seeing Brilliantly* 36

Chapter 3: BRIGHT1—Verbal Height *Solving Problems with Words* 82

Chapter 4: BRIGHT2—Quantitative Width *Solving Problems with Numbers* 120

Chapter 5: *BRIGHT3—Spatial Depth Solving Problems with Inventions* 150

Chapter 6: BRIGHT4—Global Insight *Executing* Decisiveness, Direction, and Speed 202

Chapter 7: Character Capacity - Integrity and Authenticity (CC) . 241

References 254

Appendix 274

Postscript: Developing Bright to the Fourth Power: The High-Tech, Educational Pathway to Brilliance 276

About the Authors 303

Acknowledgments

We have many people to acknowledge and thank for their research, assistance, and support, and their time given so freely. In our early attempts to discover thinking *brilliance* among leaders, we found it especially awkward to make connections between research in the disciplines of executive development, cognition, and neuroscience. This relationship also perplexed our colleagues as they worked through their own authorial uncertainties and tested our assertions that breakthroughs in neuroscience could enhance thinking capacity through technologies such as visual-spatial processing.

Our own learning journey was especially enhanced through interactions with some dear colleagues, executives, football quarterbacks, and professors, and a host of talented neuroscientists and organizational folks along the way. Notable in this regard are: John Raven of Raven & Associates (John's father developed Raven's Advanced Progressive Matrices—Scotland, UK); Professor R.W. Revans (UK author of *Action Learning*), Colonel Leslie Dow— Former Executive Director of the Edinburgh Military Tattoo; Chris Argyris of Harvard University; Stephen R. Covey of Franklin-Covey; Glenn Muranaka (G.M.) of Meadow Gold Dairies-Hawaii; Linda Silverman of the Gifted Development Center in Denver (author of *Upside Down Brilliance)*; Steven C. Wheelwright—a former Dean of Harvard Business School and presently President of Brigham Young University-Hawaii; Jack Hoag—former President of First Hawaiian Bank; the late Professor Ruth Kingsley (University of Arizona); Mayor Mufi Hannemann of Honolulu; Lee Kuan-Yew, former Prime Minister of the Republic of Singapore; and scores of executive minds on three continents.

We feel considerable gratitude for the meticulous scholarship of John Raven, Daniel L. Shea, Frank Schmidt, John Hunter, Robert Kail, and especially, David Lubinski, Camilla P. Benbow, and Jonathan Wai

(Vanderbilt University) for their 20–35 year longitudinal research, and meta-analysis of 50 years on spatial ability (2009) with precocious youth into adulthood. Given the ever-increasing importance of quantitative and scientific reasoning skills in our era, their research findings on mathematically gifted individuals who choose to pursue careers outside engineering and the physical sciences was a significant break-through. Most confirming was the finding that our best graduate business schools select their students from verbal-mathematical scores and not spatial ability—the single best predictor for career success. We discovered clear "spatial" mountaintops above the familiar cloud cover of general mental ability that excited this work. We equally appreciate a report issued by the National Academy of Sciences (2005), *Rising above the Gathering Storm,* which highlights the importance of these trends for all countries concerned about their future prosperity and the importance of developing intellectual talent. We dedicated our postscript to committed educators in search of a new smart-brain science and the tools to develop brilliance in their students.

Finally, we have the deepest thanks to our loving families who also allow us to love science.

PREFACE

Realizing Bright to the Fourth Power

Our beginnings with *Executive Thinking* came out of two happenings: a post-doctorate (Graham) in organization development with Professors Colin Ingleton and John Raven at Edinburgh University (Scotland) in the 1980s; and comprehensive research and development (Baize) in visual-spatial processing science in Colorado in the early 1990s. Before the start of the new century, a Graham-Baize research consortium was established to integrate two unique practices and create a hybrid discipline. Spatial ability batteries and the Raven's Edinburgh Assessments were administered to executives on three continents to evaluate how they mentally tackle or think through and solve their difficult problems. Formative and fledging ideas about thinking capacity were fire-tested through interviews, assessments, and consultations. Most managers, be they in the United Kingdom, Israel, United States, or Singapore, would approach their "thorny" challenges at best with some problem-solving methodology, and at worst with mental knee-jerk reactions—only later to reap the penalties of shallow thinking. In other words, many executives were tackling tough problems without enough usable potential—the thinking capacity needed to spatially assimilate and accommodate new data in their environment with earlier experience.

Here we echo the Swiss psychologist Jean Piaget's definition of intelligence:

> Intelligence is assimilation to the extent that it incorporates all the given data of experience within its framework. There can be no doubt either, that mental life is also accommodation to the environment. Assimilation can never be pure because by incorporating new elements into its earlier schemata the

intelligence constantly modifies the latter in order to adjust them to new elements. (1963, pp. 6–7)

In our early attempts to assimilate groundbreaking neuroscience research and technology into the psychology of executive thinking, we accumulated experimental evidence on two hemispheres of the brain—each with different, specialized capacities. We acknowledged both the left (verbal, logic, quantitative, sequential, and analytical thinking) and the right (holistic, spatial, imaginative, integrative, emotional, intuitive, and spontaneous) in equal proportion. When thinking through the right brain, a person is capturing experiences that significantly resemble his or her real-time experiences. It is as if we have two brains looking at the world in different ways, and only our left brains enable us to name what we see. Another understanding about visual or picture thinking is that although external images are processed normally by both brain hemispheres, the two hemispheres process them in different ways. The capacity to name everything comes mostly from the left hemisphere (Gazzaniga, 2005).

The research also cites students with above-average math (quantitative width) abilities better able to interact and share information than average students because they used both the right and left halves of their brains. Some researchers have concluded that giftedness in math may be the spin-off of a brain that has functionally organized itself in a different way (Wai, 2009). The striking ability of the brain to change its organization by processing experience was a major breakthrough for us. By working with whole-brain research, we were better able to study what kind of neural processing would allow connectivity to draw from both the brain's right and left hemispheres (lateralization) and thereby boost executive thinking ability.

We pondered: Michelangelo was a stonecutter's son, and Shakespeare was the son of a middle-class businessman. What causes some people to soar free of their limited lives and make astonishingly creative contributions? How would it feel for an executive to think like an Albert Einstein without having to get a BS, MS, and PhD in the hard sciences? Why do most executives with business degrees find it easier to formulate problems than to produce the thinking processes needed to solve problems? Our research suggested that the few who demonstrated extraordinary problem-solving ability were loaded with insight, plasticity, and directionality—able to hold objectively the multidimensional streams of consciousness required in a higher level of complexity. These few executives were able to view their linear world of unseen multiple options in three- and four-dimensional frameworks. They were like quarterbacks, able to take a backfield vantage point, where unfolding dynamic systems were simultaneously perceived in spatial combinations of height, width, and depth and directed with insight, decisiveness, direction, and speed.

Our assumptions were confirmed by more recent research that posited that the left and right hemispheres do not process the same information. In most of us, the brain's major functions are performed separately—not allowing interference with one another (Goldberg, 2009). Interestingly, neural scientists discovered that in some brain disorders such as dyslexia, cross-connectivity/communication can occur between normally distant brain regions. Here we found that turbo-charging both hemispheres of the brain for greater cross-connectivity to occur is more than promising. In other words, an executive's creative abilities could be ultra-activated by increasing his/her capacity to connect normally disconnected thoughts, memories, feelings, and ideas. That means a person could learn to mentally process in a way that she or he could proceed from different starting points, change direction as needed, and spontaneously generate many unusual, possible solutions or distantly associated answers—each of which could be correct, useful, relevant, or effective and appropriate. Such a capacity for hyper-connectivity could be at the heart of all forms of brilliant thinking.

We finally concluded that the most powerful brains are the ones where many parts of the brain are ultra-activated and processing simultaneously on a regular basis. So how do we achieve this? Exercise! Brain exercise—giving all the different parts a workout to develop new mental muscles so that they will join in on the everyday processing to make our brains more hyper-connected and smarter. The more we exercise the different parts of our brains, the more we get all the spatial sparkplugs of our brains firing and contributing, thereby creating more capacity. For us to advance to brilliance, we had to discover, beg, borrow, and invent "spatial" processing workouts for the right hemisphere. Both hemispheres are needed to help executives learn to think insightfully in three and four dimensions, the way geniuses do.

Looking back, we were very fortunate to embrace a neuroscience of creativity and inventiveness and the practice of visual-spatial processing to build thinking capacity.

During this past decade we were privileged to develop bright leaders into brilliant, thinking executives who were able to assimilate the wealth of their own experience and spatially incorporate their current environments into three-dimensional frameworks because they had developed the spatial capacity to do so. Our own executive trainees, in less than a year, spatially possessed higher dimensions of thought to assimilate and accommodate their one- and two-dimensional frameworks into three- and four-dimensional thinking. Higher, wider, deeper, and accelerated processing capacities for thinking enabled them to (three-dimensionally) hold competing and conflicting ideas simultaneously, grasping and integrating important pieces in their minds at once. They were quickly able to resolve the irrelevant issues and decisively craft superior global frameworks with four-dimensional insight, velocity, and direction. In truth, they welcomed complex and challenging problems because they believed that could gain better insights and deal with problems more wisely through the crush of opposing views. Interestingly, these ordinary-to-extraordinary executives gave little credit to any current management practices or training programs to which they had been exposed earlier.

Four significant clusters were factored out from our executive "bright" problem-solving data: (1) verbal height; (2) quantitative width; (3) spatial depth; and (4) global insight that sustained decisiveness, direction, and speed. Thinking capacity increases with added height, width, depth, and speed. We were quick to observe that executives in possession of all four of these bright powers plus a stronger spatial capacity to process multiple dimensions had a conspicuous intellectual advantage in their workplaces. They differentiated themselves from the mental masses by being able to effectively tackle tough problems and produce a vast range of creative imagery and solution insights. Thus the Baize-Graham Thinking Postulate states: *Reasoning and problem solving abilities are no stronger than one's visual-spatial processing capacity that incorporates information on what is going on in real time and space.*

Spatial ability is the engine that drives the creativity and invention motorcade escorting US companies.

Our strong spatial thinkers, as leaders, didn't hope to keep abreast of all developments in their rapidly changing and diverse workforces; instead, they adopted a more inclusive, collaborative style. They became comfortable with sharing their thinking and generous in doing so. They also developed the spatial capacity to capture multiple perspectives from their team members and make decisions with a balance of idealism and pragmatism. They were not afraid to rise above segmented, sequential reasoning to the global, integrative thinking needed to creatively resolve the tensions in order to make smart decisions. They didn't break down their problems into separate pieces and segment or sequester them, but rather saw the spatial height, width, and depth of a problem—how the various parts of it fit together, how a single decision would simultaneously affect another. They became highly integrative in their thinking. Their work environments were distinctively demanding, challenging, and often stressful. But foremost, it was their spatial capacity to sustain three- and four-dimensional thinking that trumped the mentality crowd and differentiated them as brilliant leaders.

CEO Steve Jobs and his team at Apple exemplify some of the most spatially gifted thinkers and leaders in the international tech industry. Apple's extraordinary ability for three-dimensional thinking in height, width, and depth with creative challenges is perhaps their greatest strength. Apple's willingness to abandon the past makes for better products. Nothing holds it back, so it can always stay on the edge of what's technologically possible:

Don't be surprised if Apple someday unveils a "desk-free" computer—a machine that lets you slump on the couch with a wireless keyboard while surfing on a giant projected screen. Or a surface that can recognize handwriting gestures, in order to let you sign your name on a touch screen without using a stylus. There may also be a bright future in three-dimensional computing. Instead of fusing with flat windows on your iMac, cubes, prisms, and pyramids would represent apps, and you'd rotate one in 3-D space to interact with different parts of the program. (Manjoo, 2010, p.76)

Finding the Link between Visual-Spatial Processing and Thinking Capacity

After 9/11, we studied a handful of highly competitive, innovative American industries whose product/service generation was rapid and unrelenting and whose executives clearly demonstrated high-level thinking (i.e., experimental thinking and rapid spatial thinking). The industries studied were information technology, automotive, and medical equipment. They all invested in developing new technologically sophisticated products needed to sustain greater market share. We especially scrutinized their innovation activity, such as starting a fully resourced project to launch a new product in the marketplace. More importantly, for each of these products—Toyota Lexus, Honda Acura, Apple Mac, IBM laptop, Newton Orthotics, or American Home Care System—we tried to identify episodes of brilliant thinking in decision-making, from idea conception to approval to launch. It was difficult to get senior executives to identify these episodes, but there was enough data to confirm three- and four-dimensional thinking—especially global processing activity—to differentiate talented executives.

Here we discovered that most senior executives were relatively bright in verbal (crystal) intelligence and somewhat positive on quantitative (fluid), but weaker in visual-spatial intelligence. Those few who were high in both verbal and visual-spatial were wired for brilliance—that we knew. What we also knew was that our executive research was incomplete and that the thinking dimensions needed for business acumen were not yet fully understood and delineated, especially within some of our best American industries. We fell back on our earlier observations—that certain cognitive dimensions needed to create executive brightness came more from our MBA students who had undergraduate backgrounds similar to the background of Lee Iacocca, Bill Hewlett, David Packard, or Jack Welch (i.e., engineering/chemistry/physics) Likewise, in the field, especially in Singapore, we found that executives with strong hands-on science backgrounds, exhibited high levels of visual-spatial thinking. Singapore's Prime Minister, Lee Kwan Yu, had such a background, which helped him to create the global processing needed to remove barriers, tackle problems, and execute strategies in a timely fashion to sustain an annual 7–8% GNP.

Affirming Neuroscience, Connectivity, and "What should go on in our heads?"

Another co-occurring phenomenon for us has been the rediscovery of the mind by cognitive neuroscientists who linked their attempts to analyze the processes involved in thinking and learning to their dissatisfaction with the concept of one measurable form of intelligence. The basic principle of connectivity holds that the establishment of new connections between prior learning pathways is the essence of growth and development and that the condition of the connection points, like the condition of the gap in a spark plug, determines how well we function (Kotter, 2004).

As our research and ideas converged and gelled into an integrative holding model, we went back out to field test and confirmed our own constructions and best practices across multiple settings. This proved to be a truly rewarding experience—to see something of great promise created from a collage of ambiguity and uncertainty—factored into four thinking dimensions and simply making sense to our executives. Our four thinking "powers," plus a character dimension, we believe, are the best of cuts in grouping executive thinking brilliance.

We hope that our interweaving of neuroscience and executive capacity does not make our writing highly complex or inaccessible. We have tried to minimize the highly technical and make things clear and practical whenever possible. However, what we have regretfully observed in the past decade is a huge and irresistible penchant for executives and consultants to oversimplify and to sell less rather than more, both in substance and in form. We set out to tell it like it is and ask the Lee Iacocca question: **"Where have all our leaders gone?"** We then move to present a fresh voice against a national decline in adequately assessing and preparing executives in higher-level thinking capabilities. What goes on in the head, we believe, differentiates whether executives, presidents, or countries will ultimately succeed or fail in the global arena.

Finally, cracking the code for "increasing capacity" required us to begin with what neuroscientists claim is needed for any of us to be strong in spatial-cognition—where many parts of our brain could be connectively activated and processing simultaneously on a frequent basis (i.e., ultra-smart activity). Our clear objective had become: Build visual-spatial ability, or the ability to mentally visualize, invent, construct, and manipulate three-dimensional figures holistically through hyper-connectivity.

The code for increasing thinking capacity is visual-spatial processing the brain with best practices (i.e., neural workouts) necessary to create more hyper connectivity and whole brain receptivity. This is crucial to building spatial depth, thereby creating more plasticity, insight, and speed of thinking.

Recent studies on the neuroscience of creativity and capacity-building focus increasingly on originality, fluency, flexibility, elaboration, and divergent thinking (Meyer & Damasio, 2009). Creativity requires a novel understanding and expression of orderly relationships, which in turn requires individuals to disengage from the expected and develop alternative solutions and abstractions. They must be able to take different directions from the prevailing modes of thought or expression. Extraordinary creativity is qualitatively different from ordinary creativity. The underlying neural processes are distinct. They proceed by tapping into more hyper connectivity in ways that possessors of ordinary creativity alone are usually unable to realize.

Brilliant individuals are gifted with an unusual capacity for creativity that permits them to see and think in ways that are not accessible to ordinary executives.

In the realm of neuroscience applications, visual-spatial processing clearly creates more capacity for the working memory and for inventiveness. The most creative factor would seem to be the mechanics of supplying informational input from external sources. One example of a method we already use to increase the efficiency of an external source input is the use of some of our visual-spatial techniques cited in chapters three and five. A fuller visual-spatial processing technology will specifically develop cognitive connections, systems thinking, inventiveness, and spatial memory. Learners are programmed to see the whole, gestalt picture before they can understand the parts. They see the forest and initially often miss the trees after training. Programming utilizes color, layout, and spatial organization; mind maps; system diagrams (replacing words with pictures); visual journeys or story techniques; peg words and events (the ability to visualize helps peg content quickly); and the swish techniques that rely on visualization. Once spatial learners learn to create a mental picture of a concept and see how the information fits with what they already know, their spatial processing paths are permanent. Repetition is completely unnecessary and irrelevant to their learning styles (Bear, Connors, & Paradiso, 2006).

Look at it this way ...

A supermarket is "loaded" with ideas about what to eat, most of which we could not remember if we were not in that environment. But as we walk through the aisles, each item reminds us of what we might have for dinner. As a result, we can generate many ideas in a relatively short period of time. The more things we can generate as ideas, the more options we have to work with. If we were to include in our nutritional selection antioxidants and omega-3 fatty acids, we would better feed our brains over time. Likewise, differences in information-generation capacity—sourcing, retrieving, and processing—should not be static, but can be significantly improved with practice.

The so-called leader who doesn't invest time in "building capacity" might be compared to the student who was asked by the teacher to define "vacuum." The student replied, "I have it in my head but I can't express it." We have every potential capacity within us, and we must process differently to get it out. It's important to keep our brains stretched with "mental workouts." Like any muscle, the brain needs stretching for optimal performance, and we can keep ours limber, even with games and puzzles that challenge us. Crossword puzzles, Sudoku, or learning a new language, for example, are all ways to keep the brain growing and learning—and our thinking capacity increasing. Neural information-processing technology can accelerate the process. We now have the science to build thinking capacity. It has long been known that each of us has a different way of processing information. However, as computers and other technological devices are being developed to assist us in our daily lives, the gap between those who easily navigate their way through complexities and those who get lost in a muddle of confusion widens. It is, therefore, becoming increasingly necessary to understand the basis for these individual differences so as to lessen this gap.

A journey from bright to brilliant begins with an understanding that our current thinking levels juxtaposed with our day-to-day leadership challenges may not continue to serve us well. Being able to more rapidly digest competing information, massage and distill it down to the most relevant and substantive elements, simultaneously evaluate the inconsistencies in thinking and actions, and be decisive, we become better wired to creatively ignite needed changes, improvements, and innovations to move our world forward. Our fervent hope is that the time that Douglas McGregor envisioned in the 1950s, when significant changes in leadership philosophy and practice would become a requirement for survival, is fast approaching. Significant changes will not only enable us as leaders to build more capacity and more thinking teams, it will also enable us to enrich the lives of every person who gives us permission to lead.

Twenty-first-century America demands ultra-smart leaders—those who securely possess both the thinking capacity and skills to come to grips with accelerating and unpredictable changes in complex, often chaotic environments. These brilliant leaders should know how to think in verbal, quantitative, and spatial dimensions simultaneously to get the most out of emergent trends, resolve seemingly intractable contradictions, discern insight from perplexity, and design futures through decisiveness, direction, and speed. They should be "wired in" to the idea spaces of our uncertain times. With nimbleness, connectivity, and inventiveness they should come up with new ideas rather than hoping that ideas will fortuitously arrive.

Here in Hawaii, windsurfing is a popular sport that uses some principles useful to executives. Our concept of capacity and brilliance can be illustrated by the processes of windsurfing on a gusty day. Successful windsurfers learn to visual-spatially assimilate multifaceted information simultaneously into three-dimensional frameworks. We can observe (1) the windsurfer—our brain (*capacity*); (2) the surfboard—our leadership performance (conscientiousness); and (3) the wind and waves—our surrounding environment (*visual-spatial information*). The windsurfer's ability to quickly and accurately make sense of what he visually sees and processes helps him to interpret and navigate wherever he needs to go. So much of a windsurfer's success hinges on his visual and spatial ability to assimilate and accommodate his/her surrounding environment. Visual-spatial ability, for windsurfers and executives, is the ability to see things from many different perspectives. It's having the capacity to construct and deconstruct three dimensionally to invent novel solutions to problems.

Over the years, it's been our privilege to identify executives who, like windsurfers, possess extraordinary visual-spatial thinking ability. They are able to navigate easily through their "gusty" seas, characterized by greater information-processing demands. Our unfolding passion has become one of working with executives who conscientiously seek opportunities to increase their navigational brilliance through the assistance of visual-information processing—the neural technology that remarkably enhances visual-spatial thinking capacity. We firmly believe that executives who are bright and conscientious can significantly increase their spatial ability and be better equipped to see and decisively manipulate their spatial oceans. We also believe that this is vitally important for American leadership; otherwise we run the risk of being blown off course, weakened by strong winds, rain, waves, and riotous sails, and conspicuously driven into the rocks or out to seas of uncertainty.

Finally, we're on the cusp of peculiarity by introducing a brain-stimulating neuroscience approach to executive development. At first blush, we may seem somewhat out of the box, out of our heads, or in another box. Our "come-windsurfing-with-us" text is an active invitation to "come and see" how to build thinking capacity through four dimensions or powers of brightness to increase navigational smarts rather than just learning specific tacking skills and drills. We believe that much of our survival as Americans will ultimately rest in the hands of leaders who possess the capacity for brilliance.

Morris Graham and Kevin Baize

INTRODUCTION

A Journey from Bright to Brilliant through Visual-Spatial Thinking

Lito Alcantra has not forgotten his beginnings and his opportunities as a Filipino immigrant to Hawaii 38 years ago. In the Philippines, he had been a civil engineer and dean of a university's college of engineering—steeped in hard sciences. In Hawaii (1973), facing language and licensing barriers, he found work as a janitor and laborer in a Hawaii construction company. As a new janitor, Lito was quick to observe that the offices and floors of this prominent construction firm were deplorably dirty. He could visualize three-dimensionally in his mind what it could be and should be, and how cleanliness would boost employee pride and morale. On his own, he searched out and acquired janitorial knowledge of cleaning agents and learned how to strip and wax floors, the proper way to clean or bonnet a carpet, and the proper way to buff a floor and operate a floor buffer, a carpet extractor, a floor furnisher, and a heavy-duty wet-dry vac. While cleaning a conference room for estimators, Lito paused to study a three-dimensional architectural drawing of floors, walls, and ceilings for a new high-rise construction that was left on a countertop. He was quick to discover errors in the calculations that would ultimately result in serious mistakes and cost overruns. He left a note of correction for the estimators to review in their morning meeting.

Rising quickly within one year to a chief estimator and vice president of this Hawaii construction company, he saved $1000 and brought together six trusted friends who shared his vision of a Hawaii-based Filipino company. Lito founded Group Builders, Inc. (a high-rise interior construction company) 36 years ago as a group enterprise and has upheld that vision with a current $125 million annual worth and employment for 560 Filipino employees statewide—estimators, engineers, and builders. Group Builders, Inc. sustains a sterling reputation for outstanding creativity, workmanship, on-time reliability, and honest cost estimates. In 2008, Group Builders, Inc. was cited as one of Hawaii's most prominent and successful Filipino-owned companies—the tenth largest contractor in the state. The company was honored as one of Hawaii's Best Places to Work.

Lito's Global Processing Index (GPI) or his visual-spatial ability is in the top 5% on our Global Decisiveness Assessment Battery. He has the keen ability to perceive the visual world accurately, to perform transformations and modifications upon his initial perceptions, and to be able to re-create aspects of his visual experience, even in the absence of relevant physical stimuli. Lito's ability to spatially visualize in three-dimensions what could be, as demonstrated by his inventive practices in the business, are legionary. As Lito says, "We are like one big family … coming together, staying together, and working smartly together with a shared future vision is success."

CEO Lito Alcantra taught us much about how a spatially gifted person sees the world of opportunity differently. As he put it, "If we want to make a new contribution in our work and life, we've got to do new preparation. From the vantage point of greater height, we should be able to see things we or others have never seen before—ones only made visible at the top of a high-rise. We should set our sights on personal possibilities and begin our visual climb. In the climb, our vistas and thinking about the business and the world around will continually change. But, imagination is our intelligence having fun."

It is obvious that Lito Alcantra possesses an unusual kind of ability, one that is at the core of being inventive and brilliant. The power of his visual-spatial thinking—the ability to see things from many different perspectives and formulate new, fresh frameworks—is readily apparent to anyone who works with him. Our comprehensive assessment identified Lito as high in his ability to relate, combine, and integrate separate pieces of information into a new framework—or see how various parts are related as a whole. As a three-dimensional thinker, Lito would mentally question the validity and merits of two contending options and formulate a new alternative integrating the best from each option. The world to Lita Alcantra is essentially a three-dimensional living laboratory that allows him to be self-regulating and inventive.

Visual-spatial thinking is the hallmark of imagination, creativity, and inventiveness. Strong visual-spatial learners usually gravitate to the creative professions (e.g., art, design, architecture, computer programming, graphics, animation, physics, chemistry, aeronautics, pure mathematical research, engineering, computer programming, and photography). However, this style of learning may not be understood or appreciated in an executive boardroom, which rewards logical thinking and having the "right" answer. Often, visual-spatial thinkers develop their own businesses or become CEOs, as Lito Alcantra did, because of their inventiveness and ability to see the "big picture"—the relationships of large numbers of variables. The need is for more individuals with highly developed visual-spatial abilities to advance in technology and business. These are the creative leaders/executives of society who take something that exists and align it with market needs. They understand the behavior of the marketplace and do not stick to a business model or plan when the market resists. These individuals need to be protected from traditional educational settings and need extra help from others to develop supportive environments.

We add that it is this power, or visual-spatial ability to see and think three-dimensionally and take decisive action in a fourth dimension, that this book is about. Readers will discover that the neuroscience of creativity and inventiveness is now demonstrating that visual-information-processing technology can significantly enhance the way any of us could and should smartly process our world. We can increase our capacity to think without going back to school and majoring in engineering or slogging through the hard sciences. The power to discover our expansive intellects lies in our ability to holistically think higher, wider, and deeper with the spatial capacity to yet take on more light. Latent and underdeveloped, a spatial capacity to realize more brilliance and greater opportunity lies within all of us and most definitely can now be developed through the assistance of visual-spatial information-processing technology.

CHAPTER 1

Increasing Our Capacity to Think

> *We cannot solve problems by using the same kind of thinking we used when we created them.*
>
> Albert Einstein
>
> *Today's revolutionary advances in neuroscience will rival the discoveries of Copernicus, Galileo, and Darwin.*
>
> Paul Churchland

Life is about how much we think. Thinking is about how much capacity we have to process information. Capacity, in addition to our abilities and consciousness, is about how much we can simultaneously process combinations of verbal, quantitative, and spatial dimensions with decisiveness, direction, and speed.

Brilliance is about how much we can *increase* our capacity to think.

"Life" said Emerson, "consists in what a man is thinking all day." No matter where we go or what we do, we take our thinking with us. To a great extent we are what we think about. What we think about molds our aspirations and attitudes and what we will accomplish during our lives. Our lives are influenced more by our own thoughts than anything else.

> *How could a person possibly become what he is not thinking? Nor is any thought, where persistently entertained, too small to have its effect. The divinity that shapes our ends is indeed in our self.*
>
> Spencer W. Kimball

Contrary to established dogma, our thinking capacity is not locked into an IQ score or set in genetic immutability. IQ scores cannot possibly tell the whole story about thinking capacity—not even close. Our capacity to think is uniquely dynamic, plastic, and changeable. None of us need be dead-bolted into a closed-door belief in a predetermined, fixed level of intelligence, and a limited life. We are today where our thinking has brought us, and we will be tomorrow where our thinking will take us. The dilemma for most of us is that we also filter our thoughts through the lens of limitations, fears, anxieties, and irrationality.

A widespread, oversimplified myth is that only a handful of us are capable of making inventive contributions to our lives. This bell-curve thinking is not supported by a new era of neuroscience research. Brilliant thinking can be observed in almost all intellectual activity. We discovered, after our extensive executive research on spatial ability/capacity, why the engine of inspiration and inventiveness seems always to be in high gear in some leaders while others struggle. High scholastic aptitude is not the crucial ingredient here, because it is not the only criterion determining a leader's *capacity* for brilliance. Language is a marvelous tool for communication, but it is greatly overrated as a stand-alone tool for thought. Scholastic intelligence tests primarily involve verbal (language) and numerical thinking, whereas more brilliant leaders will measure high in spatial thinking with a good grasp of concepts. They are able to free themselves from conventional thought streams; instead, distant areas of their brains converse simultaneously and more robustly than is normal. Their creative abilities play out with a hyperconnectivity of normally disconnected thoughts, memories, feelings, and ideas. Brilliant leaders are able to mentally visualize and process in such a way that they can proceed from different starting points, change direction as needed, and spontaneously generate many unusual, probable solutions or distantly associated answers—each of which could be correct, useful, relevant, or effective and doable.

Some of us are privileged in life to gain more light and knowledge than others. Some are discouraged with life and/or do not continue to stimulate our minds with mental pursuits. Some attend school for a dozen or so years and then find employment only to provide an income until retirement. Our living patterns usually move toward routines and slowing down until we quietly fade away. Many of us assume that we were born with a certain number of brain cells and thereby have a genetically predetermined intellectual *cap* (somewhat false); that our brains start to slow down fairly early in life (somewhat true); and that there is little we can do about changing this pattern (false). We can't change the fact that we're older, but we can compensate for the cognitive changes that happen as a consequence (true). Although scientists still believe (for the most part) that we cannot grow new neurons, they now believe that the brain can grow new dendrites—the connections between neurons that create memory and learning (Koob, 2009). In other words, the human brain is like plastic. It is molded, at least in part, by its environment (true). We are not hostages of fate, but only hostages of our own thoughts (true). We are what we are because of our capacity to think (true). And the way we think, the way we take on our challenges, will influence our whole lives (true).

Think back … way back! What happened when you first learned how to walk? Almost half of your brain's cortex spent a lot of spatial-processing time trying to figure out how to prevent you from falling. But once you got the hang of it, you no longer thought about it at all. Now, when you walk into a board room, you don't think about which foot to move next or which muscles need to be told how to react in order to do so. You are thinking about what's on the agenda, what you might contribute, how you might avoid failure and embarrassment, and generally of more important things. As executives, we are all learning experience by experience, but also precept by precept. Subsequent experiences confirm and reconfirm what we already know intellectually. However, unless our insight sustains ongoing spatial expansiveness (connectivity among distant brain regions) and changeability, we will not survive the erosion that naturally will occur with the passage of time.

Brilliance is about creating more *connectivity and plasticity.*

The world we have created is a product of our thinking; it cannot be changed without changing our thinking.

Albert Einstein

All of us have remarkable powers of changing (plasticity) our own thinking (creative connections between ideas) and functions through simultaneously processing, thinking, and acting. Recent neuroscience research confirms that *neural* plasticity, or cortical re-mapping—the capacity to be consciously remolded—exists from the cradle to the grave (Stein, 2008). Likewise, radical improvements in cognitive functioning—how we learn, think, perceive, and remember—are possible throughout life (Osberg, 2010). The science and practice of information processing, under the right conditions, has possibly changed hundreds of millions and possibly billions of the connections between the nerve cells of individuals. Our brains have the ability to integrate pieces of disparate data in novel ways. There is a lot of brain potential to be realized!

We can change the way we process information. Our brain selectively refines its processing capabilities to fit each task at hand. Think about what you are doing right now—reading this book. You most likely have become unaware that you are sitting in a chair or that there are objects around this book that are in your peripheral vision. You are screening out information that has been shown by experience to be less important from the welter of data that streams into your head each moment through your sensory system. Your screened data, unavailable to your thought process, take up none of your capacity, lessening the burden on your neurons.

Our brains do not simply screen out and learn selectively, though they are enhanced by challenge and inhibited by threat. They are always "learning how to learn." The brain has a processor in which thoughts, experiences, and emotions can be simultaneously processed in height, width, depth, and *space*. Insightful learning should engage most of our mental machinery and consciousness and involve both focused attention and peripheral perception. When learning occurs in a way consistent with the laws that govern brain plasticity, the mental machinery of the brain can be improved so that we learn and perceive with greater insight, precision, speed, and retention.

Furthermore, our brains are not inanimate vessels that we fill; rather they are more like a living creature with an appetite—one that can grow and change itself with proper nourishment and exercise. Our brain's processing ability can change as we do more mental work—it can regenerate itself throughout our life span. *Processing* can be appropriate or faulty. Briefly, simultaneous processing can serve to stimulate the faculty we possess to integrate bits and pieces provided by our senses that are needed for reasoning. Our reasoning serves to establish abstractions from abstractions and so forth, in an ever-widening sphere of *thinking* and *conceptualizing*. Exercising our brains keeps them young and fit!

Did you ever stop to think, and forget to start again?

A. A. Milne, *Winnie the Pooh*

No matter where we go or what we do, we live our entire lives within the confines of our minds. Everything we hear, feel, see, and think is processed by our brain. It allows us to cope masterfully with our everyday environment and is capable of producing breathtaking athletic feats, sublime works of art, profound scientific insights, and innovations in business and life. But its most amazing achievement may simply be thinking.

Think left and think right and think low and think high. Oh, the things you can think up if only you try.

Dr. Seuss

Thinking is the process of thought—to consider, judge, or believe. It is the process of exercising the mind to put together creative connections in order to construct or deconstruct, to make the mental choice between options and make a decision. Our capacity to think, reason, and decide makes us unique. Since reality is what it is and not some indiscernible haze, we can attempt to understand it, and this allows us to change, adapt, or improvise the things that make up a *reality* for our own survival. Through the faculty of *reason*, we can exploit a *reality* around our desires and dreams. We can make it an extraordinary world, where we make greater contributions, and enjoy greater well-being, health, and life—and where we can apply our productive *capacities* to achieve our noblest dreams.

Yet, few of us are taught in our early years how to exploit our mental *capacity* or *usable potential* (e.g., greater height, breadth, and depth of judgment and character to deal with ambiguous and ethical complexities in life). Inevitably, most of us develop limited, inept thinking that does not and will not serve us well. Life with limited thinking capacity, as we now have, *need not* be our handicap in the game of life. Only in the last few years has there been sufficient research to create a neuroscience that promotes visual-spatial processing technology for increasing mental capacity or usable potential.

Brilliance is about processing and thinking in multiple dimensions.

Capacity is like a four-wheel drive vehicle with extra gas in the tank. Each set of wheels allows us to get to more remote places. Most senior managers use their front wheel capacity (verbal and numerical power) more than they take advantage of the added boost that could come with the rear wheels (spatial and decisive power). When managers develop their executive "rear wheels" power, they subsequently increase their higher-order mental processes (overdrive velocity) to reach more remote places in terms of height, width, and depth and, with extra gas (reserve) in their tanks. They realize greater profitability, productivity, and confidence in their ability to better lead their businesses.

> *"Executive Thinking Capacity" is the ability to holistically and simultaneously think in height, width, and depth, and do so decisively in order to navigate with insight and velocity. It is the ability to sustain thinking in:* **high verbal levels** *(reading and writing, listening and speaking);* **wide quantitative levels** *(numbers and equations, measurements and graphs);* **deep**

spatial levels *(integration of information in three-dimensions needed for break-through and invention); and* ***global levels of decisiveness*** *(recognize and scrutinize, visualize and prioritize) needed to speedily direct and execute informed decisions.*

These four powers of thinking, we believe, differentiate brilliant executives from merely bright ones. Whether working alone or in teams, executives get more perspectives on the table, better results in less time through higher, wider, deeper, and thicker thought dimensions—all needed for informed thinking. With four full cylinders to drive our *mind-vehicles* we can discover a new order of higher speeds, road mastery, and freedom to travel anywhere.

No problem can withstand the assault of sustained thinking.

Voltaire

It is clear to us that the most critical priority for any organization or nation is the development of its thinking *capacity* so that it can tap into higher levels of thinking with key decision makers. Although many voices and vendors promote their problem solving/decision making/innovation programs, few understand the multiple connections needed to make it happen. How many different ways we can think can be more important than how much we know how to plug a problem into programs.

Never be afraid to sit awhile and think.

Lorraine Hansberry, A Raisin in the Sun

America: Where have our brilliant leaders gone?

Where have our brilliant leaders gone? Where are America's educational initiatives to develop highly capable and resilient leaders? In the quest to find and develop brilliance, one should not look for high verbal or mathematical ability as much as *deep spatial ability*—a prerequisite for graduate scientific and engineering education. Our top American graduate business or law schools may not be the place to look. They are locked into the premise that General Mental Ability (GMA) is more predictive of job performance and ultimate occupational level attained than any other ability, trait, or disposition, and believe it is better than job experience. However, when we select the top 3% of verbal/math talent in America, we ignore 50% of those students in the top 1% of spatial talent—future scientists, engineers, or leaders, like Thomas Edison, Henry Ford, or Walt Disney.

Individuals like Lee Iacocca, Bill Hewlett and David Packard, Andrew Grove, Jack Welch, and other great executives in recent history were not just people with good verbal skills, but also individuals with high spatial capacity. Their spatial thought processes enabled them to better access complex financial information and multiple perspectives and come up with alternative responses to vital issues. When problems arose, they could accurately discover the causes and quickly take curative action. They formulated good decisions, balancing the benefits and risks associated with their choices. And they effectively put into action their chosen course by working around insignificant problems and seizing opportunities.

We found other executives gifted with the ability to visualize the world with great accuracy. They were able to think in three-dimensional terms and could re-create an idea into a working visual model. They were also able to adapt and modify that model prior to any physical construction. Such individuals had an amazing ability to create a mental map of a new territory, providing a strong sense of spatial awareness for where they were positioned in relation to the world around them.

We need more than ever to develop leadership in ways that focus on a readiness to adapt and modify, move up and out, forget personal accomplishments, and keep figuring it out. Executives today need to be probing, interconnecting, asking the right questions, testing assumptions, and simultaneously integrating collective thinking so that they can make better business decisions, day in and day out. How then can we develop leaders of the highest caliber who have neither the time nor the wherewithal to take years off to augment their educational base with science, engineering, and an MBA? Yet the spatial intelligence to cope with complexity, amorphousness, and uncertainty at all levels of management is needed more than ever.

Conscientiously building thinking capacity is supersizing the brain.

We all differ in how we process our life's experiences. Are we not about *how* we think, how much ability or capacity we have, and how conscientious we are? Research suggests that great accomplishment, and even what we call genius, is typically the result of years of conscientiously building thinking capacity, and not something that flows naturally from some inherent gift. Fermi, Wright, Edison, and Ford were not simply born with talent; they cultivated it through a tremendous, sustained effort. The kind of supersized profile we found among the best thinkers across a span of organizations is a passion to make a difference, a conscientious desire for greater mental space in the way they think, and the ability to work with and through others.

> *The kind of commitment I find among the best performers across virtually every field is a single-minded passion for what they do, an unwavering desire for excellence in the way they think and the way they work. Genuine confidence is what launches you out of bed in the morning, and through your day with a spring in your step.*
>
> Jim Collins

Recently, we were in Atlanta at a national business conference talking to an executive from a distinguished consulting firm. When we asked her to describe her outlook on the future, she told us that the future of her business could be expressed in one word. That work, she told us, was no longer "skills" to create peak performance in her clients. "The word today," she said, is "capacity." She told us that almost all organizational failures could be tracked to leaders who lacked the capacity—not necessarily the skills—to address and tackle crucial challenges, tough issues, and prickly problems, and that her organization was going to emphasize thinking capacity above all else. When we asked her what she intended to do differently, she outlined a program of executive development that would require clients to go outside the box when tackling problems. Interestingly, there was no mention of *how* her clients might better process information outside the box. She went on to explain to us how executive development must become more practical and behavioral.

The fundamental flaw with this approach is that it miscasts "capacity" as linear (i.e., lock-step) strategies that supposedly get people out of the box by using tools already in the box. Recall Audre Lorde's famous words: *"The master's tools will never dismantle the master's house."* We cannot hope to break down problems using only the same methods that created them (i.e., functional height, width, and depth). We can only hope that she will not advance her message without consideration of some serious neuroscience research about what is needed to process and navigate space outside the box. It is not that executive development, knowledge, and skills don't matter. They do matter. It is that over time, our knowledge, skills, and performance will always follow our thinking capacity—always!

Spatial ability is the *single* best predictor of career performance over time.

Traditional executive development emphasizes know-how and skills as most important for peak performance. This focus had its heyday with the development of competencies in the executive training community through the 1980s. Now, personality and related concepts, such as emotional intelligence, have come to the forefront of this discussion. The requirements for success in business, such as problem solving, innovation or the ability to deal with ambiguity, were assumed to be driven more by personality.

GMA (General Mental Ability) and conscientiousness are evidence-based predictors of executive performance and career success (Mackintosh, 1998). However, graduate schools in general appear to be losing many spatially gifted candidates by restricting assessments to quantitative and verbal abilities, such as those of the Scholastic Aptitude Test (SAT) and the Graduate Record Examination (GRE). Verbal and quantitative dimensions plus conscientiousness do not constitute a full desk for *brilliance*. Something is seriously missing.

> *Complacency with our traditional judgment-based thinking methods is not enough. Our existing thinking habits are*

> *excellent just as the rear wheel of a motor car is excellent but not enough. We need to put far more emphasis on creative and design thinking. Judgment and analysis are not enough.*
>
> Edward de Bono

Creative and design thinking are spatial abilities that engineers, designers, and bright-to-brilliant executives depend on. When a mountain climber pauses with map and compass, it is his spatial ability that conceptualizes the path ahead. Through spatial ability, an artist feels the tension, balance, and composition of a painting or musical arrangement. Spatial ability is the more abstract ability of a chess master, a military strategist, or a theoretical physicist. The ability to see at all is an act of spatial ability, and strong spatial capacity transforms mental images and molds the foundation for bright leadership that is based on observation or description. Bright leaders and talented speakers or speechwriters convey a wide variety of mental images to their audience. Uniquely, spatial ability is more than visual; it includes abstract, analytical abilities that go beyond seeing images.

It is estimated that contemporary talent searches bypass approximately half of those who score in the top 1% in spatial ability, by exclusively restricting talent identification to mathematical and verbal abilities (Shea, Lubinski, & Benbow, 2001; Webb, Lubinski, & Benbow, 2007). Our findings suggest that modern talent searches should be augmented to include *spatial* intelligence in the selection process. The most current research concurs that capacity—made up of quantitative, verbal, *and* spatial ability—is the best composite predictor of occupational level attainment and performance within one's chosen occupation and does so better than any other ability, knowledge and skills, or personality disposition, and better than job experience. Spatial ability is the *single* best predictor of career performance over time (Lubinski & Benbow, 2006).

Spatial ability can be developed and can provide unlimited vocational options.

Visual-spatial ability is the capacity to mentally manipulate two-dimensional *and* three-dimensional figures. It is intimately connected to our emotional intelligence and rational intelligence and occupies almost half of our brain's cortex. If percentage of cortex is any measure, then visual-spatial "intelligence" is a major facet of who we are as people, and its understanding is a key to what we might become. *Executive Thinking* speaks to executives who want to utilize greater thinking capacity to figure things out and step up to more brilliant careers.

A primary focus on *what* a leader *does* is primitive. The more productive and more challenging approach is to focus on *how* a leader *thinks*—that is, to examine the antecedent of doing, or the capacity (weak or strong) of leaders to think—and act.

Weak spatial *capacity* will limit thinking and action when confronted with: (1) complex cognitive processes such as reasoning and decision-making; (2) novel tasks that have not developed schemata; (3) life threatening or single, difficult tasks; and (4) functions that require the suppression of habitual responses. Weak spatial capacity is inherent in linear regression, decision trees, compensation systems, and other business infrastructures *du jour*. We can begin our space travel by first challenging our own assumptions about how we work through problems to solutions. Then, we should encourage other significant co-workers to test our thinking (i.e., conclusion, assumptions, reasoning, and data).

Strong spatial *capacity* must be present for high-level thinking skills because:

- Knowledge based upon rote learning has been discredited, as it is recognized that executives cannot store sufficient knowledge in their memories for future use.

- Information is expanding at such a rate that executives require transferable brain power to allow them to address different problems in different contexts at different times throughout their careers.

- The complexity of modern jobs requires executives who can demonstrate comprehension and judgment as participants in the generation of new knowledge.

- Modern organizations require active contribution where executives can assimilate information from multiple sources, determine its veracity, and make judgments.

- The cognitive approach suggests that leaders must take on an awareness of themselves as thinkers and learners and develop the capacity and practices for higher-level thinking.

- Organizations must find ways to identify and cultivate future leaders with the capacity to set direction by implementing inventive strategies.

Strong spatial capacity predisposes executives to grasp two to three oppositional or competing ideas in their heads at once (e.g., "It was the best of times, it was the worst of times"). It means staging our minds to creatively grasp, hold, and resolve tensions between contending ideas by crafting a novel, superior idea that contains the better elements of each. It is this simultaneous, integrative, insightful, decisive thinking—not a seamless strategy or flawless execution of skills—that is the defining signature of strong executive capacity.

Smart Brain Research and a Smart New Science

Our brain is the most complex, sophisticated, and powerful information-processing device known. Neuroscience research has shown that substantial changes occur in the lower neocortical processing areas, and that these changes can profoundly alter the pattern of neuronal activation in response to experience. Thinking, problem solving, learning, and acting actually change the brain's functional anatomy from top to bottom, as well as its physical anatomy. "Please hold onto these thoughts as we take this a little deeper."

Neuroscience research attests that there are 100 billion nerve cells in the brain, as many as there are stars in our galaxy. In general, the nerve cells do not divide after birth, but the glial cells do divide. Glial cells are the metabolic and structural support cells for the nerve cells. They produce growth and tropic factors, playing a key role in regeneration and plasticity. They increase in number in response to enriching experiences. Keeping an active mind does have anti-aging benefits, in addition to elevating everyday function.

The laboratories of Joseph Altman at Purdue and Marian C. Diamond at Berkeley found that the cerebral cortex from rats living in enriched environments had more glial cells per neuron than the cortex from rats living in impoverished environments (Diamond, 2001). Active cortical neurons need more support cells. We need challenging activities (enrichment) that stimulate nerve cell development. We all have the potential to continually ask questions that stimulate nerve cell development (Diamond, 1988).

Just because our brains are alive doesn't mean our minds are being used for smart capacity. In a sense, the best definition of "mind" is that it is the state that occurs when the brain is alive and at work. The recent rediscovery of the concept of the mind provides two new dimensions for examining executive thinking: (1) the attempts of behavioral neuroscience to analyze the processes involved in acquiring the skills of learning; and (2) the dissatisfaction with the concept of one measurable form of intelligence (IQ). That being said, the daunting challenge for corporate America is to be able to harness new developments from brain science to best access unusable human potential.

Smart Brain Science: A Scaffolding to Build Thinking Capacity

One of the greatest frontiers in modern science is the study of the functions of the smart brain and the complex qualities of the mind. Our thoughts, emotions, perceptions, and behavior all originate in the complex chemical interactions of the brain. Smart brain capacities created Homer's *Odyssey*, Michelangelo's David, Leonardo's Mona Lisa, Shakespeare's *Hamlet*, Newton's calculus, Beethoven's *Ninth Symphony*, NASA's "to the moon and back," Sam Walton's Walmart, UCLA coach John Wooden's 10 championships in 11 years,

Einstein's E=mc2, and all the miraculous technological, industrial, and athletic achievements of the twentieth century.

In the early part of the twentieth century, behavioral scientists assumed that people were born with their brains fully intact, with a fixed intelligence that never changed by more than a few IQ points throughout their lives. By the end of the twentieth century, the assumption held that intelligence was a unitary homogeneous ability—even though different people varied greatly in their areas of cognitive excellence. We now know, thanks to recent developments of brain-scanning technologies like PET and MRI, that our brains change throughout our lives and that not all brains work in the same way. Behavioral neuroscience has recently provided clues as to how we all can enhance mental capacities to become more effective learners and efficacious performers to fulfill our potential and destiny.

Interestingly, in 1997, world authorities on intelligence meeting in Singapore for the Seventh International Conference on Thinking admitted to being only on the edge of understanding the inner magic of the smart brain.

These experts confirmed:

- Although specific areas of the brain are associated with particular functions, large parts of the cerebrum (known as the "thinking cap") appear to have a more general function.

- There appears to be a two-way relationship between the working of the cerebrum and the tasks upon which it is engaged: while the connections within it are necessary for higher-level activities to be undertaken, those connections also develop if stimulated.

- The brain understands and remembers best when facts and skills are embedded in spatial memory.

- Thinking negative thoughts secretes inhibitor chemicals that block or limit the flow of electrochemical impulses. Thinking positive thoughts secretes neural transmitters that facilitate thinking, learning, and creativity

Currently, most learning institutions are concerned with raising educational standards. But we suggest that the minimal requirements of schooling (i.e., mastery of the basics—reading, writing, and mathematics), however excellently taught, is *not* sufficient to meet the demands of twenty-first century leadership. A broader range of abilities, redefined as smart thinking *capacity*, is required more than ever. Our speed in responding to our world is about how many mental *connections* we simultaneously *process and execute*.

All this presents a new educational challenge to develop capacity sufficient for individuals in the new workplace, where not just elite leaders can become competent thinkers. Our own meta-analysis of the smart, adult brain literature would suggest a single imperative: If the adult brain strives to create connections, patterns, consolidations, and assimilations, then effective executive development programs should be about how to build thinking capacity needed to maximize connections, patterns, consolidations, and assimilations.

Building thinking capacity is one of the most important, yet inadequately implemented, areas of executive development programs to date. Helping executives develop and improve their thinking abilities must be connected in significant ways with processing combinations of verbal height, quantitative width, and spatial depth simultaneously with insight, decisiveness, direction, and speed. These variables that directly relate to thinking *capacity* are themselves quite daunting unless better understood.

The simple act of thinking changes our brain-body.

The Dalai Lama invited Richard Davidson, a Harvard-trained neuroscientist, at the University of Wisconsin-Madison's W.M. Keck Laboratory for Functional Brain Imaging and Behavior, to his home in Dharamsala, India, in 1992 after learning about Davidson's innovative research into the neuroscience of emotions. *Could the simple act of thinking change the mind?* Most scientists believed that it could not, but they agreed to test the theory. One such experiment involved a group of eight Buddhist monk adepts and ten volunteers who had been trained in meditation for one week in Davidson's lab.

All the people tested were told to meditate on compassion and love. Two of the controls and all of the monks experienced an increase in the number of gamma waves in their brains during meditation. As soon as they stopped meditating, the volunteers' gamma wave production returned to normal, while the monks, who had meditated on compassion for more than 10,000 hours in order to attain the rank of adept, did not experience a decrease in the gamma wave production after they stopped meditating. The synchronized gamma wave areas of the monks' brains during meditation on love and compassion was found to be larger than the corresponding areas of the volunteers' brains (Davidson, et al., 2003).

Only in the last decade has behavioral neuroscience challenged existing theories about how we think and learn. This science has produced evidence as to how we can enhance our mental capacities to become more comprehensive learners and performers. The most fundamental question to a behavioral neuroscientist might be: What types of altered communication processes between neurons are responsible for dramatic changes in thinking?

> *We both (I and Warren Buffett) insist on a lot of time being available almost every day to just sit and think. That is very uncommon in American business. We read and think. So Warren and I do more reading and thinking and less doing than most people in business. We do that because we like that kind of a life.*
>
> Charlie Munger

Building thinking capacity converts directly into usable potential.

When we hear about organizations that have embraced executive training, what we often hear about are the events, the practices, the activities that those organizations have developed by following the fundamentals of business. The best of what we have learned from training and development over the years is that learning is not about events, not about concepts, and not about a way of acting. Learning is a capacity—meaning that capacity needs to be a part of a company's portfolio of critical decision-making assets. As leaders, our job is not to make up our people's minds, but to open minds and to make the agony of the decision-making so intense that they can escape only by thinking. When we identify thinking as a capacity, we can quickly see the factors that go together to make capacity-building an executive priority. And, building thinking capacity converts directly into usable potential.

Build thinking capacity first—then work on what needs to happen.

In this new century, to sustain competitive advantage, leaders need the spatial processing depth of a collegiate quarterback. Backfield stars are high in executive processing of decision making and decisive timing—key powers that differentiate the effective from the less effective. Each of the four bright powers presented here is a mental dimension by which learning and knowledge are obtained and acquired through higher processing and reasoning.

We have documented that the supply of verbally high, quantitatively wide, *and* spatially deep executives is small in our businesses and government. High verbal executives are found in much greater abundance. Clearly, research evidence suggests that high-level capacities are essential for executive success. We are not arguing that knowledge and skills are unimportant, but emphasizing the importance of *capacity*. It increases significantly at the higher executive levels.

Developing executives who become effective thinkers must become an immediate priority. If we are to function successfully in a highly technical society, then we must be endowed and wired with a lifelong thinking capacity necessary to acquire and process information in four bright powers. Our good news is: we can now build greater self-awareness and mental capacity through the neuroscience of visual processing technology.

The Four Powers of Capacity: BRIGHT1 + 2 + 3 +4 (Verbal + Quantitative + Spatial + Decisive Speed)

BRIGHT1—An Executive's *Verbal Height—Sequential (step-by-step) Processing*. Grounded more in liberal arts (reading and writing/listening and speaking), verbal height is understanding and reasoning using abstract concepts framed in words. It aims at evaluating ability to think constructively, rather than simple fluency or vocabulary recognition. Rational decision making is linear, and it is what we do when we put our facts in order. A liberal arts education has the potential to provide verbal reasoning skills that we use throughout our executive lives. Our thinking height is primarily determined by these dimensions. Reading and writing are fundamental, but speaking with reasoning ability "on our feet" is the most neglected area of a university education. What future leaders and politicians need is training in the arts that is Socratic in nature, similar to instruction in law schools.

Language and verbal thinking without BRIGHT1 height are more or less the essence of being human. Once we have language, we tend to categorize and translate almost everything into words, giving a name to everything. We prefer words to images because it is easier to control words than to control images. We fundamentally ignore everything that doesn't fit in our categorization and is *de facto* too much stimulus coming from our visual reality. Surely we lose the capacity to remember those vivid images called eidetic that have great realism. The "images" that we remember are often only verbal categorizations. The saving grace here is: verbal language in connection to visual-spatial thinking (thinking with mental images) becomes our programming language; it helps us run simulations in our brain.

BRIGHT2—An Executive's *Quantitative Width—Symbolic Processing*.
These are numbers and equations/measurements and graphing. Executives strong in BRIGHT2 dimension use symbolic reasoning. In other words, they relate well to time, learn by trial and error, progress symbolically from easy to difficult material, are analytical thinkers, have the ability to solve mathematical word problems, work with numbers, and think in a mathematical way in general.

Unfortunately, in American education, too much emphasis is placed on mathematical computational skills and not enough on applying math to real world problems (width). In the IEA Second International Mathematics and Science study, the United States was near the bottom (15 out of 16 nations) in advanced math and dead last in physics. Contemporary talent searches miss many intellectually talented candidates by restricting selection criteria to mathematical and verbal ability measures.

BRIGHT3—An Executive's *Spatial Depth—Simultaneous/Integrative Processing.* BRIGHT3 is the ability to perceive the visual/spatial world accurately and to perform connections and transformations upon those perceptions. BRIGHT3 involves sensitivity to color, line, shape, space, form, and the relationships that exist between these elements. It includes the capacity to visualize—to graphically represent visual or spatial ideas, and to orient oneself appropriately to a spatial matrix—as with geometry and physics. Leaders strong in the BRIGHT3 dimension think primarily in pictures, relate well to space, are whole-part learners, learn concepts all at once, and learn complex concepts easily. They struggle with easy skills, are good synthesizers, see the big picture but may miss details, are better at math reasoning than computation, create unique methods of organizing, arrive at correct solutions intuitively, learn best by seeing relationships, have good long-term visual memory, learn concepts permanently, are turned off by drills and repetition, develop their own method of problem solving, generate unusual solutions to problems, and are creatively, mechanically, and technologically gifted.

Three-dimensional thinking is posited most in science and engineering—laboratories and breakthroughs; invention and manufacturing. Scientific reasoning skills cannot be acquired sitting in a room studying textbooks. A future scientist must have hands-on practical, laboratory experience. A future CEO or US president must also have hands-on practical experience, in at least a three-dimensional laboratory, and must develop the capacity to mentally navigate the movement of objects and concepts in three dimensions.

The BRIGHT3 world is essentially a three-dimensional living laboratory where we communicate new thoughts by linking the unknown with the known and valued past.

The BRIGHT3 thinker must be able to hold a three-dimensional object in memory while simultaneously and holistically transforming it. A lab provides the opportunity to think like Albert Einstein (spatially) in a divergent-convergent fashion (replicating an experiment). A lab stimulates divergent thinking or the getting out on the outer fringe to investigate from a wider, higher position the cognition going on in the smaller, inner center. The thinker is then able to mentally return to the convergent, smaller, inner center and create a new experiment that may never been attempted and which may lead to an innovation appropriate to the time and situation.

There are two levels of spatial ability:

Spatial I ability (construction) is what Thomas Edison used to construct the first commercially practical incandescent light bulb, and spatial ability propelled him to become the world record holder for patents (1093).

Spatial II ability (deconstruction) is what Henry Ford use to deconstruct an engine and determine how it could be designed better and made faster (the assembly line). Spatial ability is what a physicist uses to figure out the relationships between all physical things in the universe. Spatial ability is what made Albert Einstein's brain so unique—with Spatial I & II ability, he discovered $E=mc^2$.

Spatial I & II ability supports the thinking to discern similarities across diverse domains; organize the external world into the pieces that can be processed; construct and deconstruct; think and manipulate in three dimensions; and formulate solutions in real time.

It is significant to note is that *Time Magazine* chose the physicist Albert Einstein as "The Person of the Twentieth Century." Albert Einstein was thinking spatially three-dimensionally when he discovered that light consists of particles. He also hypothesized that an atom ready to rearrange itself and thus give off light of a particular frequency can be stimulated to do so by introducing an identical neighbor in its vicinity. By lining up these particles, a steady coherent emission of light that is extraordinarily pure and intense can be produced. Before Einstein's theories, physicists had supposed that light consisted simply of waves—but its behavior puzzled them because it was inconsistent. When the first laser was built in the early 1960s, Einstein's principles were fully realized and completely reconciled the conflicting views of light as particles or waves. Put the vibrant particles in step with one another and they make a regular wave. The rest is light history.

Before Jack Welch began his meteoric rise at General Electric, he first received his PhD in chemical engineering. Lee Iacocca, with a Masters degree from Yale, started at Ford in a drafting room and 24 years later became the president of Ford. Future leaders need laboratory experience for developing spatial ability that includes creativity, innovation, and problem-solving. All basic research begins in the hard sciences. Every BRIGHT3 candidate needs lab experience in 3-D creativity, innovation, and problem-solving.

BRIGHT4—An Executive's *Spatial Judgment: Decisiveness & Speed—Global Processing.* This dimension is necessary for executing decisiveness, direction, and speed. Football quarterbacks are provided excellent training in this fourth-dimension by having to respond to time and pressure demands. Likewise, basketball at UCLA under John Wooden utilized many of the same team dynamics. The ability to make rapid decisions in real time (such as on a football field or basketball court) is essential training for any executive and high-capacity team.

As we think about how much training in decision thinking goes into developing a collegiate quarterback, we can compare that with the lack of training provided by universities in rapid and flexible, micro- and macro-decision-thinking ability. Being flexible allows us to see challenges from more than one perspective, allows us to reframe complex problems so that solutions become clearer. It allows us to read, question, listen, think, and test underlying assumptions about a problem and facilitate the generation of an array of possible solutions.

BRIGHT4 executives are able to assess and make rapid decisions the way quarterbacks do when assessing alternatives and potential problem situations all over the playing field. They are wired to make high passes to wide receivers with keen spatial judgment, direction, and velocity. They can make decisions with certainty in an atmosphere of increasing backfield time pressures and conflicting movements on the playing field that create challenges for any executive quarterback. Making sound leadership decisions in crisis situations like a fourth down, seven yards to go for a first on the 50-yard line is even more demanding. Too long a pause or too much contemplation can redirect attention from the most relevant execution and ultimately yield uncertain outcomes—like being sacked in the backfield and losing the ball.

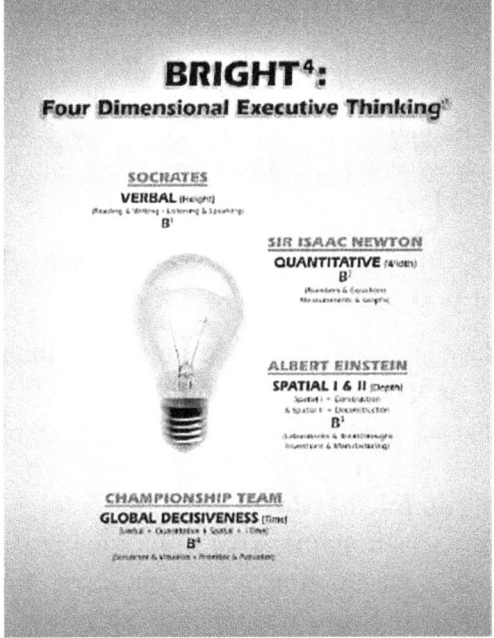

In a global economy, integrated decision speed is beyond conventional thinking paradigms.

Executives need to take ideas and do something with them. The idea of cell phones was introduced in the Buck Rogers serials in the 1930s, but the commercial phenomenal success of cell phones didn't come until a half century later. We have learned that integrated decision speed has to go beyond conventional paradigms and be an examination of traditional constraints using nontraditional thinking. The executive goes outside his/her own frame of reference and *finds another perspective or dimension to look at a problem.*

BRIGHT4 thinkers have the *capacity* to utilize 1+2+3+4 thinking powers and *process* multiple perspectives *at once and instantaneously*, whereupon insight, understanding, energies, and resources become infinite.

BRIGHT1+2+3+4 is the capacity to insightfully anticipate, visualize, and verbally articulate alternative futures from multiple perspectives; identify patterns and indicators through quantitative means; holistically recognize likely choices that could lead to gaps between desirable and undesirable futures; explore strategies that address the gaps; understand enhancing and inhibiting factors; and integrate and execute fresh strategies to rapidly respond to these factors with a sense of direction and velocity.

The Question: How do we get to the place of our greatest capacity—most potential?

Twentieth-century leadership was sustained, for the most part, with one and two powers of thinking (BRIGHT1+2). However, BRIGHT1+2 is less potent, with little staying power for the new challenges facing our current spatial *souk*. American graduate business schools, through GMAT selection scores, were and are accepting individuals strong in verbal skills and in mathematics. They are producing average-to-competent managers, but not brilliant leaders. We need leadership who can think higher, wider, and deeper, and transform their organizations to meet the changing needs of the increasingly competitive global environment.

Unfortunately, the current US pool of **BRIGHT1+2+3+4** leaders is miniscule. Few college graduates have had much exposure or experience with hands-on laboratories that build spatial ability (i.e., rapid, micro, macro, and global decision-making). Are we able to:

- recognize via Internet and the search business when we have enough information, the right information, or when we need to do more research;

- structure more complex challenges to ensure that we are addressing the right and important issues;

- involve the proper people at the right time in the right way; and

- conceptualize and craft environments that foster continual feedback, test assumptions (advocacy and inquiry), and realize smart decision thinking?

The composite of 1+2+3+4 powers of thinking is a full deck that allows an executive to reach his/her greatest potential. He/she should be able to penetrate a problem from every dimension (linear, quantitative, spatial). Most of us need more *capacity* in decision time and we need a way to get this capacity without having to play quarterback for the University of Southern California. A time-honored path to leadership was to start in engineering (BRIGHT2+1), and then transfer into sales (BRIGHT1+2), learning decision time (BRIGHT4) at corporate headquarters. After more than 20 years in the company, we are ready to lead (BRIGHT1+2+4). If we are working for a BRIGHT4 thinking leader and we have considerable spatial capacity (BRIGHT3), we are in a better place to understand the issues and problems at that level, and be at a place of our greatest most capacity and highest potential.

If we have not followed this path, do we know there is another path that will help us arrive at the place of greatest potential?

The Good, the Bad, and the Best News

Is it true that superior intelligence and graduating from a top school is the very track to success in this country? Yes and No. We shouldn't have to go there if that is not us. Why? Because more than three decades of research have proved that an overemphasis on intellect and academic talent over well-built thinking capacity is counterproductive. The implication that intellectual capacity is innate and fixed and the best schools matriculate only the most promising leaves many of us with flawed thinking, unmotivated to stretch and be at the place of our most potential.

It is not about intelligence. It is about capacity. Intelligence is fixed, but thinking capacity is not.

What if we aspire to be a higher-level executive and we are not satisfied with our current level of academic preparation, experiences, and conceptual capacity? We most likely have neither the time nor the luxury to take two or more years off to augment our educational base with an MBA or other advanced degrees. Yet, the heady demands on us (at all levels) are greater than ever.

The **good news** is that thinking capacity can be enhanced over time through an approach that encourages a focus on development rather than a singular fixation on intelligence. Just having the personal discipline to broaden our professional reading program and serve on special high-level planning groups can help. Recent research from Harvard Medical School reveals that mental-skill exercises benefit the brain by improving the blood flow and spurring cell growth. A recent report by the Mayo Clinic also concluded: "Just as physical activity keeps our body strong, mental activity keeps our mind sharp and agile. One way to do this is to continually challenge our self by learning new skills. If we continue to learn and challenge our self, our brain continues to grow, literally." ("Exercise, Estrogen, and Mental Function," 2008).

The **bad news** is that our capacity may not increase at a rate that will equip us to function effectively at the demanding strategic level anytime soon.

The **best news** for executives comes from the field of neuroscience. There is now available visual-spatial processing technology that can ratchet up our brain power—accelerate high-level thinking processes associated with three-dimensional analysis and synthesis. Visual-spatial portable laboratories with advanced programming tools can significantly enhance executive thinking capacity.

What are technology companies (Google, Microsoft, Amazon) and consulting companies (McKinsey, Boston Consulting Group, Accenture) looking for? They want employees with good so-called executive functions: visual-spatial intelligence, three-dimensional problem-solving, cognitive flexibility, planning, working memory, decision making, and emotional self-regulation.

We can build our thinking capacity by using Global Processing Technology.

Global Processing Technology (GPT) is a whole new neuroscience and practice of visual-spatial information processing that stimulates brain receptivity by activating and strengthening our neural pathways needed to build thinking capacity. GPT boosts our (1) visual memory, spatial relations, and visualization; (2) hard science processing; (3) processing speed (perceptual speed); (4) decision/reaction time and speed; and (5) ability to conceptualize, formulate, and decisively execute at higher levels of complexity.

As executives we can now build our thinking capacity as never before with the assistance of enriched, visual-spatial science technology. Over the years, our own practice has evolved from borrowing technology from visual-spatial therapy practices to selectively collecting and inventing best-practices—neuroscience tools that are now time-proven with portability. GPT offers remarkable hope for those struggling to get their mental elevators up to higher floors, where they will have greater capacity to tackle the tougher problems and invent needed changes.

We have found that the very key to crafting programs to sharpen and sustain the ability to think abstractly and analytically—together with skill in visualizing spatial relations in two and three dimensions—is to neutrally **process** the brain with the best visual-spatial cognitive exercises and brain-sharpening tools.

BRIGHT3+4 thinking executives are not born that way. Again, the good news is we can develop and expand our spatial ability. As good as we are at present, we can get smarter and better. It is a process similar to preparing to run our first marathon. Daily conditioning increases our physical stamina and capacity, which in turn increases our mileage until we can run a 26-mile course with relative ease. Likewise, our brain conditioning, through GPT enhancement, will increase our mental capacity and thereby allow us to increase our power to better access information from previous and present experiences that seem relevant to the problem at hand. Our brain will spatially generalize and fill in missing parts from its new capacity to create hyper-connections, make credible assumptions, and be up to fast, approximate solutions. New information will be better incorporated into existing experience and knowledge, allowing us to make quicker assumptions, fill in the particulars, and add sense to a looming situation. As a result, we will make cleaner, smarter, faster decisions—essential for brilliant leadership.

Additionally, we discovered secondary benefits that accrued with our own visual-spatial programming practice:

- *Improves mental acuity*: Better memory, reaction time, and concentration levels

- *Improves confidence*: Better mental strength, stamina, and emotional well-being. This in turn improves self-image and boosts self-confidence.

- *Increases mental energy and endurance*: Visual processing also can make us feel much more awake and energized afterward. We who work out our minds regularly have more energy, strength, and endurance to get through our positional task activities than non-exercisers.

- *Reduces stress, depression, and anxiety*: Diminishes wasteful mental activity. In addition, visual processing boosts mood and promotes relaxation.

And, when we come to know ourselves in a higher, more examined way, we will activate our deeper resources and unique potential to draw from an unlimited *thinking capacity*. We then will live life more richly with greater brilliance and passion to take on our challenges conscientiously.

Finally, think about this:

We Americans need to be shocked by the fact that our long worldwide supremacy is challenged as never before. Without being strong in thinking capacity as a country, we will not continue to advance as in the past. If we are attempting to help ourselves and others deal with home issues and worldwide complexities in production, energy, global warming, peaceful co-existence, etc., then we need to consider a new science that will give our society more bench strength to invent, to innovate, to lead with brilliance, and to positively affect jobs, health, prosperity, and our future.

This new science and practice will produce ultra-smart leadership with the capacity to simultaneously think in verbal height, quantitative width, and spatial depth to help others avoid making poor decisions or otherwise performing mindless actions. They will be mindful of mental traps and limitations and will invest in nourishing their own brainpower, needed to free themselves from the grip of dingy realities at hand and invent what should be happening. They will be able to grasp emergent challenges before they come into being, recognize patterns that are neither spatially contiguous nor logically related, and see around corners to anticipate high-risk and high-impact events. These mindful, **BRIGHT1+2+3+4** leaders will know intuitively where to focus their attention and thus how to seize immense unforeseen opportunities to advance their organizations and the country to a higher place.

CHAPTER SUMMARY
Key Points

- **Life is about how much we think.** *Thinking* is about how much *capacity* we have to process information. *Capacity*, in addition to our abilities and conscientiousness, is about how much we can simultaneously *process* combinations of verbal, quantitative, and *spatial* dimensions with decisiveness, direction, and speed.

- All of us have *remarkable powers to change (plasticity) our own mental combinations (creative connections between ideas) and function through simultaneous processing, thinking, and activity.* Recent neural science research confirms that *plasticity*—the *capacity* to be molded or modeled—exists from the cradle to the grave.

- Our speed in responding to our world is about how many mental *connections* we quickly *process and execute* with insight and brilliance.

- Our current ability to think *need not* be our lot in life. Only in the last decade has there been sufficient research to create a timely neuroscience and Visual Information Processing Technology for developing *our capacity*.

- "Executive Capacity" is the ability to simultaneously think in height, width, and depth, and decisively act. It is the ability to sustain thinking in high levels of verbal (reading and writing, listening and speaking), quantitative (numbers and equations, measurements and graphs), spatial (laboratories and breakthrough inventions and manufacturing), and decisive teaming aptitudes (recognize and scrutinize, visualize and prioritize) needed to speedily execute informed decisions.

- The most current research concurs that *capacity*, made of quantitative, verbal, *and spatial ability,* is the best composite predictor of occupational level attainment and performance within one's chosen occupation and predicts better than any other ability, trait, or personality disposition—and better than job experience. Spatial ability alone is the single best predictor of group membership in a profession. Spatial ability is linked to creativity, can be developed, and provides unlimited vocational options.

• *Visual-spatial ability* is intimately connected to our emotional intelligence and rational intelligence and occupies almost half of our brain's cortex. If percentage of cortex is any measure, then visual-spatial "intelligence" is a major facet of who we are as people, and its understanding is a key to what we might become as executives.

• The composite of BRIGHT1+2+3+4 powers is an executive's *capacity*, which can penetrate a problem from multiple perspectives.

• Without mental *capacity*, we would not advance. Everything associated with progress comes from ideas, and the best ideas come from people using the proper tools and processes. No matter where they happen, new ideas and the waves they create will affect our jobs, health, prosperity, the world.

• *Global Processing Technology* (GPT) is a whole new neuroscience and practice of visual-spatial information processing that stimulates brain receptivity by activating and strengthening the neural pathways needed to build three- and four-dimensional thinking capacity. There is a whole new science to explore!

CHAPTER 2

Visual-Spatial Capacity
Seeing Brilliantly

> *The soul never thinks without a picture.*
>
> Aristotle, 384–322 B.C.E.
>
> *Here is the world of imagination, hopes, and dreams. In this timeless land of enchantment, the age of chivalry, magic, and make-believe are reborn and fairy tales as rewritten by talented writers come true. Fantasyland is dedicated to the young-in-heart—to those who believe that "when you wish upon a star, your dreams come true."*
>
> Walt Disney

Fantasyland, cleverly hidden behind Sleeping Beauty's Castle was, out of the five Disneyland lands, the one most important to Walt Disney himself. Walt's flare for spatial wonderment was played out here at what was once the core of the Magic Kingdom experience. The height of Sleeping Beauty's castle is only 180 feet above the moat but looks taller through a forced perspective where things are actually smaller as they are higher – thus making them look even further away. Behind the castle guests enter into a fairytale world were dreams were dreamed, ideas were spun out without restrictions, story boards were crafted to create make believe structures, characters and events all seem real. "I can never stand still. I must explore and experiment. I am never satisfied with my work. I resent the limitations of my own imagination." - Walt Disney

Three and half summers during college years, I (Graham) worked as a supervisor in Disneyland's Fantasyland. Nightly, the music from the Disney movie *Pinocchio* was repetitively piped out from the castle:

"When you wish upon a star"

After I'd spent several weeks in Fantasyland, a guest asked me, "What is the title and words of the music coming from the Castle?"

My response: "What music?" Being a psychology major, I realized that "auditory adaptation" had had its effect on me over time. I no longer could differentiate background sounds from what I was overwhelmingly attending to—the needs and expectations of our guests and "on-stage" cast members. I was *spatially* selective and missed so much of the "hidden magic" in the hidden spaces around me.

As readers, we expect the lyrics above to say, *"When you wish upon a star"* because we've heard this phrase before. Most of us will not see that there are two *a's* in the sentence. We see the sentence according to our expectations, not based on what is in front of us. As a consequence, **we don't** *see* **a lot of the** *space* **around us and thereby limit our** *capacity* **for greater brilliance.**

I and other employees were privileged to be instructed by Walt Disney himself and I will forever cherish examples of his spatial thinking:

"Fantasy and reality often overlap."

"Animation can explain whatever the mind of man can conceive."

"I don't want the public to **see** the world they live in while they're in Disneyland. I want them to feel they're in another world."

"Disneyland will never be completed. It will continue to grow as long as there is imagination left in the world."

"Imagination stimulates creativity."

"I always like to look on the optimistic side of life, but I am realistic enough to know that life is a complex matter."

"Mickey Mouse popped out of my mind onto a drawing pad 20 years ago on a train ride from Manhattan to Hollywood at a time when the business fortunes of my brother Roy and myself were at lowest ebb and disaster seemed right around the corner."

Walt had an extraordinary capacity to process spatially in dimensions of height, width, and depth simultaneously with keen insight, decisiveness, and direction. He had brilliant three-dimensional sight, while his brother Roy was gifted with numbers and budgets (BRIGHT2). Walt Disney was gifted with the ability to visualize the world with great accuracy (BRIGHT3+4). He was able to think in two- and three-dimensional terms and could re-create an idea into a working visual model or cartoon character that he was able to adapt and modify prior to any physical construction in the Disney industry. Walt had an amazing ability to create a mental map of a new creation/territory—providing a strong sense of spatial awareness for where he was positioned in relation to the world around him.

Walt's greatest spatial rejoinder was: "I only hope that we don't lose sight of one thing—that it was all started by a mouse." His picture thinking was a real phenomenon. He had the *capacity* to truly think spatially; come up with novel ideas using pictures to the exclusion of linear thinking language; find or create new opportunities, new endeavors, new adventures; and maintain a humble, down-to-earth, personal style that set an overall organizational tone of competence, optimism, integrity, and inspiration.

The ability to re-create our own visual experience is a gift to be acquired.

Visual-spatial intelligence is defined by Gardner (1984) as the ability to perceive the visual world accurately, to perform transformations and modifications upon one's initial perceptions, and to be able to re-create aspects of one's visual experience, even in the absence of relevant physical stimuli.

The following skills represent the core abilities of individuals with visual-spatial ability:

- Spatial Awareness: The ability to solve problems involving spatial orientations and moving objects through space, such as finding one's way around, or maneuvering a car.

- Working with objects: The ability to use strategic eye-hand coordination to construct, arrange, decorate, or fix things.

- Artistic Design: The ability to carry out tasks or projects that require aestheticism, judgment, and design.

One of the advantages that visual-spatial capacity has over time is that with distance, we can actually see and traverse the space to the horizon and know that the telephone pole on the horizon is not of miniature size. Because this is subject to our experience and thinking, we have learned to compensate for it. Effective spatial thinking regarding depth is when the imagination, as with Walt Disney's *Fantasia* or James Cameron's 3-D *Avatar*, paints distant objects so large in our consciousness that they seem to us even more important than those that are closer. Figuratively, this can mean that distant goals take on greater importance than short-term goals. Our imagination is capable of running ahead and focusing light on the future so that it stands out like a beacon to brighten our way. The capacity for visual-spatial processing means the capacity for greater light. The more light we can get on the objectives, the better we see.

We don't see enough, clearly enough, or soon enough.

We all have the capacity to desire and acquire more light, greater vision, and deeper thought. Visual-spatial capacity may be the thing we need more than anything else in leadership. We need the ability to see, we need understanding, and we need appreciation for sight and clarity.

We should view *capacity* as a core resource for our survival—an innate mental reservoir to be developed by education, enhanced by experience, and applied within almost every conceivable context.

Simply put, it's about *our potential for processing "light" and our reaction speed with that light.*

Much of our brain capacity is devoted to visual processing, and half of our cortex is involved with sight. In addition, when visual inputs conflict with clues from other senses, our vision tends to dominate. And, the sensory areas of our brain are not the passive recipients of signals from our sense organs. Instead we should think of them as being in a state of dynamic equilibrium with the outside world, an equilibrium that is constantly in response to the changing environment. Most of us don't see far enough, clearly enough, or soon enough.

To demonstrate: We can stand in the middle of an open doorway and use our arms to apply outward pressure on the two sides as if we were pushing them away from our body. After about 40 seconds, we suddenly let them go and relax, stand normally and just let our arms hang by our sides. If we are like most people, our arms will involuntarily rise up as if pulled by two invisible helium balloons. The reason? When we apply continuous outward force, our brain gets used to this as the "neutral state"—so that when the pressure suddenly disappears, our arms drift outward.

Spatial ability is essentially the ability to think on the fringe, as Albert Einstein did. It is the ability to see outcomes not only from a sequential step-by-step standpoint, but also from a multidimensional, simultaneous viewpoint.

Spatial ability has come of age in the research literature and within the perplexing changes since 9/11. In many challenging marketplaces, the *capacity* to think, collaborate, and innovate gives leaders and organizations their bench strength—the advantage that differentiates them from their competitors. We believe that for organizations and nations to remain in a continuous state of innovation, a perpetual free flow of ideas is necessary. Developing BRIGHT3+4 executives will unleash a wealth of talent to effectively process new ideas.

From the Spatial Realms of Polynesian Voyagers to Modern Executive Navigators

As we move closer toward being an "enlightened" rather than an "enactive" learning society, the opportunity and necessity for practice in the spatial realm—like mental imaging and multiple viewpoints—has been minimized. Our multidimensional viewpoints can be communicated in built space and real time, where spatial behavior is manipulated as a form of visual-spatial thinking and non-verbal communication. Navigation for earlier peoples without navigational instruments, like Polynesian voyagers, was possible because they learned to read the position of stars, the color of the water, migratory birds, and various weather patterns. As their journey progressed, navigators had to envision the position of islands as they sailed, mapping their locations in a mental picture of the journey.

Howard Gardner, a psychologist at Harvard University, is a strong supporter of visual-spatial ability and its relationship to other intelligences and cognition. Gardner initiated a new way of thinking about intelligence and began an educational revolution when he published in 1993 *Multiple Intelligences,* in which he identified seven different types of intelligence that are relatively autonomous and vary in individuals. Gardner determined that each individual has multiple faculties that are to a significant degree independent of each other, and that are manifested as a collection of aptitudes in which the total is greater than the sum of the parts. He states that spatial ability and spatial cognition are the basic building blocks that an individual needs in order to develop higher-level thinking skills, specifically those that complement verbal processing skills.

What Gardner called spatial *intelligence*, we call visual-spatial ability. We believe that it is more likely that visual-spatial intelligence derives from the concomitant workings of several intelligences, including an eighth one that we have identified as our BRIGHT3+4 powers—spatial depth and global processing intelligence. We also believe that an executive's ability to pull together parts into meaningful, unified, whole images of the way things work is vital to their higher-level perception and abstract thinking. Our BRIGHT3+4 powers have the capacity to divine meaning out of the complex—the separate and disparate elements. High levels of abstract reasoning work the same way perception (information processing) works. Abstract reasoning reflects a holistic logic that has its grounding in perceptual/informational processing and reaches out into new creative domains. More than a single dimension, visual-spatial intelligence is a totality for seeing the world and embraces all four of our BRIGHT powers.

An executive with strengths in verbal, quantitative, and spatial ability sustaining multi-dimensional viewpoints has a huge competitive advantage in the business world. We know that graduates with degrees in physics, chemistry, and engineering have demonstrated excellent spatial ability. We also know that many famous business executives, including Lee Iacocca, Bill Hewlett, David Packard, Andrew Grove, and Jack Welch, had science and engineering backgrounds that required spatial ability. Clearly, spatial ability is the engine that drives the creativity and innovation motorcade escorting US companies.

Visual-spatial capacity refers to our mental ability to represent the outer world internally in our mind. It's the ability to hold the world visually in our minds the way a sailor or pilot navigates the large spatial world, or the way a chess player or sculptor represents a more circumscribed spatial world. It gives us the capacity to know where we are in space. If we find it easy to visualize things as though we were an observer taking up different positions, like a fly on the wall, then we are strong in this ability.

Visual-spatial thinking is a group of visual-spatial processing strengths that, when practiced with rigorous discipline, results in the production of fresh and original graphic ideas needed for high-level thinking construction, direction, and velocity. High visual-spatial thinking capacity is usually found in pilots, chess players, painters, architects, sculptors, chemists, theoretical physicists, war strategists, navigators, illusionists, fiction writers, graphic artists, designers, cartographers, and film makers. Some famous examples include: Pablo Picasso, Leonardo da Vinci, Thomas Edison, Henry Ford, Frank Lloyd Wright, Steven Spielberg, J.K. Rowling, James Cameron, and some great football quarterbacks and extraordinary architects, engineers, carpenters, and executives.

Disney's Submarine Voyage: A visual-spatial thinking "skipper" saves his crew.

Disneyland's Submarine Voyage in Tomorrow Land was inspired by the US Navy's nuclear submarines of the 1950s and the Disney film *20,000 Leagues under the Sea*. US Navy officers attended the ceremonies June 6, 1959, and rode the 52-foot-long submarines to compare them with the real thing. The ride was designed to take about 1,400 people an hour on an eight-minute journey into "liquid space." Halfway submerged, the fleet lumbers around a lagoon filled with 9 million gallons of water and decorated with plastic plants.

Some of us who were seasonally employed at Disneyland in the early 1960s knew of a potential disaster (a possible worst-case scenario) on the submarine ride. One of the eight subs was just launched from the loading dock with 56 guests on board when an undetected defect played out. On the aft starboard side, a porthole was cracked and under water pressure imploded, and the sub began taking in water. Air bubbles were detected from the dock and a crisis response team enlisted. Because these subs didn't have emergency hatch releases for evacuation, no outside intervention was possible. The sub had to run the balance of its six and half minutes of programmed track, and onlookers could only pray that none of the 56 guests or the skipper would panic, be injured, or drown in the malaise.

Inside the sub, a young adolescent boy seated in the damaged rear quickly ran fore and alerted our Disneyland "skipper"—a 21-year-old university physics major—of the water gushing in. At that moment, most of the guests were fixed looking out portholes at the adventures under the sea, but a few became aware that their feet were getting wet from water gushing down the aisle. The skipper quickly surveyed the situation and broke from his standardize spiel. Grabbing his microphone he bellowed out: "Now hear this; Now hear this … Code Red, Code Red. We have just been hit by an enemy torpedo … sustaining damage on our aft, starboard side and taking in water.

Prepare for battle! Man your porthole stations—we are going after the enemy. Each of you will need to fix your eyes on anything moving and anybody trying to board our vessel."

Our skipper then performed a dramatic and thrilling five-minute monologue of high adventure, energy, and visual imagery that including launching four torpedoes, taking out the enemy, and keeping everyone totally enlisted and entertained. There were no screams of panic but cheers of "Victory at sea!" as the water rose to waist levels. "I am so proud of this crew … you folks are the best! Please hold your children up … we are momentarily docking and going in for repairs … This is the finest crew I have ever had."

When the sub hit the dock, the hatch tripped its release with 56 guests coming out looking like drowned rats from the necks down and flashing wide smiles from the necks up. Disney wardrobe people were there with towels to transport and put these guests into dry Disney uniforms and had their cloths laundered and pressed by the end of the day.

There were no complaints or legal suits, only complements about our skipper, who took their minds and imaginations into another realm of space. Within a week, letters were received expressing thanks and appreciation to the Disney personnel for their expertise. One lady from that ride wrote from Gary, Indiana, "I have told everyone here in Gary to go to Disneyland and take the submarine ride. I realize that the 'sea battle' doesn't happen every day, so I have expressed hope to my friends that they are on the ride when they do it. Thank you all for the best ride of my life."

Over the years, when we have asked our strong visual-spatial executives to describe their world of tackling problems, they usually begin with pictures in their mind of what they are trying to communicate, and then use visual words and metaphors to get across what they saw. By doing this, they are connecting with their own visual models—and helping others make their own visual models for their ideas. Given that our brains process ideas quickly, this translates into our people visually processing faster—as our Disneyland submarine skipper did.

Inventiveness consists of seeing what everybody has seen, and thinking what few people or nobody has thought.

Harry Potter and the Deathly Hallows, the seventh and final Harry Potter book by J.K. Rowling, sold 11.5 million copies in the USA during its first ten days on sale in July 2007, and was subsequently selected as the international book of the year. Rowling gave her Harry Potter story an ending that was as graceful, unpredictable, and satisfying as the series itself. Rowling's visual-spatial capacity through fictional awareness and imagery exemplifies the highest form of visual-spatial ability, using unique description, metaphor, and organic form. A voracious reader growing up with an active, creative imagination, she expressed herself through innovative writing, rose above her humble condition as a single parent in Edinburgh, Scotland, and left her imprint on the world of literature as very few have in history. At her 2008 commencement speech at Harvard University, she urged the graduates to speak out on behalf of the powerless:

> We do not need magic to transform our world. We carry all the power [capacity] we need inside ourselves already. We have the power to imagine better. Imagination is the fount of all invention and innovation ... If you want to see the true measure of a man, watch how he treats his inferiors, not his equals.

Visual-spatial capacity relies on the sense of sight and being able to visualize people, objects, and imagery. It is the ability to understand spatial relationships and to perceive and create images like wizards and pictures (visual art, graphic design, charts, maps, etc.). It is activated by presenting the mind with and/or creating unusual, delightful, and colorful designs, patterns, shapes, and pictures, and engaging in active imagination through visualization, guided imagery, and pretending activities. Furthermore, we who are strong in spatial capacity can better recognize relationships between objects and manipulate images.

Outstanding quarterbacks are outstanding at visual-spatial thinking.

Acknowledged as the thinking man's quarterback during his brilliant 14-year NFL career with the Miami Dolphins (1967–1980), Bob Griese, the 1971 player of the year, was renowned for his poised leadership and ingenious play-calling during the Dolphins' dominance of the NFL in the early 1970s. He used the pass only sparingly. But when the defense clogged up the Miami runners, Bob quickly and efficiently opened things up spatially with his accurate aerials. Griese helped lead Miami to a perfect 17–0 record in the 1972 season, when the Dolphins won their first Super Bowl title, and the following year, led Miami to a second consecutive Super Bowl championship. Bob Griese was inducted into the Pro Football Hall of Fame in 1990, and subsequently became one of network television's most respected football analysts, especially as the expert commentator on the main game of the week during coverage of College Football for over 11 years.

What makes an effective, thinking quarterback? "First, we need to be quicker in reaction time and more spatially coordinated than everyone else," Griese says. He counsels:

> Try playing basketball and handball on a regular basis, and we will get into fantastic shape. Second, we want to be fresh in the fourth quarter when everyone else is exhausted. Third, we must be able to read the defense and know what type of coverage our opponent is going to run against us. How many zones? What type of man coverage? What type of blitz? Study the corner back, look to see if he is eying the receiver or quarterback. If he is eyeing the receiver, he is in some type of man coverage. If he is eyeing the quarterback, he is in zone coverage. If he is lined up outside the receiver, he is in zone coverage. If he is lined up inside the receiver, he is in man coverage. If he is lined up in a low focus position, he is in man coverage. If he is standing tall, he is in zone coverage. And, if he is lined inside and looking into the line of scrimmage, he is coming on some kind of stunt.

Make sure we have someone pick him up or he is going to hand us our head (Griese, 2000).

A consistent running game follows many of the same spatial principles as a successful passing game. It's important to field the right personnel, capitalize on mismatches, counter defensive alignments, and execute the play properly. The final element of the run play comes from our skill with agility moves. The spin move is one of the most lethal and important for gaining even a few extra yards. If we're approaching a single defender, perform a spin move to the outside just as the defender reaches our position. At worst, we'll gain a few extra yards; at best, we've dodged the defender and are now in the open field with nothing but field in front of us. Jukes and stiff arms are also excellent for dodging or breaking tackles and gaining a few extra yards. All this is part of the complexity of the three-dimensional football game.

As the play develops, good quarterbacks *see* and gauge where blocking is holding up as well as where free defenders are moving. If blocking is holding up inside and free defenders are to the outside, turn up field with your quarterback. If blocking is weaker inside and defenders are charging the quarterback, pitch to the running back and turn him up field along the sideline. You can pitch the ball even after crossing the line of scrimmage. Do so carefully, however; don't pitch just because you're about to be tackled. A gain of five to six yards is a solid play, and a few extra yards isn't worth the fumble risk.

Whole-to-part relationships, as in football, are needed to construct and deconstruct complex objects, developing an understanding at both the micro and macro levels. Visualization is the ability to construct, manipulate, and interpret images in the mind. Creative problem solving is the external manifestation of all of the above activities coupled with reason. That's what an excellent quarterback is all about.

Don't play with an old playbook.

The brain is constantly trying to automate processes, thereby dispelling them from consciousness; in this way, its work will be completed faster, more effectively and at a lower metabolic level.

Consciousness, on the other hand, is slow, subject to error, and expensive. (Roth, 2004)

The normal thing to do is the thing we have always done. Every time we approach a problem in the workplace or life we bring our old playbook—accumulated experience, knowledge, and training—to bear on it. But this includes our accumulated assumptions, inferences, and biases, conscious and unconscious. Any piece of information that comes along, whether it's a new face, a new way of thinking about ourselves, or a new business idea, gets fundamentally the same treatment when it comes into our brains. It doesn't matter whether the data is in the form of a sound ("When you wish upon a star"), a smell, a taste, a form, or a texture, the process is that the new data is compared to our existing visual-mental models, to see where the connections are. We then attempt to accommodate the data into our existing mental models. If any data doesn't quite fit, we try harder to make the connections fit. The more experienced and expert we are, the more likely we are to assume outcomes by extrapolating from the known facts and experiences to predict a result. Our old mental models can limit us from seeing clearly the new opportunity.

Often the way we frame a problem contains an embedded assumption that prevents us from solving it. In the Middle Ages, the definition of astronomy was the study of how the heavenly bodies move around the Earth (i.e., the Earth was considered to be the center of the universe). This resulted in a chain of wrong explanations of various phenomena. Similar ideas exist in most businesses—inferences that underpin most strategies and decisions, and that are so fundamental that they are never challenged. The downside is—our brain is already hardwired for the most part.

- Changing the way we think is one of our tougher challenges; we tend to defend, and fight hard to hold onto, our view of the world.

- When external realities change, our internal realities often don't change as quickly.

- Our visual-mental models may be antiquated.

- Given that our visual models are all so different, any group of people will see the same situation from substantially different perspectives.

The fact that our mental hardwiring drives our perception, thinking, and feeling, and informs our behaviors, has far-reaching implications. Our brain truly sees the world according to its own wiring. For two of us to really connect/communicate, the picture must be the same.

Language and verbal thinking are basically the essence of being educated in America. What is the cost that we pay for this focus? Part of the cost is that once we have language, we are inclined to categorize and give a name to everything. This means that we ignore everything that doesn't fit in our categorization, being de facto blind and deaf to many stimuli coming from reality. Certainly we lose the capacity to remember those vivid images called eidetic, that have great realism. The "images" or "pictures" that we remember are often only verbal categorizations.

Once we learn verbal language, we start ruminating with it, and quickly learn verbal thinking. Probably before language, our "thinking" is made only by images. But after we learn language, it's as if an inner voice starts speaking in our brain and continues throughout life, speaking about every experience we have and every aspect of reality. We translate almost everything into words, giving a name to everything. We prefer words to pictures because it is easier to control words than it is to control pictures. Verbal thinking functions in connection with visual thinking to become our programming language—it helps us run movies in our brain. This is something impossible for an animal. When my (Graham's) Siamese cat sees my daughter going toward the refrigerator, she gets excited and most likely is "seeing" the open refrigerator full of food. I, with my spoken language ability, can start anytime and anywhere a "movie" and see myself opening the refrigerator and taking out the cat food. To run this mental movie far away from the refrigerator, my language is essential. Visual thinking, however, has a feature that makes it superior to verbal thinking: it can be easily understood by people with different languages and cultures.

To see is to process; to process is to make whatever we are sensing or thinking fit into our existing visual models.

Thinking, in order to have something to think about, must be based on images of the world in which we live. As I write this, I (Graham) am looking out my second-story window at the Pacific Ocean less than a thousand yards away. I see lots of rough wave action and begin to visualize if it will be a safe condition for kayaking within the hour. I determine whether I will go out in heavy, turbulent waters with my narrow kayak and paddle around scary Laie Point and then paddle a mile out to Goat Island. I visualize capsizing, smashing against a reef, and becoming shark bait. Then I begin thinking about my commitment to Kevin Baize, my family, and to finishing this book. I decide to forego any extreme-sport kayaking.

Without gathering and processing visual information on what is going on in real time and space, our brain cannot work. It is as simple as that. ***To see is to process. To process is to make whatever we are sensing or thinking fit into our existing visual models.*** And thus, we feel more comfortable surrounded by order; we feel better inside symmetry, where we can see how everything is connected.

The human brain is able to continually adapt and rewire itself into new playbooks (visual models). Multitasking is a good example. Our brain's neural playbook is not initially designed to perform two different tasks at the same time and with the same level of efficiency. But it can, with new informational processing. The modern military has witnessed young recruits who have come to the service with considerable experience playing video play games that require a lot of eye-hand coordination and plasticity. They are so good at this that they have been able to outperform someone who is of a higher rank and with longer military experience.

The dictionary defines "plastic" as the capacity to be molded or modeled. The word "neural" refers to nerve cells. Our brain contains more than 100 billion nerve cells. The ability of the brain to change in structure and in function—like plastic—throughout our life is known as brain plasticity. Neuroscience is now affirming that an enriched environment can stimulate nerve cell development, resulting in increased brain size and weight.

The work of Marian Diamond and Michael Merzenich, along with other researchers, has demonstrated that the capacity of the brain is guided by a "use it or lose it" principle. When we use neural pathways, they become reinforced and strengthened—larger neurons, with more dendrites and glial cells. When we don't use a neural pathway, that pathway is subject to atrophy. There is a competitive plasticity constantly going on for any given area of our brain.

> Let's say we manage a bank. Our top marketing person comes to us with an idea to redesign the service areas of the bank. He says, "We want the bank to be less formal—hipper and more inviting to our young professional customers." **Quick: How do we envision the new space?** *What do the light fixtures look like? What color are the walls?*
>
> *Our mind is probably a blank. Perhaps that's what people seek when they recommend an outside-the-box, "blank slate" approach. But the blank is not helping us create a less formal lobby. After all, our team might sit at the conference-room table and nod vigorously that the goal is to be "more inviting to young professionals," but secretly, the team members are envisioning success differently. Jon imagines Alicia Keys's music piped into the lobby, Brenda ponders adding a playroom for young children, and Sonny thinks all the customers would be happier if the clerks would just smile more ("We should develop a smiling policy").*
>
> *What if our marketing person had said this instead: "We want the space to be more like a Starbucks and less like a post office." Suddenly, it's easier to picture (***see***) the goal (and to answer the light-fixture and color questions). Notice, though, that the Starbucks vision is constraining. It takes options off the table. The Starbucks vision is judgmental—it says yes to Alicia Keys and no to the playroom. It's helpful—it constrains freedom, yes,*

but it also dramatically improves the chances that our team will hit the target. (Heath, 2007)

Imagine that the US Department of Transportation has found that a particular Japanese car is seven times more likely than a typical family car to kill occupants of another car in a crash. The US government is considering restricting sale and use of this Japanese automobile.

ANSWER THE FOLLOWING TWO QUESTIONS:

Do you think sales of the Japanese car should be banned in the United States?

Do you think the Japanese car should be banned from being driving on American streets?

Perceptually, this thought problem can be spatially presented in a different way: The Department of Transportation found an increased risk of fatalities, not in a Japanese car but in an American one.

What's happening in our head? It could be more.

Regretfully, because most leaders don't read and exercise their thinking much, brilliant leaders are rather uncommon. The fact is that putting our brains to work around tough issues makes us apprehensive. Many of us avoid complexity and ambiguity and seek out the comfort of simplicity and certainty. We desire the confidence of choosing between well-defined alternatives and the closure that comes when a decision is made easy.

For more than three decades, Dr. Michael Merzenich has been a leading pioneer in brain plasticity research. Dr. Merzenich found that in the process of thinking anew and learning a new skill, the brain responded by using many neurons at first to perform a given new activity. Eventually the brain would become more efficient and use fewer neurons to do the exact same activity. In addition, he found that the neurons involved in the activity would increase in speed and clarity and in their ability to work with other neurons as a direct response to the learning process.

Dr. Merzenich used his brain research to develop specific training programs aimed at improving language-impaired subjects. He found that lasting changes (long term plastic changes in the brain) occurred with intense training experiences that required the subject to pay very close attention to the activity. He discovered that long-term plastic changes were occurring after 50–70 hours of this intensive training. The goal of this focused attention is to model the learning experience of a young infant. Young children are like sponges, absorbing the surroundings of their environment with unparalleled attention. In contrast, Dr. Merzenich found that passive and observational experience did not create long-term plastic changes in children.

What can we do to actively promote mental acuity?

According to Dr. Merzenich, we must continue to learn in our lives. We must be active learners. This can be achieved in a variety of ways. One major problem is that most of us understand that we need to be active, but we think that being active means getting up every day.

Dr. Merzenich also states that we can be active learners by learning in new forms and in new domains. It's not just being active and getting up every day and going through the motions. Our brain is a learning machine, and it needs to be engaged in new learning of different dimensions. The best kinds of exercise are those that challenge us. For example, to master a musical instrument at an older age is a wonderful thing. Or seriously undertaking the mastery of a second language is a wonderful thing to do. One of the problems with such exercises is that it's very hard to maintain the skills and abilities necessary to continue a mental fitness program.

Our brain can indeed be retrained to process verbal information faster, more clearly, and with greater power. Intense sensory retraining experiences can improve virtually every aspect of our verbal learning process. Serendipitously, Dr. Merzenich found that not only did speech, language, and auditory processing improve, but also IQ.

Morris A. Graham, PhD and Kevin Baize, OD

Visual abstract thinking is high-level critical thinking conducted by imagery.

Some years ago an essayist, John A. Kouwenhoven, wrote a book called *What is American about America?* He asked himself what the following had in common: the Manhattan skyline, the gridiron town plan, the skyscraper, the Model T Ford, jazz, the Constitution, Mark Twain's writing, Whitman's *Leaves of Grass*, comic strips, soap operas, assembly-line production, and chewing gum. In his personality profile of our country, each feature of our country was considered a legitimate *abstraction* ("the land of Mark Twain," "the land of skyscrapers") but together they are a jumble of information until they are welded into some macro unifying feature. This was accomplished by further *levels of visual abstraction*, which brought a trait common to all 12 micro features, namely "a concern with *process* rather than product." If this diagnosis is valid, the *abstraction* has yielded an enlightening concept by revealing something important about the thing *abstracted*.

> *Boutique hotelier Chip Conley has used visual abstraction ingeniously in creating his antique properties. He told his team: Let's bring magazines to life. His company, Joie de Vivre Hospitality, designed the Hotel Vitale in San Francisco to be "Real Simple meets Dwell." That's a crystal-clear box. And it makes it easy for his team to brainstorm features of the new hotel. The architects elevated the yoga studio to a prime top-floor location, rather than tossing some token yoga mats next to the elliptical machines in the gym. The front-desk clerks waged war on clutter: Imagine a countertop with no pen cups or frequent-stay rewards-club brochures. The house-keepers don't just clean the rooms, they organize them. Other Conley hotels feature a Rolling Stone theme or a New Yorker theme. We can all be grateful that he hasn't yet unveiled the Economist hotel, where staffers continually remind us of our ignorance of foreign affairs.*
>
> *As we've seen, a well-constructed box can help people generate new ideas. Imagine if, as in the case of the Hotel Vitale team,*

you could flip through hundreds of pages of Real Simple magazine for strategic inspiration. Research tells us that brainstorming becomes more productive when it's focused. As jazz great Charles Mingus famously said, "You can't improvise on nothing, man; you've gotta improvise on something." (Heath, 2007, pp. 74–77)

Begin first with mental pictures—then use visual words, ideas, and metaphors to get across what we see.

It was Aristotle who said, "The soul never thinks without a mental picture." The thought elements in our perception and the perceptual elements in our thoughts are symbiotic. They make our thinking a seamless *process* that leads without break from the simple acquisition of sensory information (mental pictures) to the most generic high-level words, ideas, metaphors, and memory. The indispensable trait of our *thinking process* is that at every level it involves *abstraction*. Coming to an informed generalization on anything should not simply be a matter of collecting an infinite or big or complete or random number of instances. Instead, we should approach the task with a groundwork notion of what the concept might be like. Then we look for examples. We are channeled by a sense of where characteristic aspects of the phenomenon might reveal themselves. We discard weak, unclear instances and negative unnecessary repetitions. We match each example with the tentative concept, thereby completing, rectifying, and rimming it. It is this gradual shaping of abstraction that we mentally process as a sorting apparatus with the alertness and intelligence of a functional mind to an articulate tongue.

Visual-spatial thinking is a process of idea-finding, synthesis, and formulation.

Our sequential system involves analysis, progression from simple to complex, grouping of information, and linear deductive reasoning. It is influenced by hearing and language and an awareness of time. In contrast, spatial thinking involves synthesis, an intuitive grasp of complex systems, (often missing the steps), simultaneous processing of concepts, inductive reasoning (from the whole to the parts), use of imagination and generation of ideas by combining existing facts in new ways (creative thinking). It is influenced by visualization and images and an awareness of space.

Thinking in the visual-spatial is a process of idea-finding and formulation that uses pictures, colors, abstract plans, diagrams, etc.—where the accumulation of ideas influences the whole. Visual-spatial thinking is a close cousin to brainstorming and *improvisation*. By seeking to discover visual forms that fit our underlying human experience, through our visual thinking we come to know our world.

> *Keith Sawyer, author of the insightful book* Group Genius, *spent years studying the work of jazz groups and improvisational theater ensembles. He found that structure doesn't hamper creativity; it enables it. When improv comedians take the stage, they need a concrete stimulus: "What if Romeo had been gay?" The stimulus can't be, "Go on, make me laugh, funnyman."*
>
> *"Improv actors are taught to be specific," Sawyer says. "Rather than say, 'Look out, it's a gun!' you should say, 'Look out, it's a new ZX-23 laser kill device.' Instead of asking, 'What's your problem?' say, 'Don't tell me you're still pissed off about the time I dropped your necklace in the toilet.' The paradox is that while specificity narrows the number of paths that the improv could take, it makes it easier for the other actors to come up with the next riff."*
>
> *So don't think out of the box. Go box shopping. Keep trying on one after another until you find the one that catalyzes your thinking. A good box is like a lane marker on the highway. It's a constraint that liberates.* (Heath, 2007, pp. 74–77)

Visual abstract thinking is high-level critical thinking manipulated by imagery. Visual thinking executives can come to conclusions in an intuitive way—as through *improvisation*, without reasoning with language. Instead, they manipulate with visual symbols to form answers to problems. We have found that professionals in science, technology, engineering, and mathematics who are strong in visual thinking and find themselves in executive positions have unique leadership development needs not fully appreciated in mainstream businesses. They usually are long overdue for leadership skills-building and training in basic business acumen.

In Search of Visual-Spatial Talent

Why do graduate business schools not assess the spatial ability of their applicants who take the Graduate Management Assessment Test (GMAT)? Perhaps conspiracy theory is alive and well. *Spatial ability is the engine that drives the creativity and innovation motorcade escorting US companies.* Chief executive officers need global ability to compete in a global economy. To be more competitive globally, US executives must think more globally. The CEO of the new century needs verbal, quantitative, *and* spatial ability.

Students with spatial strengths and verbal deficiencies rarely have the opportunity to demonstrate their gifts in American high schools or go on to become a J.K. Rowling. Many of the tests used to identify gifted students or judge achievement in students value performance speed over the careful and reflective thinking that is characteristic of learners with spatial strengths (Gallagher & Johnson, 1992). For example, college admission tests (such as the Scholastic Aptitude Test [SAT] and the Graduate Record Exam [GRE]) are traditionally used to determine entrance to undergraduate and graduate programs but do not assess spatial ability (Gohm, Humphreys, & Yao, 1998).

The emphasis on mathematical and verbal abilities on college admissions tests and other high-stakes testing may cause high school personnel to emphasize these areas when teaching and advising students. As a result, individuals identified as having spatial gifts or talents are disproportionately undereducated and underemployed relative to their ability levels when compared with equally gifted individuals with strengths in mathematical and verbal areas (Gohm et al., 1998). Individuals with high spatial abilities are more likely to drop out of school, are working in larger proportions in traditional blue-collar occupations, and hold a smaller proportion of credentials at every educational level beyond high school (Gohm et al., 1998; Humphreys, Lubinski, & Yao, 1993). The underemployment and under-education of gifted students with spatial strengths is of concern because they are ideal candidates to become America's future executives, engineers, scientists, and innovators. Our current system would never identify Thomas Edison or Henry Ford (See postscript for a detailed discussion).

The Ability to Comprehend and Communicate about Visual-Spatial Properties

Fast Company reported that executives at Home Depot were surprised by the fire-safety statistics: Fewer than half of US households have a fire extinguisher, and the majority of people who have one can't remember where they store it. Home Depot executives realized that people hide their fire extinguishers from view because they look terrible. Orange Works, a new visual design lab set up by Home Depot and the Arnell Group, a self-described "invention" firm visually processed the problem: "The design challenge was to create a kitchen fire extinguisher that people would proudly keep on their countertops." The solution, the "Home Hero," which looks aesthetically like an upright iPod. Once the Home Hero's pin is pulled, you just press a simple switch to trigger the foam (McKeough, 2007).

Visual-spatial ability is not simply a visual process of instantly inventing a home fire extinguisher; it is a multifaceted, multi-perceptual sequence of events. Wiley (1990), though focusing primarily on the visual component, has developed a relatively broad model of spatial cognition. He has developed a "Hierarchy of Visual Learning" model, that provides a structural framework for how one learns through the process of "visual cognition, visual production, and visual resolve." These stages are dependent upon one another, and represent one's ability to mentally comprehend, store, retrieve, create, edit, and communicate spatial information.

In essence, what Wiley describes is one's ability to comprehend and communicate spatial properties. Our research gives attention to the highest level (e.g., visualization). Particular emphasis is placed on visualization, as it is at this stage that an individual must mentally manipulate images. Performance (externalization, transmission, reception, and resolution) is a result of the individual's ability to successfully complete the visual-spatial processes.

Visualization and imagery is the "inner landscape of our perceptions."

> *Perception is strong and sight weak ... In strategy it is important to see distant things as if they were close and close things as if they were distant.*

Miyamoto Musashi, legendary Japanese swordsman 1584–1645

Visualization has been described as the "inner landscape of our perceptions." (Samuels & Samuels, 1975). It is the personal process of internally perceiving the essence of an object, person, concept, or process (Kosslyn, 1983). With regard to cognition, establishing a base understanding, or essential knowledge, allows the individual a firm platform from which to explore permutations of that knowledge.

Visualization is a more complex version of simple imagery. Imagery consists of those mental images that are produced by memory or imagination (Samuels & Samuels, 1975). Visualization takes these mental images and adds an affective, almost visceral component, making the image stronger and potentially more meaningful. In other words, the process of visualization has the ability to generate physiological and emotional responses similar to that which we experience during "real-time" perceptions (i.e., those that are occurring as we are experiencing them), as opposed to those that we reconstruct in our minds. For example, the fear that we feel while having a nightmare is just as real as the fear we might experience if what we were dreaming were actually happening to us.

Visualization is a directed process that we can undertake toward our goal of greater understanding or making meaning. It opens the door to creating a dialogue with our perceptual senses. In Gagné's Memory Model (Gagné, 1985), sensory input is illustrated as a mono-directional flow. In contrast, an expanded model would recognize that by using visualization, we can actually *create* perceptual sensations that embody experiences created entirely in our minds.

Since visualization is a directed activity, does this mean that it is a *conscious* activity? Not necessarily; some of our best problem solving is done while dreaming, a state under the domain of the unconscious (Samuels & Samuels, 1975). There are also substantial questions about the hypnotic state; is it conscious or unconscious? Can we visualize when in a hypnotic state? Most of the literature seems to indicate that, indeed, visualization and cognition relate to one and other. The key, then, is to determine the relationship, as well as other criterion that will facilitate use of visualization as a cognitive aid.

Visualization can be used to enhance many aspects of our life physically, spiritually, and mentally. In a cognitive sense, it can be used for developing focus, establishing connections and relationships, and creative problem solving, concept enhancement, and memory enrichment. (Kosslyn, 1983). When we visualize something step by step, the connections between the brain cells are physically formed and we have created a physical pathway to success.

First, create a pictorial version of the goal that we want to achieve, and then draw it and paste it at a place we can see it. When there is a clear target, the right details are easier to find.

The relationship between visualization and cognition really rests on the concept of *representation*. Gagné describes at least three types of representative knowledge; propositions, productions, and continuous knowledge (such as images and sounds) (Gagné, 1985). Regardless of how these representations are stored in long-term memory, they can be recalled in their representative form to short-term memory for contemplation or action. Visualization can use information from long-term memory as well as new information gleaned from the environment to create new knowledge and understanding. Denis (1991) states:

> *It will come as no surprise that in the context of a discussion about imagery the definition of "thinking" used here will hinge on the notion of representation. A convenient distinction is often made between long-term and transient representation. Long-term representations are the constituents of individuals'*

permanent knowledge, and transient representations are built up from new informational inputs. Representations are the locus of application of processes, which manipulate and transform their content in order to derive new pieces of information. Thinking is that set of mental activities involved in the manipulation of representations with the construction of new pieces of information as outputs, which can enter into an individual's knowledge base. (1991, p. 103)

Dynamic mental "simulations and manipulations" have been used to solve intensely complex problems by creative individuals throughout history. By shifting perspective, and by determining whole-to-part relationships, critical questions have been answered. For example, the mathematician Poincaré and the physicist Feigenbaum used such a technique when developing their respective descriptions of geometric space and universality. In art, the same relationship holds. Tufte quoted the artist Paul Klee as saying:

It is not easy to arrive at a conception of a whole which is constructed from parts belonging to different dimensions. And not only nature, but also art, her transformed image, is such a whole. It is difficult enough, oneself, to survey this whole, whether a nature of art, but still more difficult to help another to such a comprehensive view. This is due to the consecutive (linear) nature of the only methods available to us for conveying a clear three-dimensional concept of an image in space, and results from deficiencies of a temporal nature in the spoken word. (Tufte, 1990, p. 15)

Visual-Spatial Ability Tests

Visual-spatial ability tests have been included in many prominent aptitude batteries, such as the General Aptitude Test Battery (GATB) used in federal agencies to predict job performance. Research on several instruments has shown a link between spatial ability and visual careers such as architecture and engineering **as well as managerial problem-solving** (Hunter, 1994).

Count the number of "Ys" in this text:

Yesterday, Lucy went all the way to Boston. She wanted to buy new shoes. She had to go into many shops before she found the shoes she wanted. She was happy to stop at a restaurant to have some tea and cookies before she took the train back home. (The answer is at the end of this chapter.)

Critical visual-spatial power can be developed in order to think more creatively and to better comprehend the pattern of forces that govern our world.

Network TV problem solver, President and CEO of Network and Entertainment Services Andrea Wong said in an interview with Newsweek (October 15, 2007):

> *While in college at MIT (the hardest four years of my entire life), I was taught how to look at a problem, figure out how to break it down and attack each part on its own with a disciplined approach. I know that I will never solve harder problems than I did while I was there. I am now dealing with the challenge of coming into Lifetime and growing this company and growing this brand. It's the same approach, the same mental confidence that allows me to know how to look at the issues. Whether it's breaking down the marketing issues, the issues with respect to programming, the building of the right team and putting the right team in place, or making our advocacy work for us, I break it down like I did in college.*

Problem solving is an active concern of the mind, as Andrea Wong would attest. Picture thinkers can come to conclusions in an active, intuitive way, without reasoning with language. Instead, they manipulate with visual symbols to form answers to problems. As one of the two most common modes of thought and learning styles, visual-spatial thinkers are to be found in all walks of life but may be overrepresented in occupations requiring good visualization skills. This should not be confused with logical thinkers, who think mathematically and in systems, but may not do so pictorially.

A Profoundly Dyslexic Executive—a Visual-Spatial Thinker—a BRIGHT Clue

Organizations and their executives who steer straight-line courses do so at their own peril. Paths must be continually flexible and constantly recharged. So it is for Ford. The company provides financing for more of its customers, more profitably, than anyone else in the business.

Donald Winkler, Chairman and CEO of Ford Motor Credit Co., struggles to process the world in ways that the rest of us do. Winkler often sees the world in disjointed ways that we don't or won't. He was hired to run Ford's enormous financial arm (with more than ten million customers and $165 billion in receivables). His remarkable success speaks to his productive harnessing of something most would consider a disability. It also speaks to how business today must be done and how we must utilize greater mental capacity to survive the complex, the chaotic, and the unexpected.

Winkler's language is the language of communicating *on the fringe*. It is way of thinking that was born of his need, as an engineer and as a dyslexic (difficulty in reading or in comprehending what is read), for extreme systemization, and of his need for perpetual reexamination and continual improvement. Some people must "think with images" because they don't master language. Breakthrough leadership, Winkler states, is about creating "something that would not have happened otherwise and something that will never go back to the way it was. Leadership is about taking people to places that they wouldn't have gotten to be themselves."

Winkler teaches seminars using a box paradigm to explain how we limit our thinking and constrain our growth. "There are lots of reasons we stay in the box, but the number one reason is fear of failure. To break out of the box, you have to ask questions—power questions." What comes out of the box is a translation of vision into strategy. "That is the hardest thing to do—If we are to accomplish this, what four or five key areas do we need to go after?"

Every morning, Don Winkler wakes up at 3 AM. He begins each day with 20 minutes of mental calisthenics: simple exercises that help point his brain in the right direction. It is not something that he particularly enjoys, yet he requires himself to keep at it. He feels he cannot be effective otherwise. Winkler's fringe thinking for seeing and moving ahead: "When you're best in class you risk standing still. It's easy to be too content. You need to take the paradigm that you're in and turn it upside down" (Hammonds, 2000).

Dyslexics seem to excel in visual thinking because of their reading problems. Donald Winkler's dyslexia (disorganized circuitry in the left temporal lobe), or his difficulty with problems in perception, where his brain misinterprets sensory input (the visual-word-form area does not develop fully), can now be helped or corrected with brain exercises. Actually he is partly helping himself and has greatly helped us understand how we or anyone can build their sensory processing ability. Three BRIGHT insights were given here to help our own visual-spatial technology: (1) learning disabilities such as dyslexia may arise in part from faulty sensory processing; (2) good visual-spatial assessments (our Global Decisiveness Assessment Battery) can identify sensory deficits in anyone, including executives; and (3) our own Global Processing Technologies augment a new neuroscience and practice of increasing capacity of height, breadth, and depth of visual perception along with the accompanying visual-spatial speed and visual memory components.

Said differently, we can now significantly improve sensory processing and thereby improve spatial ability with almost anyone because of a neuroscience breakthrough with dyslexia. Researchers have found that dyslexics possess a greater ability to notice the presence of symmetrical patterns. The evidence suggests that this skill was helpful in a group of astrophysicists to detect the symmetrical spectrum of black holes. This skill is also embedded in our highest powers—three- & four-dimensional thinking (BRIGHT3+4).

Exercise: "Fifty Pages"—a Visual-Spatial Workout

Let's pick a simple executive topic—things like creating an effective/green office, logo design, caring, market growth, or cost savings. Next, we set aside fifty 8½ by 11 inch pieces of paper. We begin by coming up with five visual representations of an effective office. Over the course of two weeks (ten days), we re-imagine our topic in as many different ways as possible. Our only rule is to not repeat any of the ideas. Take about ten minutes each day. The point where we feel unproductive should be the point where we start thinking, really thinking about something different and inspiring. We begin to realize how powerful this visual representation process can be.

The more time we spend progressing our ideas and building off of our past concepts, the more our brain has no other course but to look for something less obvious.

When we were doing the Fifty Pages experiment ourselves, we would have to challenge ourselves not to repeat any ideas. One of the best ways we found to do this was to start asking questions of ourselves. How would Batman design his effective office? How would a deaf person set up an effective office? What could power an office besides electricity? How "green" could we be to reduce damage to the environment? These indiscriminate thoughts may not seem applicable, but this is how the creative mind operates. It stands to reason that the more difficult the problem gets, the more creatively our mind will have to labor to solve it.

A common approach we use with executives is "logo design." There is a great need for organizations to distinguish themselves. When paired with things like metaphors, irony, and juxtaposition, symbols and iconic representations become substantially more memorable because we are embracing a level of meaning and depth. This process can create intrigue and garner attention from viewers, which often translates into brand recognition and awareness. Organizational and technical prowess in laying out a page is not always about new designs or decorations. Considerable thought needs to go into the message behind the design. Visual thinking always begins with understanding our problem. Fundamentally, the thinking becomes the game plan to visually solve the problem.

In our example, the problem was to create a more effective/green office. The sketches that we were generating didn't need to be elegant renderings because we were just working through a fast iterative process of idea gathering. Some of us have trouble breaking ourselves of the need to thoroughly render an idea before moving forward. If this is a problem for us, introduce some lighter constraints such as only working with ink Sharpies, or strictly limiting ourselves to sixty seconds per drawing. Polished designs have their place in the process, and it is not here.

Visual-Spatial Thinking: How We See, What We See, How We Process and Interact

Visual-spatial research is at an inspiring time in its evolution. Currently, communication, art, perceptual psychology, and neurobiology are exchanging insights into a cross-disciplinary dialogue that is revolutionizing our understanding of how we see, what we see, and how we process and interact within visually dominated environments. There is a plethora of research on non-linear dynamics emerging under the cover of "Chaos Theory," from fractals to fluid dynamics, to the application of "fuzzy" logic in "smart" washing machines and self-focusing and stabilizing camcorders. An exciting shift in focus has yielded revolutionary new insights into visual (thinking in pictures) problem solving. Chaos Theory has helped us view perception and the mind as non-liner and dynamic.

The neurologist Ian Robertson, in his book *Opening the Mind's Eye*, argues that the "cold network of language" has destroyed our ability to think in pictures. For instance, if we are able to describe the experience of eating a mango, the real experience has been lost, replaced by an abstract and cold verbal description. What we remember and describe is more or less a pale shadow of the real thing, an abstract categorization.

Visual thinking is processing in pictures rather than words; ideas are interconnected (imagine a web). Linear-sequential thinking—the norm in American business—is particularly difficult for individuals high in spatial ability and requires a translation of their thought processes that takes extra time. Spatial intelligence is the ability to digest, often with the help of others, large amounts of information in order to form important decisions. Some of our executives were obviously more intelligent than their IQ scores revealed. Gifted executives can have immense ability in visual-spatial processing and marked weaknesses in auditory-sequential processing. As children, these to-be executives were not identified as gifted and often struggled at school because their intelligence and learning styles were not recognized and/or appreciated. Many were "at risk" students because their learning environments did not understand strong visual-spatial thinking and compatible learning styles.

All of us have thinking and learning style dominance: intrinsic information-processing patterns that represent our typical mode of perceiving, thinking, remembering, and problem-solving. Behavioral scientists are increasingly recognizing the process of visual processing in the way that quarterbacks and executives think and learn. Our executives who scored high on an WAIS (IQ) test did so because of their great ability with tasks using visual-spatial processing and those requiring auditory sequential thinking processes. In our laboratory setting they prefer to use their dominant and commanding visual-spatial thinking but could fall back on their auditory sequential thinking when they perceived the need to do so.

To get more visual light and reflection, a sun roof is worth the extra cost.

Alertness refers to awareness—the sunlight on our thinking—including our commitment for, attitudes on, and attention to light. *Reflection* leads to pondering the light on thinking about needed improvements. Reflection is the ability to think on and accurately assess our own behaviors and skills as they are manifested in any situation. It is an important ability for ultra-smart leadership. As we understand what cognitively influences our decisions, we are better able to manage and influence our own thought processes.

Reflection differentiates effective thinkers from less effective. Executives can no longer succeed on the unexamined repetition of established formulas. Individuals at all levels of the organization should be asked to think in new ways about themselves, their work, and their organization. Executives can learn a variety of strategies to encourage higher-level thinking skills within their organization and ensure that critical thinking is subsidized and protected.

Reflection is thinking about thinking.

Reflection is the mental faculty or process by which knowledge is acquired through perception, reasoning, and intuition. The basic process of acquiring knowledge is simply learning. This includes the creation and management of aggregated knowledge in the form of complex cognitive structures or mental maps.

It is reflection directed at monitoring and controlling the process of thinking. Reflection is thinking about thinking. The result of reflection is the conscious regulation and rearrangement of how we think in the face of complex problems requiring novel solutions.

Reflection is both a process and a skill. As a *skill*, cognition is about reflection and strategic management of self. As a *process*, reflection involves conscious, self-directed investigation of one's mental processes. This includes perception and understanding of context as well as the notions of perspective-taking and multi-frame thinking. The process of reflection often involves temporarily de-centering—suspending assumptions, including one's own values and belief systems.

Information processing occurs at two levels. At the "lower" level, a closed system accepts input, processes it, and produces output without any feedback. At the "upper" level, a control system acts as a feedback processor with a capacity for both rewriting the rules used at the "lower" level and providing feedback to the "lower" level. The action process, reflection, merely executes, resets, and executes again. The executive process, reflection, can edit or adjust the action process after considering feedback.

Smart creativity and inventiveness come only after ample visual-spatial capacity.

Research by Gallup reported that less than 30 percent of employees are truly engaged in their jobs. Other polls have shown that an additional 25–40% of the work done by most organizations is waste or non-value added. This means that nearly 40% of every payroll dollar is lost. With the advent of true global competition, can we afford to lose 40% of our time as a company and the loss in creativity that otherwise could be in place?

In "fast"-thinking organizations, the flow of product is the measure of efficiency. But in knowledge-based organizations, it is the flow of *creativity* that drives effectiveness. Relatively soon, access to capital and technology will be equal around the planet. Commodity-based companies will disappear in western society. Only knowledge-based enterprises that can tap into latent creativity will survive. Employees are the only sustainable competitive advantage. Creativity is the new coin of the realm and trust is the cornerstone. Mass is out; lean is in!

We know that creativity does not prosper under pressure. That is why so many strokes of genius have occurred outside of the laboratory or office, in situations that have nothing to do with work. Creativity requires an openness to unrelated activity, new ways of seeing the world, and a willingness to explore possible connections. Creative revelations come to most people when their minds are involved in unrelated activity. The brain continues to work on a problem (mental fermentation) once it has been supplied with necessary raw materials. A little relaxation and distance changes the mind's perspective on the problem—without our being aware of it.

Legend has it that Greek mathematician and mechanical wizard Archimedes was stepping into a bathtub when the principle of fluid displacement came to him. Organic chemist Friedrich August Kekule had a dream about snakes biting their own tails. His creative moment came when he depicted the chemical structure of benzene as ring-shaped.

Creative thinkers are very knowledgeable about a given discipline. Coming up with an impressive idea without ever having been closely involved with an area of study is not impossible, but very improbable. Albert Einstein labored for years on rigorous physics problems, mathematics, and even philosophy before he formulated the central equation of relativity theory: $E = mc2$. As legendary innovator Thomas A. Edison, author of 1,092 patents, noted, "Genius is 1% inspiration and 99% perspiration." New ideas need preparation, nurturing, time, and support. Having an idea is good but acting on it is more important. Results are what count.

Once a problem is identified, a leader who wants to solve it has to examine it from all perspectives, including new perspectives. The process should look like an intellectual voyage of discovery that can go in any direction. Fresh insights result from disassembling and reassembling the Lego blocks in an infinite number of ways. That means the problem solver must thoroughly understand his Legos.

Mindscapes and Mind Mapping: Powerful tools to awaken our visual-thinking ability.

Brain research has shown that our brain organizes information by making patterns. Mind mapping, a method of visually representing ideas and of aiding the brainstorming free-association process, has been used by some of history's greatest brains, including Michelangelo, Mark Twain, and Leonardo da Vinci. Mind mapping is a spatial activity that will awaken our creative side as well as our analytical side. Mind mapping will also help us generate new ideas when needed. It doesn't matter whether we're using it for personal goal setting, problem solving, or simply to become a more creative, spatial thinker. Our mind works in pictures, associating one idea to the next. Mind mapping allows us to continue this natural thought process on paper.

A mindscape is a visual "storyboard"—a spatial method of displaying the gestalt organizational structure of a thought. For example, a team could use a drawing of a trek up a mountain to depict their development of a departmental mission statement. A road could symbolize the path to the group's objective, and rocks could represent potential obstacles along the way to the goal.

Mind Maps provide us with a platform to throw related ideas onto paper in a jumbled but semi structured manner. We aren't forced into creating ideas hierarchically. Instead we can jump from one idea to another simply and easily. These maps are formulated by first getting a blank sheet of paper and putting one thought in the middle of it. We then put ideas related to it onto the paper, joined to it by lines. Quite quickly we'll be able to generate a spider type diagram which has multiple points on it.

As we develop the diagram, we think of points that are related to the points already written on the paper. We simply draw a line to the related point and then write the idea down. The free-flowing nature of the diagram means that we can jump about. It's easy to move from topic line to another topic line. So if an idea is sparked as we are writing about one topic then we can easily switch and add it. We should only put one word on each line, or we should use color and drawings to stimulate the different sides of our brain.

Building a mind map begins with a blank sheet of paper—preferably unlined. Put in the middle of the paper the idea we're going to focus on. Write the idea in the middle of the page in capitals and draw a square or circle around it. Next, think of a related point. Let's take an example: "Open Office Honolulu." Some related points might be: "Hire staff" or "Find office." We write down the ones that come immediately to mind to the side of the main topic. In this case, we'll write one on each side. Now start to think of ideas around "Hire staff." Perhaps: "find recruitment agency"; "advertise in local paper"; "do field trip in Honolulu"; "ask customers."

We continue to add in this way until we've exhausted our ideas. However, we should be cautious not to force ideas. Often I find that mind-map thinking works better if I limit my time. So I think of how long I think I'll need, and then I reduce the time a bit. Think of a mind map as being a vehicle to move our thoughts about so that we can deal with them.

Mind mapping not only stimulates creativity and inventiveness by drawing upon the visually-oriented right side of the brain, it's also a very efficient way to do a "mental core dump" of our thoughts and ideas onto paper in a matter of minutes. Forward-thinking executives increasingly realize that creativity and innovation are quickly becoming mission-critical business skills for coping with a world of accelerating change.

Creative minds, from Madison Avenue to software designers, have recognized in recent years that symbols are everywhere and are powerful communication tools. Mind mapping can stretch our thinking beyond our usual "in the box" to "big picture," capture complex ideas quickly, and easily identify relationships between ideas and processes.

Building a mind map typically consists of the following steps:

1. Start from the central concept or issue.

2. Create branches and sub-branches to capture all related ideas and issues.

3. Add pictures, documents, hyperlinks as needed to each branch.

4. Arrange the branches logically.

5. Create visual links between related branches.

6. Present or distribute your mind map.

A mind map is a diagram used to represent concepts, ideas, tasks, or other items linked to a central theme. In a mind map, the central theme is often illustrated with a graphical image. The ideas related to the main theme radiate in a clockwise direction from that central image as "branches." Topics and ideas of lesser importance are represented as "sub-branches" of their relevant branch.

Mindmap

By presenting the relationships between ideas in a non-linear graphical manner, mind mapping encourages a brainstorming approach to the handling and organization of information. Mind maps have numerous applications, both in the education sector, where they are used as an aid to studying and learning, and in the business sector, to facilitate critical thinking, problem solving, and decision making.

Concept mapping with visual models is the process of rendering tacit models visible and shareable by the use of representational mapping. This mapping is done by means of a variety of techniques, which are like moving diagrams. They exploit both basic wisdoms: a picture is worth a thousand words, and thinking includes the power to influence patterns of ideas. Visual models create a flexible medium where change of pattern is facilitated.

1. Each unit of meaning (statement, fact, opinion) is recorded on one single object.

2. Any object in the model that is persistent throughout the process and is movable at any time thus encourages flexibility.

3. Objects can be added, subtracted, revised, and moved at any time; they can be augmented with clusters, arrows, and text overlays.

4. Various conventions, especially color, can be used to create additional layers of meaning especially about connectivity and significance.

5. These conventions can carry meaning in terms of both frameworks of thought (e.g., a planning concept) and of the nature of a particular thought (e.g., a cognitive mode).

6. The process can be carried out simultaneously by more than one person in collaboration, interrelating their thoughts in common models.

7. The representations of maps are practical control tools for: a) live discussion; b) group memory; c) task organization; d) building of shared models; e) decision support; and f) information retrieval.

Concept mapping is more than an extension of brainstorming and mind mapping. It is much deeper in its scope and implications.

Conceptual mapping is a flexible medium that:

- increases the brain's capacity to handle complexity;
- enables people in groups to share their thinking aloud;
- provides a basis for new dynamic user-determined computer interface;
- enables computer based methods and information to be run from individually configured mind maps.

The combination of these aspects with suitably designed methods, skills, and computer software, creates a new visual-spatial working environment that enables a bridge to be built between implicit visual models and conscious modeling techniques like system dynamics.

Five essential characteristics of concept mapping are:

- The main idea, subject, or focus is crystallized in a central image.
- The main themes radiate from the central image as "branches."
- Each branch includes a key image or word drawn on its associated line.

- Topics of lesser importance are represented as "twigs" of the relevant branch.
- The branches form a connected "tree-like" structure.

What are thinking maps?

The concept of thinking maps, while similar to previous generations of graphic organizers, is fundamentally different in that a specific *visual organizer* was created for eight thinking processes. Educational research confirms that consistent use of thinking maps increases IQ scores, SAT scores, and reading & writing scores. Thinking maps help students and executives become independent, reflective, life-long problem solvers and learners.

Thinking maps are a common visual language for learning individually and in teams. They have a consistent design, but are highly flexible. Each map is based on a *thinking process*. With consistent use, the brain develops a pattern that connects the process to a specific thinking map. There are eight maps that are designed to correspond with eight different fundamental thinking processes. They are supposed to provide a common visual language to information structure, and are often employed when executives take notes and visually organize their notes to communicate patterns and processes to their teams.

Eight thinking maps include the Circle Map, Bubble Map, Double Bubble Map, Tree Map, Brace Map, Flow Map, Multi-Flow Map, and the Bridge Map.		
Circle Map: used to define in context.		http://www.tangischools.org/schools/kes/circle_map_info.htm
Bubble Map: used to describe qualities.		http://www.tangischools.org/schools/kes/bubble_mapinfo.htm
Double Bubble Map: used to compare and contrast.		http://www.tangischools.org/schools/kes/double_bubble_mapinfo.htm
Tree Map: used to classify or sort information.		http://www.tangischools.org/schools/kes/tree_mapinfo.htm
Brace Map: used to define in context.		http://www.tangischools.org/schools/kes/brace_mapinfo.htm
Flow Map: shows the sequence of events.		
Multi-Flow Map: shows the causes and/or effects of an event.		http://www.tangischools.org/schools/kes/multi_flow_mapinfo.htm
Bridge Map: used to show analogies.		http://www.tangischools.org/schools/kes/bridge_mapinfo.htm

Stuck in a rut? Try reframing the visual picture

A bow and an arrow costs $1.10 in total. The bow costs $1 more than the arrow. How much does the arrow cost? Is it 10 cents? Please reframe our thinking here. Ten cents cannot be right: The bow would have to cost $1.10, for a total of $1.20. The initial summation is in error.

Reframing is changing the way we understand a statement, situation, or behavior to give it new meaning, Reframing enables us to make better choices that are more congruent with our goals, values, and desired outcomes. For instance, if we were given some negative feedback, would we see the feedback as: An assault on our competence and/or ego? A learning opportunity? A chance to explore new options? A glitch on the screen? The other person's problem? Or something else?

The frame we choose (the meaning we give) sets off a series of beliefs, thoughts, attitudes, and behaviors. Each frame leads in a somewhat different direction. It's important to choose the frame that will take us and our team where we want to go. If we're not headed there, reframe.

The more visual frames we and our team can generate, the more choices we have and the more innovative and creative our thinking becomes. With each new frame comes a reservoir of previously untapped choice. Options and opportunities are discovered where none existed before. Our decision-making skills improve as we choose the frame that will serve us best.

Visual-spatial communication vitalizes all dimensions.

Visual-spatial communication supports and sustains creative problem solving that originates in visual-spatial information processing. The communication is simply using as few words as possible and focusing on using visual pictures and words. Visual-spatial communication should have logic and a life of its own that resonates with usable potential. It should operate on every level of awareness, from emotional processing to three-dimensional thinking. Visual-spatial communication should enrich and enable by expanding awareness through analogies based on our experience. Specifically, we should exercise visual-spatial communication to:

- advocate our position and combine it with self-reflection and humility while encouraging inquiry from others;

- improve picture-reasoning skills, including the ability to use graphical and other representations of information for decision making purposes;

- enhance the ability to understand relationships among variables to improve decision making;

- increase our ability to comprehend new situations and adapt to new tasks;

- develop an understanding of the typical biases and decision traps that we and our people fall into when we/they try to interpret information, and provide tools to overcome these biases and decision traps; and

- develop an approach for framing problems appropriately in order to make effective and responsible decisions.

Visual-spatial communication skills should be an indispensable part of any executive's professional practice. The difference between an executive who contributes toward a competitive advantage and one that does not can be discerned by anyone whose natural responses to visual-spatial information have been cultivated to the higher levels rather than stifled.

In summary, being more visual-spatial requires us to think like a quarterback before the snap, to decide quickly on the essence of what we want to communicate, and say it in as few words as possible, focusing on using visual pictures and words. By giving out our visual model or mapping up front or in the huddle, we keep our people's attention and interest. This process allows our people to craft their own visual models that connect to the ideas we are trying to share. When we are attempting to raise performance levels, knowing that our people first need insights for themselves, we give them the space to craft their own visual mapping of our ideas and thereby made insightful changes.

Solution: There are **seven** "Ys" in *"Count the number of 'Ys.' in this text"*.

CHAPTER SUMMARY
Key Points

• Thinking, in order to have something to think about, must be based on images of the world in which we live. Without gathering and processing visual information about what is going on in time and space, the brain cannot work. *To see is to process. To process is to think and believe.*

• Neuroscience is now affirming that an enriched environment can help to stimulate nerve cell development, with a resulting increase in brain size and weight.

• The brain can indeed be retrained to process verbal information faster, more clearly, and with greater power. These intense sensory retraining experiences can improve virtually every aspect of the verbal learning process.

• Visual thinking is a group of generative skills that, when practiced with rigorous discipline, results in the production of novel and original graphic ideas that are needed for executive speed and agility.

• We know that graduates with degrees in physics, chemistry, and engineering have demonstrated excellent spatial ability. We also know that many famous business executives, including Lee Iacocca, Bill Hewlett, and David Packard, Andrew Grove, and Jack Welch, had science and engineering backgrounds that required spatial ability.

• Smart processing and smart reasoning come only after smart visual-spatial capacity. Information is no better than the processing that provides information on what is going on in real time and space.

• Mind mapping not only stimulates creativity by drawing upon the visually-oriented right side of the brain, it's also a very efficient way to do a "mental core dump" of our thoughts and ideas onto paper in a matter of minutes. Forward-thinking executives increasingly realize that creativity and innovation are quickly becoming mission-critical business skills for coping with a world of accelerating change.

• Reframing is changing the way we understand a statement, situation, or behavior to give it new meaning, Reframing enables us to make better choices that are more congruent with our goals, values, and desired outcomes.

• Visual-spatial ability supports and sustains a quality of creative problem solving that originates in perceptual-information processing and is characteristic of higher-level executive thinking.

• Visual-spatial thinking has a holistic logic and life of its own that, as usable potential, can be brought to bear creatively and analytically to solve various kinds and levels of problems. Visual-spatial intelligence operates on every level of awareness from subliminal perceptual process to holistic, high-level creative thinking. When we are attempting to raise performance levels, knowing that our people first need insights for themselves, we give them the space to craft their own mental mapping of our ideas and thereby made insightful changes.

CHAPTER 3

BRIGHT1—Verbal Height
Solving Problems with Words

> *For languages, I do something similar in terms of thinking of words as belonging to clusters of meaning in that each piece of vocabulary makes sense according to its place in my mental architecture for that language. In this way, I can easily discern relations between words, which help me to remember them.*
>
> Daniel Tammet, *Think Better: Tips from a Savant*

A Verbal Power from Higher Ground

Some years ago our young family (Graham) elected to vacation in the mountains around Yosemite National Park. Our VW camper provided excellent transportation, food storage, and outdoor gear for each family member and every wilderness experience. It was a unique time for building family relationships, close communication patterns, and memories for a lifetime. It also was a vacation of potential peril. Leaving Yosemite Park, we traveled north to higher latitudes on narrow logging roads in search of new sights and ultimately a place to camp overnight. Traveling through glacier-molded peaks, we sighted a pristine, idyllic mountain lake—nature's best performance of the day. After unanimous consensus, I pulled our van over to a narrow shoulder on the right, yards above the lake, allowing our eight-year-old son, David, his two older sisters, and my wife to wade and refresh in the cool waters below. The children within moments were in knee deep. My last communication to my wife: "Please watch the kids. I am going to sneak out the driver's side, cross the highway, and climb up over 1,000 feet to a smoothed peak, take pictures of the panorama, and be right down." The view from the top was spectacular. Pictures taken and descent begun, the view below was horrifying. I could see my son look for his father and then look up and catch sight of me. I also could see from my height and line of sight his determination to cross the highway in front of our camper, climb the hill, and be with father. Standing on higher ground, I could see a logging truck traveling some 50–60 miles an hour barreling down that highway; it would be momentarily passing our van when my son would step out from a blind spot into the road. In my mind, there was a compressed motion picture—my son hit and his lifeless body flying through space. I had only one second to pick my words, about two to three seconds to say them, and about one second to pray. "David, stay there. Do not move! Do not move!" I watched with a heightened dread the play-out of the scene unfolding below. David, feeling rejected, dropped to his knees just several feet from the unaware passing truck. David's life had been spared and my life was shaken and weakened coming off that hill. Father and son had the longest hug ever with gratitude for three things: visual height, power words, and obedience.

Language and speech serve to scaffold higher cognitive capacities.

A strong thesis has been proposed and defended by current researchers that the process of language acquisition and enculturation does not merely serve to load the mind with beliefs and concepts, but actually scaffolds our cognitive processes to some degree (Lucy, 1992a, 1992b; Nelson, 1996; Bowerman & Levinson, 2001). Children brought up speaking Korean (as opposed to English)—in which verbs are highly inflected and massive noun ellipsis is permissible in informal speech—tend to be much weaker at categorization tasks, but much better at spatial tasks such as using a rake to pull a distant object toward them (Choi and Gopnik, 1995; Gopnik, Choi, & Baumberger, 1996; Gopnik, 2001). Vygotsky (1934), argues that language and speech serve to *scaffold* the development of cognitive capacities in the growing child. Researchers working in this tradition have studied the self-directed verbalizations of young children—for example, observing the effects of their soliloquies on their behavior (Diaz & Berk, 1992). They have found that children tend to verbalize more when task demands are greater, and those who verbalize most tend to be more successful in problem solving. The idea is that language gets used, not just for communication, but also to augment human cognitive powers. We are to assume from Diaz and Berk's work that language is a necessary condition for the acquisition of certain cognitive skills and that it forms part of the functioning of the higher-level executive system.

The structure of the language we habitually use is intimately involved in the thinking process and influences the way we perceive our environment. The stronger a language is in symbolic abstraction, the higher the potential for verbal intelligence. Dialects and street languages will never facilitate higher levels of thinking. The Russian psychologist Lev Vygotsky was evangelical on the role of developing a strong language to facilitate intelligence. He was challenged by the young American psychologist Morris Graham (PhD dissertation) who measured the strength of language development and verbal intelligence with adolescents in ten language-cultural groups (English, Hispanic, Papago Indian, Chinese, Japanese, Tongan, Samoan, local Hawaiian, French, and Southwest American). Only two language groups significantly differentiated below the others with lower levels of abstract thinking—the Hawaiian speakers in rural Hawaii and Papago Indian adolescents in Arizona. Both languages were mixtures of different tongues—considered "street languages" and lacking what the Swiss psychologist Jean Piaget termed Formal Operational Thinking, where individuals develop the ability to think about abstract concepts with skills such as logical thought, deductive reasoning, and systematic planning. Deductive logic is the ability to use a general principle to determine a specific outcome. This type of thinking comes with a powerful language that can construe hypothetical situations, the ability to think about abstract concepts, and consider possible outcomes and consequences of actions—important in long-term planning. To recap: **The Graham Heightening Hypothesis:** *Verbal intelligence is facilitated by the symbolic strength of a language and by the height of its acquisition.*

Clark (1998) argues for a sort of intermediate-strength version of the Vygotskian idea, defending a conception of language as a cognitive *tool*. Chomsky, too, has argued for an account of this sort (1976, ch.2) According to this view—which Clark labels "the supra-communicative conception of language"—certain *extended* processes of thinking and reasoning constitutively involve natural language. The idea is that language gets used not just for communication, but also to augment human cognitive powers.

> *Every thought tends to connect something with something else, to establish a relation between things. Every thought moves, grows and develops, fulfills a function, solves a problem.* (Vygotsky, 1934)

Heightening drives out flat thoughts. Linear questions of purpose force us to define our task. Questions of information force us to look at our sources of information as well as at the quality of our information. Questions of interpretation force us to examine how we are connecting, organizing, or giving meaning to information and to consider alternative ways of giving meaning. However, questions with height force us to examine what we are taking for granted. Questions with height force us to check out where our thinking is going; examine our biases and invite and welcome others to inquire into our reasoning and logic; discriminate what does and what does not bear on a question; evaluate and test for truth and correctness; give details and be specific; examine our thinking for contradictions; and consider how we are putting the whole of our thought together, to make sure that it all adds up and makes sense within a reasonable system.

We must continually remind ourselves that thought begins within some context only when questions are generated by both us and our team. No questions mean little understanding. Superficial questions sustain superficial and sloppy understanding. Most project team members typically have few intellectual questions. Most will sit in silence; their minds are silent at well. Hence, the questions they do have tend to be superficial, ill-formed, and self-serving. Most of the time they are not thinking through the work they are presumed to be tackling. In other words, people are usually so busy doing their jobs, that there's often not enough time for the project team's mission, which is to energize the competitive advantage of the company.

If we want to energize our "project team" in thinking through their purpose for coming together, we must stimulate their thinking with questions of height that lead them to further questions and further height. We must overcome what previous work histories have done to blunt the thinking of our employees. As executives, we must lead out in changing minds through effective questioning that investigates, invigorates, and develops our people to tackle, invent, and advance the company.

Inner speech structures mastered become the basic structures of our thinking (Vygotsky, 1934).

Inner speech reflects a higher mental function according to the Russian psychologist Lev Vygotsky. This is speech for communication and reflects a synthesis of mental functions and denotes the ability for deep, reflective thought. Communicative speech uses the "sense" of words and sentences. This "sense" is found in the social, cultural context in which the words are being used. Prior thought, imagery, experience, and inner conversation go into framing what is actually spoken. This is much more a mental than a physical process. The goal of this final stage in speech development is to bring forth a coherent, mutually understandable thought (Vygotsky, 1934).

Vygotsky believed that writing, from its earliest forms of line drawings, is a higher mental function (1934). All drawings are based on *spatial memory* rather than actual copying from an object, and therefore represent the person's thoughts. Drawing is a non-verbal way of expressing inner speech. It is symbolic, as is writing. In the earliest school years, children put their thoughts on paper through pictures. As they learn writing symbols, they change to pictures and words, and then finally to a predominance of words. "The entire secret of teaching written language is to prepare and organize this natural transition appropriately" (1934, p. 116). As with general language learning, Vygotsky emphasized that writing should be incorporated into real, necessary, and relevant situations for any of us to realize that writing is another form of speech, a higher mental activity

Thus by writing an idea down, for example, I can off-load the demands on memory, presenting myself with an object of further leisured reflection; and by performing arithmetic calculations on a piece of paper, I may be able to handle computational tasks which would otherwise be too much for me (and my short-term memory). In similar fashion, it may be that inner speech serves to enhance memory, since it is now well-established that the powers of human memory systems can be greatly extended by association. (Baddeley, 1988)

Inner speech may thus facilitate complex trains of reasoning. (Varley, 1998)

Critical reading and language acquisition both help develop an ability to create verbal height—BRIGHT1 power.

Verbal height is positively correlated to strong symbolic-abstract language acquisition. Language acquisition shapes the way we think, and determines what we can think about. Mastery of words in any language is to have in our possession the ability to produce verbal height and order out of chaos and command a vocabulary that is a true measure of BRIGHT1 power. As Edmund Burke said, reading without reflecting is like eating without digesting. Just reading facilitates our capacity to use language in order to express ourselves, comprehend stories, and understand other people. Critical reading might focus on acquiring business-specific knowledge on business systems and mechanics, competition, and biographies and leadership principles. Verbal height abilities also include writing and our ability to employ a second language for reasoning and problem solving.

Learning a second language also enhances our verbal height and lets us experience the world from different, fresh perspectives. There is good evidence that language learning helps individuals to abstract information and focus attention, and may even help ward off age-related declines in mental performance. When we learn a second language, we let go of our own grown perspectives and experience the world from the perspective of characters and information that have been crafted and molded by another culture. We have found in our own lives that the more we keep our second languages alive, the more we want to be proficient. Command of a second language should become an insatiable desire and an unquenchable thirst.

To read critically in one or two languages is to make judgments about **how** any text is sequenced and argued. This is a highly reflective skill requiring us to "stand back" and gain some distance from the text we are reading. We might have to read a text through once to get a basic grasp of content before we launch into an intensive critical reading. The key is this:

- Don't read looking only or primarily for **information.**
- Do read looking for **ways of thinking** about the subject matter.

When reading, highlighting, or taking notes, it is well to avoid extracting and compiling lists of evidence, lists of facts and examples. Avoid approaching a text by asking, "What information can I get out of it?" Rather ask, "How does this text work? How is it argued? How is the evidence (the facts, examples, etc.) used and interpreted? How does the text reach its conclusions?"

> *A film is made up of still images flashed in rapid succession to simulate movement. Slow down the film, and the movement and meaning slows and the film's impact is diminished. Viewers won't learn as much about the film as if it were shown at normal speed. With reading the same thing can happen. When a person reads word by word, like frame by frame, they are not reading on the level of ideas. You need to read on some level that's more conversational and allows things to coalesce into ideas themselves.*
>
> Doug Evens, Institute of Reading Development

Heightened BRIGHT1 power is best acquired through extensive reading. Abraham Lincoln said, "*A capacity and taste for reading gives access to whatever has already been discovered by others.*" Our most brilliant executives are, for the most part, voracious readers in two languages. It is delightful to be audience to presidential candidates who can/will converse and think in a second or third language, e.g., Governor Mitt Romney—French and Spanish.

The ability to receive, store, process, and use information is developed through a series of cognitive ordering procedures called *sequential processing*. The two basic building blocks of learning and memory are *auditory* and *visual sequential processing*. These building blocks are essential to listening, learning, reading, and communication. They form the base of the brain's higher-order executive functions. Essentially, every mental process we perform is dependent on these processing abilities.

Our capacity to process, to learn new information or a second language, and form links and memories is realized through structural plasticity. During learning, reversible physiological changes in synaptic transmission take place in the brain. These temporary, reversible changes are referred to as short-term memory and the persistent changes as long-term memory. Visual-processing technology facilitates structural plasticity, which improves our ability to sequentially process information with height, expands our learning capacity, and improves our global brain function.

If you have knowledge, let others light their candles with it.

Winston Churchill

Sir Winston Churchill's exceptional leadership during World War II was largely grounded on his power to realize verbal height and convey power words to a terrified United Kingdom. His excellent visual-verbal and written communication abilities are detailed in the history books. Few leaders have understood the delicacies and height of language better than he did. People read his works not only for what he said but for the way he said it. He met one crisis after another by his ability to express ideas with vivid imagery and tremendous force. These he prepared in advance. Some of his neatly turned phrases were too smooth and perfect to be extemporaneous. His ability to ultimately draw out passions, sentiments, and emotions of his following, to set them on fire through the proper combinations, shading, and expression of words and meanings were why history has recorded Sir Winston Churchill as one of the world's great leaders.

We leaders leave our impact and imprint through our words of height. Those of us involved in leading ought to read and study logic, debate, rhetoric, literature, drama, language, poetry—all of which have to do with the effective understanding and power of words. Great poets have stood next to the prophets in their ability to influence lives. One who reads poetry must respond to its mood and stretch his mind to its *highest verbal* dimensions. Truly, the provocative power of words is the secret of the poet. It is especially powerful when there is added to it the influence of the character of the leader who is using the words. Even a bob from the person who is esteemed is of more force than a thousand arguments or studied sentences from others.

To envision information is to work at the intersection of image, word, number, art.

Communication that has a visual component can be far more effective than communication that does not. The psychologist Jerome Bruner of New York University has described studies that show that people only remember 10% of what they hear and 20% of what they read, but about 80% of what they see and do (2001).

Training materials used by the federal government cite studies indicating that the retention of information three days after a meeting or other event is six times greater when information is presented by visual and oral means than when the information is presented by the spoken word alone. The same materials also cite studies by educational researchers suggesting that 83% of human learning occurs visually (US Department of Labor, 1996). Information from the research suggests that while purely visual communication is more effective than solely verbal communication, the more compelling communication combines both visual and non-visual content. Charts, diagrams, tables, graphs, and other visual forms of art can bring together the visual and the verbal to add another dimension to the material and create an entirely new path toward understanding—or "seeing" its meaning.

As the researcher and academician Edward R. Tufte has observed, "To envision information—and what bright and splendid visions can result—is to work at the intersection of image, word, number, art." Color also serves this purpose of adding another dimension.

> *If you talk to a man in a language he understands, that goes to his head. If you talk to him in his language, that goes to his heart.*
>
> Nelson Mandela

Higher perspectives are better for sorting, sifting, or discriminating.

Most of us in Hawaii have experienced enough luaus to know that we must first visually walk up and down the long tables of food assortments to "surf" and see the selections before loading up our plates at the beginning of the line and running out of space by the middle table. We know the folly of rushing to the table and loading too much too soon, without glancing ahead: mounds of food that go untouched—not to mention the many delectable dishes we never try. Our plates are loaded up before we can make it to the desert table. Looking around at the big people with the big plates, I think of the need for a good diet and regular exercise to keep my weight down and help my mind function better, but, being hungry, I begin to lose ground on mental discipline!

We all have more luau food or available information coming at us than we can possibly digest or consume or fathom in this century. More and more frequently, we see executives doing the same thing with information: downloading and saving files in a great rush of data gorging that rarely includes reading, sifting, and thinking time. They accumulate scores of files and pages without sorting, sifting, or discriminating. They search the Web, find zillions of hits, and light up with elation at the finds. Confusing quantity and sheer volume of questionable information with success, they greedily scoop up everything within their reach, saving it for later.

We must be aware of a "luau mentality" as a nemesis to *verbal height* when we step up to our information feast. At the same time, we should hardly be surprised by this gorging. Many think that length and wisdom are related and pay the price. Our brilliant executives are about *height*— "selectively less is more—higher perspectives are better." Wisdom has more to do with distillation and reduction than with length and volume. While we may want to search widely, we must harvest sparingly and wisely. We must be capable of simultaneously grazing the Net and reading selectively and deeply, seeking expanded opportunities for questioning, problem-solving, researching, thinking deeply, and finally, processing sequentially with *height*.

BRIGHT1 is insight on linear processing that is imposed on nonlinear experience

The B1 thinking is insight (height) on linear processing, which is what we do with information that needs to be arranged in some order with insight. Also known as serial or sequential processing, linear processing is a term used to describe the processing that occurs in some order—like a Haiku:

> *Through the microscope,*
>
> *slice of brain stains pink and blue,*
>
> *the wonder of thought.*

(Alan, 2010)

Whenever information must be organized or kept in specific order so that the parts are correctly sequenced, successive processing is involved. A linear thinking process is one in which thoughts are associated with sequence. Therefore, a person with B1 insight or thinking would solve a problem step by step. On the other hand, dyslectics have a nonlinear thinking process, where they associate pictures with thoughts. That is why it is difficult for them to read and write.

B1 linear processing of experience can link insight with creativity and inventiveness through verbal imagery, which connects it to the nonlinear systems of art and perception. Good sequential processing (height) enables us to retain, process, and use more of what we take in through the visual and auditory channels and determines how quickly and clearly we can grasp concepts with several elements. Sequential processing is also important whenever comprehension is based on appreciation of the order of events. For instance, successive processing is involved in remembering a series of words or numbers and blending sounds to form words.

> *The most terrifying words in the English language are: I'm from the government and I'm here to help.*
>
> Ronald Reagan

Ronald Wilson Reagan, the fortieth president of the United States who launched the modern-day conservative political movement was known as the Great Communicator. He was a master at taking sequential, linear dimensions and imposing verbal height (insight) on nonlinear experience. President Reagan, in office from 1981 to 1989, helped redefine the political framework as he led the country into a new conservative view of itself. The Republican Party still draws much of its ideological authority from this period. Americans always felt they knew where he stood because he possessed extraordinary verbal abilities with height. He was an indisputable master of what his vice president, George H.W. Bush, dubbed "the vision thing."

Just five years after leaving office, by then already severely debilitated by his illness, President Reagan announced his illness in a letter, written in longhand, to the American people. It was vintage Reagan. As he worried about the impact of his disease on his wife, he also voiced his ever-present optimism.

"In closing, let me thank you, the American people, for giving me the great honor of allowing me to serve as your president," he wrote. "When the Lord calls me home, whenever that day may be, I will leave with the greatest love for this country of ours and eternal optimism for its future. I now begin the journey that will lead me into the sunset of my life. I know that for America there will always be a bright dawn ahead (1994)."

If you like my work, then I am yours for the hiring.

Living in Edinburgh, Scotland during the early 1980s as a post-doctorate student in developmental-organizational psychology, I (Graham) found myself in the midst of a national recession, evident in double-digit unemployment and tight budgets. Especially bleak was the "demise" of young adults of the rising generation—those of capacity and promise who hopelessly became physically, mentally, and linearly locked on to government welfare—the dole. Japanese imports of electronics and automobiles were winning the trade war in price and quality. Japanese think tanks were flying in and romancing some of the best minds in the UK. Prime Minister Margaret Thatcher identified the economic crisis as a crisis of the spirit of the nation.

On one of those drizzly, buttermilk-sky days, I picked up a Scottish newspaper (also cited in Scotsman.com) and read about Neal Duncan, a man who refused to go on the dole. His life vision was to work as an engineer in the car industry. After every enterprising attempt to find work in the UK, he was turned away. He wrote to the president of General Motors in the United States, stating: "I will work for you for 6 months—no charge. If you like my work, then I'm yours for the hiring." The letter—a linear (height) proposition—came to the attention of the US CEO and brought a quick response: "That's the kind of young engineer we want working for us—he thinks differently. Put him in management training and give him an opportunity to grow with the company in the United Kingdom." Neal undoubtedly thought linearly and non-linearly and was able to spatially visualize himself above contemporary entry-level, sequential thinking. He was mentally able to torque-up (heightening) or a leap into a higher state of insightful, non-linear thinking. Neal was an exemplar of *the problem is never the problem—it's how we process it with verbal insight and height.* Our hats off to Roger Smith, the CEO who recognized and sponsored a Scottish talent who could/would ultimately make a difference in General Motors.

We are here in Edinburgh; how do we get 20 miles south of London?

Our first year in Edinburgh, I (Graham) purchased a British-made car to get myself and family members to important commitments and events. Weeks followed and near-accidents were averted when I quickly caught myself driving on the American side (the UK wrong side) of the road facing oncoming traffic. My commutes were less anxious when I mapped out the entire linear course with all the critical connections and roundabouts, and put it to memory. Edinburgh possessed few highways, multiple lanes, and some dead ends that would end up at Scottish historical sites, golf courses, or farms. After a month we were visited by my in-laws from Hawaii and someone suggested that we all take a week off during holidays and drive 500 miles south to London and beyond to visit someone's old friend; I would be doing the driving. Where we were and where we ultimately had to go was clearly beyond my linear comfort zone; I did not have enough faith to make this trip.

Before leaving Edinburgh, my in-laws had to visit Arthur's Seat—the main peak of the group of hills that form a wild piece of highland landscape in the center of the city of Edinburgh and about a mile to the east of Edinburgh Castle. This craggy hill rises above the city to a height of 251 meters (820 feet), provides excellent panoramic views of the city, is quite easy to climb, and has a popular "cow trail" walk. Though it can be climbed from almost any direction, the easiest and simplest ascent is an old cow trail path from the east slope that rises above Dunsapie Loch. The trick is to find the lane that takes one to the base of the east cow trail and not to one of many dead ends at the bottom of the hill. It was my mother-in-law, who had grown up around cattle, who quickly knew where cows would come from the hills above and drink from the cool waters of Dunsapie Loch. She proudly led our party to the cow trail and up to Arthur's Seat.

I found myself driving in the front right seat, with my wife in the left front seat and my in-laws in the back. All passengers had strong opinions of what turns to make and where we needed to be. As long as I was on the M1 superhighway south, my family members were contained. We decided to say "Aloha" to my in-laws in London to let them do London as a couple and secure their connections back to Hawaii. Obviously, my wife and I eventually made it back to Edinburgh, still talking to each other.

Metaphorically, we see many of our frustrations and decisions, whether traveling or performing some other activity, as the combined result of four similar, yet widely divergent phenomena—highways, lanes, cow trails, and dead ends. Each is a linear path from here to somewhere else. Yet, each has its own uniqueness that helps form the basis of questioning: Where are we? Where do we desire or need to be? How do we get there from here?

Highways provide the relatively straight and rapid, most logical and efficient way of getting from point A to point B. The freeway or superhighway is well-paved and well-engineered. The route is tested and proven, and the guidelines are historic and easy to follow. There are signs to guide the way on and off; there are rest stops and roadside points of interest and they are posted along the superhighway.

Lanes are narrow streets, passages, or closes through the middle of a block giving access to the rear of lots or buildings. They originate from main streets and usually terminate with another main street. They sometimes are the shortest distance between two points within congested urban areas. They, too, are plotted on maps (up to a point—the smaller ones are usually ignored).

Hiking trails, or cow trails, are close to being the antitheses of the orderly progression established by freeways and alleyways. They cause our forward progress to head off in meandering directions—often on foot to get to higher, better ground. We know how cows are; they constantly make right-angle turns, poking their noses here and there, often reversing their direction. Whether foraging or fleeing, they make it difficult to predict where they are heading next. And yet, they always seem to make it back to the barn (their point B) safely.

Dead ends are for many neighborhoods a means to provide security and control of where traffic is not to go. They may bring order to an unstable terrain and often chaotic environment and make the world around more predictable and manageable. Dead ends should allow the driver to know in advance, with signs posted at the entrance, what will happen if they proceed. Otherwise, there will be feelings of frustration and helplessness unless there's a turn-around.

Like highways, every decision that we make hopefully starts out with basic research, careful thought, and the setting of goals, strategic plans, and objectives. "We are here, and this is where we want to go." We strategize the direction, the difficulties ahead, and how much time and resources are required. We can gauge our speed, and we know what and whom we have to pick up along the way. Our basic course, our linear movement from point A to point B, is set. Our challenge is to find the best sequential routes to get there.

There is an easy lesson to be learned by all of this: *We should plan our highways well, welcome the plasticity of other modes as lanes, stop, get out and be meandering hikers once in a while to get to higher ground as needed, and avoid the dead ends.*

We don't live in a perfectly linear world.

Years later, with one of my (Graham) daughters attending Lewis & Clark College in Portland, Oregon, I refused to drive to the college's freshman-parent orientation without a GPS system in the car. "Drive 200 yards, and then turn right," articulated my car's computer voice. I lit up in the driver's seat, talked back to Miss GPS, followed the directions, and reached our destination without error. Our Global Positioning System provided the shortest and most logical and efficient way of getting from the Portland airport to the college campus. My system measured the distance between the receiver and desired destination (latitude, altitude, and longitude) with accuracy within one centimeter. The through streets were well-paved and well-engineered, the route was tested and proven, and the guidelines were updated and easy to follow. There were signs to guide the way, there were rest stops and roadside points of interest, and all of these were plotted on our GPS map.

When I missed a turn and continued, the voice responded with "recalculating" and directed me back to my designated location. This

Global Positioning System directed me to within a few yards of my daughter's dormitory. Yet if the satellite service's digital maps becomes even slightly outdated—if, for example, there is new road construction—I could become lost. Then I would have to rely on the ancient human skill of navigating in three-dimensional space. I believe that my human positioning system via cognitive maps is flexible and capable of learning. Any of us who know the way from A to point B, and from A to C, can probably figure out how to get from B to C, too.

Nevertheless, we don't live in a perfectly linear "GPS" world. Our plans can never be concrete because we don't know everything there is to know. We require the assistance of avenues. From all sides comes a flow of new information and resources that we can use to make our journey more efficient in the long run. Some of these avenues move into our sphere of influence through our own efforts—it is vital to initiate inquiries that pay off in strategic data and the delivery of funding for our journey. Other avenues just happen; they find us and enrich us with unexpected help.

Still, a mental juggernaut that ignores what else is "out there" can be efficient, yet ineffective. The hyperconnectivity of normally disconnected thoughts and memories contains many individual bits of information, but we do not check to see if they are consistent with one another. As a result, contradictory bits may stand side by side without confusing us. This observation indicates that our cognitive mappings are different from reading road maps, because physical maps must be coherent. Metaphorically, that's where the planned cow trail to the top of the hill becomes an important role-player in our decision making. Intermittently, we need to roam or ramble—to move off the straight and narrow, to wander away from the beaten path. We need to explore the wilderness streams and breathe the fresh air. We need to examine the flowers and the people who live away from the freeways and out of the mainstream. *We need to question and seek what will elicit the outcomes that will define our campaign and whether or not new direction is indicated.*

Socratic Heightening: An unexamined journey is not worth making.

The most interesting and influential thinker in the Fifth Century was Socrates (470 BCE–399 BCE) whose brilliant dedication to careful reasoning (critical thinking) transformed the learning community. Perhaps his most important contribution to Western thought is his dialectic method of inquiry, known as the Socratic Method, which he largely applied to the examination of key moral concepts, such as the Good and the Just. It was first described by Plato in the *Socratic Dialogues*. A problem is broken down into a series of questions, the responses to which gradually distill the answer. The influence of this approach is most strongly felt today in the use of the Socratic Method, with hypothesis being the first stage.

Socrates' method of *insistent questioning* at least helps us to eliminate one bad answer to a serious question. At most, it points us toward a significant degree of intellectual *height and independence*. The use of the Socratic Method, even when it clearly results in a rational victory, may not produce genuine conviction in those to whom it is applied. As Socrates argued in the *Apology*, the only opinion that counts is not that of the majority of people generally, but rather that of the one individual who truly knows. The truth alone deserves to be the basis for decisions about action, so the only proper approach is to engage in careful moral reasoning by means of which one may hope to reveal truth.

Devotion to heightening through questioning is devotion to engaged thinking.

Even after he was convicted by a jury, Socrates declined to abandon his pursuit of *truth* in all matters. Refusing to accept exile from Athens or a commitment to silence as his penalty, he maintained that public discussion of the great issues of life and virtue is a necessary part of any valuable human life. **"The unexamined life is not worth living"** (Plato, 1993). Socrates would have rather died than give up philosophy, and the jury seemed happy to grant him that wish.

Socrates chose to honor his commitment to truth and morality even though it cost him his life.

One of the reasons that executives tend to overemphasize "coverage" over "engaged thinking" is that they do not fully appreciate the role of heightening or questioning in developing their subordinates. Consequently, they assume that answers can be taught separate from questions. Indeed, so buried are questions in established instruction that the fact that all assertions—all statements that this or that is so—are implicit answers to questions is virtually never recognized. For example, let us look at the statement that the most powerful force in business isn't greed, fear, or even the raw energy of unbridled competition. The most powerful force in business is love. The question may be: "What will help our business grow and become stronger?" or "What will propel our career forward?" or "What will give us a sense of meaning and satisfaction in our work, which will help us do our best work?"

Hence, every declarative statement in the communication is or should be an answer to a question. Every opportunity for an executive to develop his people could be couched in the interrogative mode by translating every business or political dilemma into a question. To our knowledge this has never been done. That it has not is testimony to the privileged status of answers over questions in organizational coaching and the misunderstanding of executives about the significance of questions in the learning (and thinking) process. Instruction at all levels of leadership now keeps most questions buried in a torrent of obscuring "answers."

> *Too often we ... enjoy the comfort of opinion without the discomfort of thought.*
>
> John F. Kennedy

Verbal brilliance is driven first by questions of height (heightening), then discomfort of thought, and then self-examination.

Verbal height is not driven by flat answers but by heightening—bright questions. Had no questions been asked by those who laid the foundation for a discipline—for example, physics, calculus, or chemistry—the discipline would never have been developed in the first place. In fact, every intellectual discipline is born out of a constellation of questions of height to which answers are either needed or highly desirable. Furthermore, every discipline stays alive only to the extent that fresh questions are generated and taken seriously as the driving force in a process of thinking. Likewise, every thriving organization feeds on questioning, discomfort of thinking, and self-examination. To think through or rethink anything, we must ask questions that stimulate some discomfort of thought. The errors that we make in our thinking often come about because we cut off the questions and dialogue.

Questions of height define tasks, articulate problems, and delineate issues. Answers, on the other hand, often signal a fragmentation in thought. Only when an answer generates a further question does thought continue its life as such. This is why it is true that only employees who have questions are really thinking and gaining wisdom. Moreover, the quality of the questions we ask determines the quality of the thinking we are doing. It is possible to give employees an examination on any organizational policy or procedure by just asking them to list all of the questions that they have about a procedure, including all questions generated by their first list of questions. That we do not test our employees by asking them to list questions and explain their significance is again evidence of the privileged status we give to answers isolated from questions. That is, we ask questions only to get thought-stopping answers, not to generate further questions.

Heightening turns on and revs up the thinking engines.

We need time for critical self-reflection to be aware of our strengths and weaknesses; our language, thinking, and emotions; and how we have been shaped by earlier experiences. Personal questions of height should put us in touch with status quo ideas, habits, and behaviors we have acquired over the years that need to be thrown under the bus. An illustration of verbal height regarding words and language is found in the words of Andrew Carnegie and Benjamin Franklin. Both men expressed their avoidance of using definitive terms such as "always" and "never," preferring instead terms as "usually" and "seldom."

Our co-workers and employees also need questions of height to turn on their intellectual engines; they must themselves generate questions from questions to get their thinking to go somewhere. A major stimulant to thinking height is focused questions. Thinking is of no use unless it goes somewhere, and again, the questions we ask determine where our thinking goes. It is only when our thinking goes somewhere that we learn anything of value.

A Russian businessman walked into a Swiss bank in Geneva and asked for a $100 loan. He offered his luxury Mercedes car as collateral. The bank manager quickly approved the loan. A year later, the Russian came back. He repaid the loan and the 10% interest and asked to collect his car. Finally, the puzzled bank manager dared to ask him, "Excuse me, sir, could you tell me: did you really need that $100 so badly? In order to get the money, you left your luxury car with us for a whole year!" The Russian replied, "That's simple—just think outside the box. Where else in Geneva could I find such a great parking place for just ten dollars a year?"

Use Socratic questioning to gain verbal altitude.

Socratic questioning is important for the critical thinker because the art of questioning is important to profound thought. Socratic questioning adds height to length in thought processing and nourishes a keen interest in assessing the truth or plausibility of things.

There is a special relationship between critical thinking and Socratic questioning, because both share a common end. Critical thinking gives us a comprehensive view of how the mind functions (in its pursuit of meaning and truth), and Socratic questioning takes advantage of that overview to frame questions essential to the quality of that pursuit.

The goal of Socratic thinking is to establish a disciplined executive oversight in thinking, a powerful inner voice of reason to monitor, assess, and reconstitute in a more rational direction our thinking, feeling, and action. Socratic discussion cultivates that inner voice by providing a public forum for it.

The Practice of Socratic Heightening

John is looking at Susan, but Susan is looking at Steven. John is married, but Steven is not. Is a married person looking at an unmarried person?

    A. Yes

    B. No

    C. Can't be determined.

Most of us will choose C. However, the correct answer is A. Our logic and reasoning need to be founded on asking the right questions. Susan is the only person whose marital status is unknown. We need to question both possibilities—either married or unmarried—to determine whether we have enough information to draw a conclusion. If Susan is married, the answer is A. Logically, she is the married individual looking at an unmarried individual (Steven). If Susan is not married, the answer is still A: John is the married person, and he is looking at Susan, the unmarried person.

Good logic should complement sound reasoning that comes from sound questioning of all possibilities. While there are numerous ways in which Socratic questioning can be effectively executed in the organization, there is a set of principles that guide a Socratic dialogue.

Executives engaged in a Socratic/thoughtful dialogue should:

    • Respond to every answer with a further question (that calls upon the respondent to develop his/her thinking in a fuller and deeper way).

    • Seek to understand—where possible—the ultimate foundations for what is said or believed and follow the implications of those foundations through further questions.

    • Treat all assertions as a connecting point to further thoughts.

- Treat all thoughts as in need of development.

- Recognize that any thought can only exist fully in a network of connected thoughts. Stimulate audience through questions to pursue those connections.

- Recognize that all questions presuppose prior questions and all thinking presupposes prior thinking. When raising questions, be open to the questions they presuppose.

Executives engaged in thoughtful dialogue should systematically raise questions based on the following recognitions and assumptions of thought:

- ***All thought reflects an agenda.*** We do not fully understand the thought until we understand the agenda behind it. ("What are you trying to accomplish in saying this? What is your central aim in this line of thought?")

- ***All thought presupposes an information base.*** We do not fully understand the thought until we understand the background information that supports or informs it. ("What information are you basing that comment on? What experience convinced you of this? How do you know this information is accurate?")

- ***All thought requires the making of inferences, the drawing of conclusions, the creation of meaning.*** We do not fully understand a thought until we understand the inferences that have shaped it. ("How did you reach that conclusion? Could you explain your reasoning? Is there an alternative plausible conclusion?")

- ***All thought involves the application of concepts.*** We do not fully understand a thought until we understand the concepts that define and shape it. ("What is the main idea you are putting forth? Could you explain that idea?")

- ***All thought rests upon other thoughts.*** We do not fully understand a thought until we understand what it takes for granted. ("What exactly are you taking for granted here? Why are you assuming that?")

• *All thought is headed in a direction.* It not only rests upon something (assumptions), it is also going somewhere (implications and consequences). We do not fully understand a thought unless we know the implications and consequences that follow from it. ("What are you implying when we you say that? Are you implying that ...?")

• *All thought takes place within a point of view or frame of reference.* We do not fully understand a thought until we understand the point of view or frame of reference. ("From what point of view are you looking at this? Is there another point of view you should consider?")

• *All thought is responsive to a question.* Assume that we do not fully understand the thought until we understand the question that gives rise to it. ("I am not sure exactly what question you are raising. Could you explain it?")

• *All thought has three possible functions: to express a subjective preference, to establish an objective fact (within a well-defined system), or to come up with the best of competing answers (generated by competing systems).* We do not fully understand thinking until we know which of the three functions is involved. Is the question calling for a subjective or personal choice? If so, let's make that choice in terms of our personal preferences. If not, then, is there a way to come up with one correct answer to this question (a definite system in which to find the answer)? Or, finally, are we dealing with a question that would be answered differently within different points of view? If the latter, what is the best answer to the question, all things considered?

• *All thought emerges within a human context.* We do not fully understand the thought until we understand the context that has given rise to it. ("Tell us more about the situation that has given rise to this problem. What was going on in this situation?").

How to Prepare to Lead a Thoughtful Discussion

One of the best ways to prepare to lead a Socratic discussion is by pre-thinking the main question to be discussed, using the approach of developing prior questions. Prior questions are questions presupposed by another question. Hence, to settle the question, "What is a cross-functional work team?" we should be able to first settle the question, "What is a work team?" and to settle that question, we should be able to settle the question, "What is the basis of a team?" Accomplishing anything in business more complicated than opening the mail requires teamwork. "How do we build a team that is made up of members from different departments around a shared problem? What might happen if we get a bunch of folks from different disciplines and throw them all together?"

Construct a List of Prior Questions, Focus on the Alpha and the Omega

To construct a list of prior questions, simply write down the main question that we are going to focus our discussion on and then pose a question we would have to be able to answer before we could answer the first. Then take the second question and do the same for it (i.e., determine what question we would have to answer to answer it). Then, continue on, following the same procedure for every new question on our list.

As we proceed to construct our list, keep our attention focused on the first question on the list as well as on the last (the Alpha & the Omega). If we do this well, we should end up with a list of questions that probe the logic of the first question, and hence, a list of questions that are relevant to a Socratic discussion of our first question. During the Socratic dialog, we should loosely follow our list of logical prior questions, using it primarily as a guide for deeply probing the issue at hand.

A Sample List

As an example of how to logically construct prior questions, consider this list of questions that we developed in thinking through key questions intended for use in conducting a Socratic discussion. The question was, "What is leadership development about?"

- What is leadership?
- What do leaders lead?
- What is the difference between leaders and managers?
- How does one become a responsible leader?
- What do leaders do and not do?
- How do leaders grow their people?
- How do leaders know where they need to go with their organizations?
- How can leaders know who is going to help them get there?
- How do leaders make sure those people understand and have bought into their vision?
- How can leaders make sure their people have the tools, training, and technology to accomplish the vision?
- How as a leader does one give constant feedback, provide coaching where needed, and changing personnel as necessary?

In summary, to create something that has never been clearly understood before, we must begin asking questions that help our people generate new thinking and ultimately create new opportunities and visions—that create new products and services targeted for specific markets, etc. We can develop a culture of Socratic questioning and idea generation needed to increase intellectual capital, intellectual property, knowledge assets, and/or business intelligence, corporate knowledge—all esteemed as the only sustainable, untapped source of competitive advantage in business today.

Hawaii Energy Dilemma: In Search of a BRIGHT Solution

Both authors have homes in Hawaii. We humorously say that whenever we fill our cars with gas, we double the value of our vehicles. As consumers, we probably take most things for granted, including accepting the high cost for energy in our middle-of-the-Pacific, East-West, community. But we stumble over the frequent, uncorrelated, unexplainable, unpredictable "spikes" in gasoline prices. What we do know is that Hawaii is heavily reliant on external forces and imports to supply basic energy needs, which continually subjects us to forces over which we have no control. What we don't know is why prices are rising higher than in any other state in the union, and whether refiners, distributors, or retailers are to blame for gouging.

There is a lack of transparency surrounding the oil industry's weekly "flat" reports, which makes it hard to use them as accurate barometers of their profitability. They do not contain any data regarding the weekly average profits or the margins (e.g., excessive profits being gained) which would directly add to the price of this very precious commodity. The fact that prices are so unpredictable and variable explains why there is considerable anxiety around random price spikes at the pump. The state is so dependent on this one commodity that frequent rises in oil prices become very problematic for the economy's stability. The lack of reliable information makes it difficult for executives and legislators to address the problem in a constructive fashion.

We are told by legislators and government policy makers that we, the public, need to address our overdependence on oil. What do we address? How are we market drivers? What are the choices? What are the clean energy sources? How are we to ask the obvious questions and contribute to the complex solution of a preferred green energy future? We are told that as consumers, we can dictate the incentives for businesses to get their investors to participate with capital. These are mostly linear questions to a more complex, systemic problem.

The solution has to be taken to a higher dimension of executive thinking. It is obvious that the government chooses not to lead this transition and represent the solution against some of the inherent barriers. The business community is not supported in developing the projects to make the case for long-term solutions of alternative energy sources.

On a linear level, the answers are simple (e.g., the government needs to encourage and not discourage business entrepreneurs from moving ahead with "green" incentives). However, thinking systemically, it all starts with money. Once we have the capital available, anything is possible. We can build a large wind farm or build a solar farm. It will take early adopters or entrepreneurs to come into the market and take the risk and demonstrate the model. Then, we can have our more prominent leaders do something about it. Momentum happens when we have one or two successful demonstrations of how the model works; it will be a cake-walk for others to declare, "Hey, these guys did it. Let's do it, too." Then in this sequence comes public awareness. The public can apply pressure on the government, the utilities, and the Public Utilities Commission.

On a global-spatial dimension, the reason prices are going up is because resources are running out on our planet, maybe in 30, 50, or 100 years. Another global perspective is that oil is located in countries where the owners are not enthusiastic about depleting their supply, because it is their main export and source of revenue. To maintain their most valuable commodity, oil-rich nations will probably only increase production *gradually* to barely accommodate the growing demands for fuel worldwide.

What do we Americans do with all our oil? Half of it is converted to gasoline to power our cars, trucks, and SUVs. In Europe, less than 15% of oil is used for gas. The four big Asian economies of China, India, Japan, and South Korea combined use less oil than the United States. Back to simple economics: when demand grows more than supply, costs go up.

A clear question with height: If we can figure out a way to spur innovation with less oil consumption, go green, insulate ourselves, and lower energy costs, then don't we in Hawaii stand a better chance as a society of giving people a better way of life? Why not have half of our homes generating electricity through mini-solar home power plants—employable for our electric cars—renewable within a decade through micro-grids? Can we creatively cut back on our second and third jobs, use electric cars or ride bicycles to work, and spend more time with our family and children? Why can't Hawaii within several years realize 50% more energy efficiency through solar technology? Why can't we support new energy technology that uses mirrors to intensely concentrate the energy of the sun. As the sun moves, these mirrors follow the sun and reflect sunlight into a pipe. There a heat-transfer liquid circulates to create steam, which in turn can create electricity. Why not? Why not more electric cars? The future can be so BRIGHT! The solution clearly begins with verbal questions of height.

New BRIGHT Energy Technology—First Solar

Fast Company listed First Solar as the sixth most innovative, thinking company in America in 2010:

> *For most of the past decade, the first renewable company to be listed on the S&P 500 had one overriding goal: driving down the cost of solar-power modules until they could compete with traditional power. It has used every strategy at its disposal, from newly patented technologies to overseas production to vertical integration at all levels of a project—all while managing to sidestep economic landmines and navigate the shifting policy landscape. The company was the first solar supplier to cross the $1-per-watt mark, putting it roughly on par with conventional power and cruised to $0.85 per watt by the end of 2009, the lowest cost in the industry.* (Kamenetz, 2010)

Energy management—using less energy and saving money—will be the next big thing!

Some problems you just can't solve; tackle them anyway through debating.

Debate—a formal way of conducting an argument in which one advocates in favor of an issue or policy, while another advocates against the proposal. Debate forces executives to think about the multiple sides of an issue, and it also forces them to interact not just with the details of a given topic, but also with one another. Debates are versatile in the range of topics possible and the format that the debate may follow.

Returning to Hawaii from Edinburgh (Graham), my wife Winnie pursued her passion and started a speech and debate program at Kahuku High School on the North Shore, Oahu. This "country" school was known for great surfers and football players. The school has more representatives in the National Football League than does any other high school in the United States. Because her program successfully competed on state and national levels over the years, nothing did more to elevate perspectives and heighten aspirations of her students than debating with the best in the country. Policy debaters (similar to British parliamentary) are Kahuku's pride, with two-member teams researching both sides of a resolution and prepared to take either the affirmative or negative case against another team from anywhere. Her students have graduated and have taken their speech and debate critical-thinking skills (verbal height) to some of the best universities, to their jobs, and to life itself.

We have found that running debates in organizations is straightforward, and after a little bit of preparation, executives quickly learn the necessary skills. Organizational debating allows exploration of unsettled issues/problems as well as developing confidence in speech and higher-order thinking skills. The ability to express our opinions (or even other people's opinions) clearly, persuasively, and in a way that will make other people want to listen to us is a very valuable skill. Debate develops powers of argument, increases understanding, and boosts critical thinking—all essential higher-order thinking skills. Executives like Glenn Muranaka, General Manager of Meadow Gold Dairies, personally take part in their executive team debates to stimulate greater preparedness, communication, and more innovative thinking.

Organizational debating attempts to bring clarity to the messy problems that take place in and around the workplace. The debate starts with a resolution—a short and simple statement that defines what both sides will argue. Each team—the affirmative and negative—tries to convince a neutral judge (executive) that their position is right. The teams do this by building up their arguments and tearing down their opponents' arguments. The central characteristic of organizational debating is that it provides rules to encourage the two debate teams to clash. It is not enough that two sides give different advocacies. Each side must directly respond to the arguments of the other team, compare their position to that of their opponents, and give the judge a reason to vote for them.

How it works:

- Executives must first be made aware of a debatable topic and of the variety of potential positions that can be taken on the topic. These topics can come from any controversial issue before the organization that needs an informed decision.

- Executives should then be given an opportunity to research the topic somehow and form their own opinions on the issue.

- Pairs or small groups should be formed where like-minded executives can share their opinions on the topic and gain information from others. During this step, executives should be encouraged to think about the potential arguments that will come from the other side and how they can respond to these arguments.

- Now some form of debate must take place where the two (or three or four) sides share their opinions and present their arguments. This could take the form of a classic debate, with opening and closing arguments from both sides and time for rebuttals, all done as an executive team. Alternatively, it could simply be small groups or pairs sharing their differing points of view with one another.

- Then the CEO should follow up with a summary of the opinions and views expressed by all sides and an assessment of their strengths and weaknesses.

- In the final step, other executives (judges) and the CEO should be allowed to express their opinions about which side made the case most convincingly. This step is important in that it helps the executives to understand that this type of thinking and debate process can lead to real results, and it provides a sense of closure on the issue.

Executive Debating Skills and Keeping the Team Verbally "In Shape"

Critical thinking skills: Understanding and assessing other people's arguments is essential in an information world. Critical thinking is the process of formulating, identifying, clarifying, and sustaining thoughts and ideas. Critical thinking is essential for well-reasoned arguments. Executives need to learn to see the logical connections between abstract ideas and events in the real world. Critical thinking allows debaters to find the logical flaws in the analysis of their opponents' positions and be able to see when an argument is not being supported. Critical thinking is the cornerstone of good debate.

Research skills: When we advocate a position, we need evidence to support our arguments. Sometimes simple logic or common examples can be used successfully to support an argument. But often the arguments will need evidence and require us to gather information from outside sources.

Organizational skills: A big part of debating is organizing our arguments into an effective speech. Organization is even more important in public speaking than in writing. Readers can always turn back a couple of pages and remind themselves of what the author is talking about. But in debate, if we are not clear and logical, we might lose the attention of our judge and then lose the debate.

Listening and note-taking skills: In debate, listening skills are essential because if a debater fails to hear or to understand an opponent's argument, he or she cannot successfully refute it.

Please commit to honesty. If we participate in organizational debating, our job as a debater is to be honest in our arguments, honest in our use of evidence, and response to questions.

Please debate with respect. Debate is not about personalities, and we should never belittle or degrade another person simply because he or she disagrees with us. Debate is about ideas, and in a battle of ideas, the only acceptable weapon is a well-reasoned argument.

Good BRIGHT1 Communication Skills: Brevity, Thoroughness, and Structure

Good linear messages have three attributes: brevity, thoroughness, and structure. These attributes should be included in every voicemail, e-mail, or memo. Remember, BRIGHT1 communication lets people briefly know everything they need to know. Messages must be thorough enough to cover the subject and follow a structure that makes sense and allow people to skillfully keep their thinking and conversations focused on problem solving, solutions, and actions.

It's important that we take time to develop good communication skills in any situation in order to have the most useful conversations and bring our people onboard. That would include providing appropriate, continuous, and positive communication to validate, confirm, encourage, support, and believe in their potential. With good communication skills, we can stretch our people more than they stretch themselves—creating new thinking and transforming performance where needed.

What are some challenges for visual-spatial thinkers living in a "Sequential Land"?

Linear thinking appears to be influenced profoundly by sequential processing while the executive who learns holistically rather than in a step-by-step fashion will employ the height of visual imagery in the learning process. Because an executive may be processing primarily in pictures rather than in words, ideas are interconnected. Linear sequential thinking—the norm in American education—is particularly difficult for this executive. Some visual-spatial learners (typically from the hard science majors) are excellent at auditory sequential processing as well. They have full access to both systems, and can resort to sequential methods of problem solving if they don't get an immediate understanding when looking at a problem.

Most visual-spatial executives do not gain access to gifted programs because of a lack of insightfulness in academia. These learners make great intuitive leaps, grasp extremely complex material, excel at mathematical and scientific reasoning, and demonstrate high levels of creativity. However, if they are weak in sequencing, they may be poor in mechanics—computation, spelling, and handwriting. Their weaknesses are often viewed as evidence that they are not really gifted, and their high abilities may be ignored.

The learning style of visual-spatial executives is paradoxical: the harder the concept, the faster they grasp it. The easier the work, the more likely they are to fail. Their abilities are frequently misjudged, because of the discrepancy between the way they learn and the way material is presented in the regular training format. They usually become frustrated with their lack of success in the workplace.

Using linear thinking only can doom an organization and/or executives.

We believe that for any executive to continue to look at something from one point of view or to take information or observations from one situation, place this data in another situation (usually later), and make a conclusion in the later situation—is a prescription for failure. Using only linear thinking can doom an organization and/or executives. Consider the company that hires new employees who have backgrounds that match those of employees who were hired in years past without any thought given to future needs and/or direction of the organization. Consider the following example:

> *You are an executive responsible for hiring a new Project Manager to manage consulting service delivery projects. You receive résumés for the position and start to comb through them. While thinning out the résumés, you run across one résumé from a candidate (#1) who has been a consultant and project manager for your closest competitor, and another from a candidate (#2) who has been a consultant and project manager in various industries but has had little experience within your industry. These two candidates have completely different*

> backgrounds, with candidate #1 having a BS in Business, an MBA, PMP certification, and ten years of experience, while candidate #2 has a BS in Computer Science and an MS in Marketing and ten years of experience. Which candidate would you choose?

Most of our students voted for hiring Candidate #1 with "industry experience" and the PMP certification. Of course, there isn't a right or wrong answer to the question, since many factors would come into play (communication abilities, culture fit, salary requirements) and a person's feelings and intuition about the candidates will always make its way into the hiring decision.

This example, though, shows an aspect of linear thinking that exists in organizations. There really is no right or wrong answer as to which candidate should be hired, but a person who is able to employ critical-thinking abilities and think in a two- or three-dimensional manner just might have looked at the candidates in a different light. Instead of hiring Candidate #1, who has similar experiences as other people within the organization, why not consider candidate #2, who might be able to bring a fresh outlook to the organization? Assuming that candidate #2 has the ability, shouldn't he/she be considered just as much a fit as candidate #1? We think so.

It's much easier to hire only those people that fit a narrowly defined job description than it is to open up the candidate search to people with a more diverse background. If the two candidates in the above example were both able to show demonstrable evidence of their ability to do the job, candidate #1 would still be the only candidate considered in most organizations, because that candidate fits the mold that the hiring manager has created for the candidate search.

In Summary: In business and politics, it's important to hire and politically elect verbally high, quantitatively wide, and spatially deep (BRIGHT1+2+3) thinking leaders who have holistic powers to sustain the ideology and economy of the country. We believe that part of the reason for the large failure rates within the project-management community (especially within IT Project Management) and a big linear "tax-and-spend" government is related to an inability to debate the issues (B1) and also to think in two- and three-dimensional fashion. If we don't find and nurture ultra-smart thinking leaders, we will experience a regression to "dumb-dumb" and lose out on stimulating the needed responsiveness, inventiveness, and opportunities that cannot be conceptualized by verbally gifted thinkers and talkers only.

How do we get beyond a "linear mentality only" within our organization? The answer: develop BRIGHT2+ 3+4 thinking.

Morris A. Graham, PhD and Kevin Baize, OD

CHAPTER SUMMARY
Key Points

- Excellent, clear, and concise verbal and written communication is a key power for bright executives. Bright1 is sequential processing, which is what an individual uses to work with information that is arranged in order. Also known as serial processing, sequential processing is a term used to describe the processing that occurs in the order that it is received.

- The ability to receive, store, process, and use information uses a series of cognitive ordering procedures called *sequential processing*. The two basic building blocks of learning and memory are *auditory* and *visual sequential processing*. These building blocks are essential to verbal height: listening, learning, reading, and communicating. They form the base of the brain's higher-order executive functions. Essentially, every mental process we perform is dependent on these processing abilities.

- Questions define tasks, express problems, and delineate issues. Answers, on the other hand, often signal a disconnect in thought. Only when an answer generates a further question does thought continue.

- Our capacity to process with height—learn new information and form memories—is realized through structural plasticity. During learning, reversible physiological changes in synaptic transmission take place in the brain. These temporary, reversible changes are referred to as short-term memory, and the persistent changes as long-term memory.

- If we work it right, our decision-making will be enriched by contributions both solicited and unsolicited. If we keep our eyes and ears open—if we truly see and listen—then our arrival at point B "on the map" will have more meaning. It will affect more people positively, and it will facilitate more than satisfactory end results.

• Thinking is of no use unless it goes somewhere. The questions we ask determine whether our thinking goes anywhere. It is only when our thinking goes somewhere that we learn anything of value to us.

• Linear thinking can doom a system and/or a person who continues to look at something from one point of view; to take information or observations from one situation; and later place this data in another situation and make a conclusion in the latter situation.

• The sequential dimension appears to be influenced profoundly by auditory processing.

• The executive who learns holistically rather than in a step-by-step fashion will employ visual imagery in the learning process. Because the individual is processing primarily in pictures rather than in words, ideas are interconnected. Linear sequential thinking—the norm in American education—is particularly difficult for this executive. We believe that part of the reason for the large failure rates within the project management community (especially within IT Project Management) and a big linear "tax-and-spend" government is related to an inability debate the issues (B1) and also to think in two- and three-dimensional fashion.

CHAPTER 4

BRIGHT2—Quantitative Width
Solving Problems with Numbers

> *The latest authors, like the most ancient, strove to subordinate the phenomena of nature to the laws of mathematics.*
>
> Sir Isaac Newton (1642–1727)

> *Not everything that can be counted counts, and not everything that counts can be counted.*
>
> Albert Einstein

> *I have always thought of abstract information—numbers, for example—in **visual**, dynamic form. Numbers assume complex, multidimensional shapes in my head that I manipulate to form the solution to sums or compare when determining whether they are prime or not. In my mind, numbers and words are far more than squiggles of ink on a page. They have form, color, texture, and so on. They come alive to me, which is why as a young child I thought of them as my "friends." I think this is why my memory is very deep, because the information is not static. I do not crunch numbers as I compute, I dance with them.*
>
> Daniel Tammet, *Think Better: Tips from a Savant*

BRIGHT2 or quantitative thinking needs to be about *width*. It was Sir Isaac Newton, the English physicist and mathematician (calculus), and the greatest scientist of the seventeenth and eighteenth centuries, who said, "If I have ever made any valuable discoveries, it has been owing more to patient observation than to any other reason." His *Philosophiæ Naturalis Principia Mathematica*, published in 1687, is considered to be the most influential book in the history of science. In this work, Newton described universal gravitation and the three laws of motion, laying the groundwork for classical mechanics, which dominated the scientific view of the physical universe for the next three centuries and is the basis for modern engineering. He affirmed the power of *quantitative width*:

> Everything that is anything can be measured in four measurements—what, where, when, and how much … what (what it is and what it is not), where (where it is and where it is not), when (when it is and when it is not), and how much (how much it is and how much it is not). (Newton, 1999, pp. 408–409)

The twentieth century belonged to verbal (symbolic) and quantitative (two-dimensional processing) thinkers and learners. Literacy reigned supreme. "Literate" and "educated" were synonymous, and "illiterate" meant "ignorant." Reading, writing, and arithmetic depend on verbal-auditory-sequential-numerical skills and develop linear sequential reasoning further. The emphasis on literacy in the schools at the end of the last century is a testament to the panic our society is experiencing as consciousness begins to shift from the linear verbal thinking of *Dragnet* ("We just want the facts, Madam") to an investigative, DNA/quantitatively driven, problem-solving *CSI* (Crime Scene Investigation).

Many Americans have a difficulty with even straightforward mathematics. Around a third of Americans adults cannot calculate 10% of 1,000. Individuals who struggle with concepts such as percentage have a difficult time with more complicated ideas, such as compounding of savings and, very relevant to our current crisis, adjustable-rate mortgages. If that reflects some of our educational background, then hope comes with broadening our quantitative abilities through asking questions that will stimulate two-dimensional thinking or "widening."

What is quantitative width?

What is and what is not the demonstration of something?

What is and what is not the pattern?

What is and what is not the proof?

What is and what is not the refutation?

What is and what is not the contradiction?

These are all questions that stimulate two-dimensional, wide thinking (BRIGHT2). It's as old as Plato's Academy and as modern as the latest demographic study, organizational assessment, or computer program. This quantitative modality permeates our professional and personal lives. A little web surfing reveals sticker and invoice prices, dealer holdbacks and incentive packages, depreciation estimates, customer satisfaction ratings, reliability statistics, expected insurance costs, crash-test results, and various accident, injury, and fatality rates, not to mention a wealth of financing data. As technology accelerates, our ability to make wise decisions, whether at work or at home, increasingly depends on our proficiency with processing quantitative information.

$y = mx + b$: From straight lines to processing in two-dimensional width

BRIGHT2 processing takes place almost every time we pay attention to a new source of information (taking it quantitatively wider or two-dimensional). It is happening right now while we are reading these lines, filtering the relevant information in order to get some width around the flow of the above equation. The terms line, linear, and linearity play a major role in mathematical thinking, although mathematics is not about linear thinking. Mathematicians have studied the "line" and "linearity" to a degree which dazzles the mind, because it is more about width. Their best known description of a straight line is the formula $y = mx + b$.

We have discovered that most executives use two-dimensional thinking (BRIGHT2), which focuses on reframing issues and contradictions to address the appropriate problem. Effective two-dimensional thinking should distinguish systemic patterns from random events, identify acceptable risks in alternative decisions, and make better decisions within group or department settings.

> *Jack Welch, early in his career at General Electric, insisted that each of GE's businesses be number one or number two in market share in its industry. Years later he insisted that those same businesses define their markets so that their share was no greater than 10%, thereby forcing managers to spatially look in another dimension for opportunities beyond the confines of a single-dimension, narrowly conceived market. Trying to learn from what Jack Welch did invites confusion and incoherence, because he pursued—wisely—diametrically opposed courses at different points in his career and in GE's history.* (Martin, 2007)

A Two-Dimensional Transmogrifier Warm-Up

The transmogrifier makes bizarre changes to those brave enough to enter it. Sam gave it a try, and he came out colored red (but otherwise the same). Then Don stepped in. The transmogrifier took a while, but Don came out blue when he was finally done. Slim took his chances next and unfortunately came out as green ooze. Sid's resulting coloring was red, but only on one side. Justin turned into a blue woman, and then Mal stepped out green—and her sex was changed, too. Tom is up next. What will the transmogrifier do to Tom? (The answer is at the end of the chapter.)

Prisoner's Dilemma—Moving through Contradiction to Two-Dimensional Thinking

We use a tool in our leadership seminars to get our executives to understand and appreciate two-dimensional dilemmas—thinking by what game theorists call "Prisoner's Dilemma." In it, two prisoners accused of the same crime find themselves in separate cells, unable to communicate. The investigating officers try to persuade them to implicate one another. If neither goes along with the officers, they will both receive a sentence of just one year. If one accepts the deal and the other keeps quiet, then the turncoat goes free while the patsy gets ten years. And if they both denounce one another, they both get five years.

If the first prisoner is planning to keep quiet, then the second has an incentive to denounce him and get off scot-free rather than spend a year in prison. If the first prisoner were planning to betray the second, then the second would still be better off pointing the finger, and so receive a five-year sentence instead of a ten-year one. In other words, a rational, self-interested person would always betray his fellow prisoner. Yet that leaves them both moldering in jail for five years, when they could have cut their sentences to a year if they had both thought in two dimensions and decided to keep quiet.

We have found over the years that linearly thinking leaders will often neglect a real problem, on the grounds that others will either solve it (x and y variables), allowing their group to become a free-rider, or let it fester (linear play-out thinking), making it a doomed cause anyway. Taken internationally, the world is condemned to a slow roasting (the "global warming dilemma"), even though global warming could be averted if everyone (countries) thought at least two-dimensionally and cooperated.

The dynamics of the Prisoner's Dilemma change dramatically if participants know that they will be playing the game more than once. In that case, they are pressed to think in two dimensions (self-investment and other's investment) and cooperate, in order to avoid being punished for their misconduct by their opponent in subsequent rounds. The most successful strategy when the game is repeated must employ a two-dimensional thinking that: (1) players should start out by cooperating ; (2) they should deter betrayals by punishing the transgressor in the next round; and (3) they should not bear grudges but instead should start cooperating with treacherous players again after meting out the appropriate punishment. The result of this exercise can be sustained two-dimensional thinking and cooperation rather than a linear cycle of recrimination.

Two-Dimensional Thinking and the Capacity to Process Quantitative Width:

E J 6 3

Four cards, pictured above, are sitting on a table. Each card has a letter on one side and a number on the other. Two of the cards are letter side up, and two of the cards are number side up. The rule to be tested is this : *For these four cards, if a card has a vowel on its letter side, it has an even number on its number side. Our task is to decide which card or cards must be turned over to find out whether the rule is true or false. Indicate which cards must be turned over:* ____ ____

Most of us will choose E (correct) and 6 (incorrect) as turnovers. Why is it wrong to choose 6? Read the rule again: it says that a vowel must have an even number on the back. But it says nothing about whether an even number must have a vowel on the back or what kind of number a consonant must have. The rule says nothing about consonants, so there is no need to see what is on the back of the J. So finding a consonant on the back of the 6 would say nothing about whether the rule is true or false. In contrast, the 3 card, which most of us do not choose, is essential. If the 3 card has a vowel on the back, the rule would be shown to be false, because that would mean that not all vowels have even numbers on the back. In brief, to show that the rule is not false, the 3 card must be turned over (Stanovich, 2009).

Few jobs involve greater contact with numbers and the need for keen quantitative thinking than that of an accountant. Accountants have the ability to digest, often with the help of others, large amounts of information in order to form important decisions. If accountants are not thorough with figures, they might miss a liability that has been excluded from a company's balance sheet or a depreciation charge that has been miscalculated. Yet how much advanced mathematics is required to assess numbers on financial statements? Likewise, large amounts of quantitative information are a feature of other professional occupations—architects, doctors, management consultants, financial planners, marketing executives. Good quantitative thinking is crucial to doing their jobs well. But matrix algebra is not required. Nor are such high school staples as quadratic equations, analytic geometry, and imaginary numbers. Contrary to popular opinion, formal mathematics is not the best way to teach quantitative thinking, and superior quantitative reasoning is not restricted to those who excelled in high school math.

What differentiates good two-dimensional/quantitative thinkers is not their skill with pure mathematics, but rather their *capacity to process quantitative information*. Two-dimensional thinkers possess certain capabilities that they bring to bear whenever they need to make decisions based on numbers. And with uncommon exceptions, these capabilities are not taught in math classes or textbooks. Good quantitative thinkers insist on empirical evidence instead of conventional wisdom, with the assumption that figures are often wrong or misleading. Good quantitative thinkers don't examine numerical information until they have a strategy for doing so. They know that some numbers are far more important than others, and they systematically shave the data in an effort to find the most revealing figures. They also make lots of rough estimates, scribble on the backs of envelopes, and use arithmetic shortcuts.

We may be confident that we probably know all the math we need (i.e., the basics—arithmetic, percentages, fractions, decimals, square roots, and exponents). Fundamentally, strong quantitative/B2 thinkers process the numerical world with greater width. When Shaquille O'Neal accepted the NBA's Most Valuable Player award in 2000, he quoted Aristotle: "Excellence is not a singular act, but a habit. You are what you repeatedly do." Excellence in anything is the product of practice. That's especially true of quantitative thinking, which doesn't come naturally to any of us. We present here some skills to practice and increase our capacity to widen our BRIGHT2 dimension.

BRIGHT2 Capacity: Making Judgments with Quantitative Evidence

Developing quantitative thinking capacity is an essential component of our B2 power. Two-dimensional thinking incorporates both qualitative and quantitative evidence and evaluation. In some fields of endeavor, quantitative approaches play a central role, while qualitative thinking dominates other fields. Despite these differences in emphasis across fields, numerical thinking skills and habits of the mind learned in one area often carry over and reinforce those learned in other areas. It is for this reason that the width and breadth of experience associated with liberal arts education prepares executives effectively to be active B2 participants and leaders in government, civil society, business, and academia.

Policy debates, scientific discussions, and personal and organizational decisions involve making judgments about claims made with quantitative evidence. To evaluate these claims, executives must have some basic familiarity with counting, measurement, and statistical analysis. Equally important is the capacity to ask and answer questions in ways appropriate to these quantitative tools and to understand when and where the use of quantitative tools is appropriate and when and where it is not. Executives should learn a group of related approaches to collecting, interpreting, and presenting information about their world built out of relatively simple and familiar numerical, statistical, and logical skills.

TARGET PRACTICE

A large circular target has a radius of 12 feet. The next ring inward has a radius of six times the square root of three. The next ring inward has a radius of six times the square root of two. The inner ring has a radius of six feet. If you shoot at this target randomly, which region are you most likely to hit?

(Answer: end of the chapter)

Executives must develop the widening capacity to:

- **Describe the world quantitatively:** B2 thinking should involve quantitative or statistical descriptions of social and natural phenomena. This includes descriptions of patterns and variations and rates of change, such as non-linear or exponential growth. Understanding descriptive statistics and the various modes of presentation of quantitative data is central. Executives should be able to distinguish when quantitative approaches are appropriate and when they are not.

- **Evaluate sources and quality of data:** B2 thinking should understand the sources of data, including the processes of collecting or producing data. This may involve understanding how to assess the reliability and validity of measurements and elements of probability and sampling, including sources of bias and error.

- **Distinguish association from causation:** The B2 thinker knows ways that associations between factors are established by observation, experiment, or quasi-experiment. It is important to be able to establish the meaning of an association or correlation and learn the protocols for weighing the statistical significance and theoretical importance of findings, including inferring causation. Most decisions, whether public or private, individual or societal, may be thought of as involving conflicting goals. Much of the debate on public issues involves disagreement about the value of the different goals. Where there are conflicting goals, quantitative thinking offers techniques for weighing the relative impact of policy options. While there rarely is a single correct outcome in the face of such conflicts, the quantitative thinkers can bring measure and balance to policy discussion.

- **Understand trade-offs, uncertainty, and risk:** Few things in life are certain; decisions and debate often revolve around unknowns. B2 thinkers possess skills that can be used to assess, compare, and balance risks, and understand the limits and strengths of these techniques. B2 thinkers know that, in the face of the unknown, if not the unknowable, we often rely on conditional statements and probabilities in making decisions and can evaluate conclusions drawn from conditional statements.

• Use estimation and modeling to evaluate claims and test theories: B2 thinkers understand that quantities vary over huge ranges; big and small are not absolute notions but depend on context or scale. B2 thinkers appreciate the value and limitations of abstracting out detail—constructing models—and know that the sensitivity of model results to assumptions can and should be reported along with the model results.

B2 capacity-widening is about applying our numerical processing to daily contexts.

A mathematician might take delight in abstraction, but the B2 thinking executive should be able to apply his/her capacity-widening to daily contexts (i.e., understanding the power of compound interest or the uses and abuses of percentages; using fundamental statistical analysis to gauge the accuracy of a statistical study; or applying the principles of logic and rhetoric to real-world arguments). Though few executives are trained to work with complex mathematical concepts, all B2 thinkers should be able to understand mathematics well enough to develop informed opinions about quantitative concepts.

Answering the following three questions requires numerical processing that two-dimensional (B2) thinking executives should be able to tackle.

1. Officials estimate that 320,000 Boston-area party-goers attended the 1995 Independence Day celebration on the banks of the Charles River. They also estimate that the party-goers left behind 40 tons of garbage. Given that a ton equals 2,000 pounds, how many pounds of garbage did the average partygoer leave behind?

2. One year ago, a person invested $6,000 in a certain stock. Today, the value of the investment has risen to $7,200. If, instead, the person had invested $15,000 one year ago instead

of $6,000, what would the investment's value be today? (Assume that the investment would increase by the same proportion.)

3. According to the Cable News Network (CNN), the number of injured in-line skaters (or "Rollerbladers") was 184% larger in 1994 than it was in 1993. Did the number of injured skaters almost double, almost triple, or more than triple?

BIG STORE SALES

The big store sales were on. Unfortunately, the $100 fancy Hawaiian quilt wasn't selling. It was reduced by 40%, but didn't sell. Then, it was reduced 20% further, and still didn't sell. Finally, it was reduced another 25%, and it sold. What did it sell for, and what percentage of the original amount was that price? (Answer: at end of chapter)

What should a basic competency in numerical processing include?

We are to understand that many executives have not learned sophisticated math skills, but all should be able to use simple math tools to reason, understand, interpret, critique, debunk, challenge, explicate, and draw conclusions. In short, BRIGHT2 executive thinkers should be able to evaluate the crush of quantitative data that comes with organizational leadership.

We affirm the following fundamentals are needed for an executive to do two-dimensional thinking—numerical processing:

- Interpret mathematical models such as formulas, graphs, tables, and schematics, and draw inferences from them.

- Represent mathematical information symbolically, visually, numerically, and verbally.

- Use arithmetical, algebraic, geometric, and statistical methods to solve problems.

- Estimate and check answers to mathematical problems in order to determine reasonableness, identify alternatives, and select optimal results.

- Recognize that mathematical and statistical methods have limits.

Expressions of B2 Thinking: Examples from Current Issues of Public Concern: None of the questions below have a single, sequentially, correct answer. All of them involve judgment, values, and ethics. All of them are strongly informed by quantitative information; most of them involve balancing competing goals. Quantitative thinking should enable executives to make informed judgments about such issues and to communicate those judgments and the reasoning behind them in discussion and debate.

- One way to address global warming is to use more nuclear and hydroelectric power. Yet nuclear power imposes risks and hydroelectric dams can have serious environmental consequences. How do we judge to what extent it is worthwhile to accept these risks and consequences?

- Opponents of immigration often claim that immigrants force down wages of American workers. Proponents say that immigrants take jobs that Americans aren't willing to do. Both arguments seem plausible. How should we evaluate these claims?

- Government statistics show that, as a group, women continue to earn less than men. How can we assess whether this reflects discrimination or different lifestyle choices that men and women tend to make?

- Some people want to take public money to give vouchers to students to study in private schools. These people claim that the private, generally religious schools produce better educational outcomes for the same money and back up these claims with standardized test results from pilot programs. Should we support an expansion of these programs?

- Would a $5 per gallon tax on gasoline derail the economy? Would it have a substantial impact on gasoline consumption and alternative energy sources?

- Might a universal health care bill ultimately bankrupt the United States, or are such claims simple fear-mongering?

- Are the risks of mass flu vaccination worth the benefits? How do we measure the risks?

- Private accounts in social security would increase payments without raising taxes, yet they are acknowledged to increase risk. How do we know whether this increased risk means that private accounts are bad public policy? Could it be true that a 1% increase in social security taxes would save the system?

Numbers and Equations, Measurements, and Graphs/Charts— Keep it Broad!

Mathematics uses numeric reasoning, which adds a unique dimension to executive thinking (i.e., the ability to solve story or word problems, and thereby understand a greater width and breadth). Executives appear much broader/weightier with good mathematic skills (i.e., facility with numbers and equations, measurements, and graphs/charts).

Years ago, McKinsey & Co. transformed what is known as industrial engineering into the fledging field of managing consulting. Today, there is no better known, sought after, and successful consulting firm than McKinsey & Co. Their consultants have trained many of the world's greatest management thinkers and business leaders in laser-sharp logic and acumen to approach and solve even the most intractable business problems. McKinsey relies on numbers, measurements, and charts—graphical representations of information—as a primary means of communicating with its clients. "The simpler things are, the easier they are to understand" fits here. McKinsey consultant Ethan M. Rasiel writes:

> *When I started at the Firm, the first pieces of equipment I was issued were a box of mechanical pencils, an eraser, and a set of ruled, plastic templates with cutouts for various shapes: circle, rectangles, arrows, and so forth. "Don't lose those templates," I was told. "They're expensive to replace and you'll need them*

to draw your charts." This was in 1989, hardly the Stone Age, and for years I had been using computer graphics to draw charts and graphs. The Firm uses charts as a means of expressing information in a readily understandable form. The simpler things are, the easier they are to understand. Therefore, McKinsey prints its charts in black and white; it avoids three-dimensional graphics unless absolutely necessary to convey the message; and it adheres to the cardinal rule of one message per chart. (1999)

One of McKinsey's favorite graphs is the waterfall chart, which illustrates quantitative flows from a lot of information in a clear, concise manner—how to get from number A to number B:

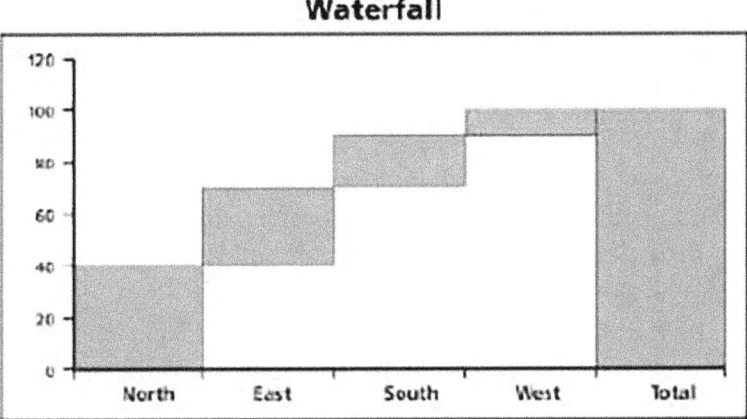

Waterfalls can help leaders think above static data (balance sheets, income statements) or active data (time series data, cash flows). An example of a usage might be an income statement, starting with sales on the left and ending with net income on the right. The chart should show the various items that lead from one to the other. The starting point (sales) is always a column that begins at zero. Positive items such as interest income are depicted as columns that start at the high point of the preceding column and reach upward. Negative items such as operating expenses are columns that start at the high point of the preceding columns and extend downward. The total is the distance from the top of the last item (or bottom if that item is negative) to the zero line. Subtotals can be included along the way in the same manner.

Start with a blank sheet of large paper, and then broaden or expand out (widening).

Most B2 thinking is done in a widening or expanding (width) mode. There is a connection to the central idea of the problem or consideration only through a final solution at a higher level of awareness. In considering a problem to be tackled, we start with a blank sheet of large paper and write the problem to be solved or decision to be made with end dates in the center. We broaden out with as many paths and descriptions as possible to give ourselves as much information about the problem as we deem needed to comprehend the meaning and significance of a wide variety of situations, data (Numbers and Equations, Measurements and Graphs/Charts), or events contingent on the problem or decision to be made. This should give us an ability to categorize, decode significance, and clarify meaning.

After establishing the multiplicity of connections and writing short descriptions along each initial path from our paper, put our problem aside and let our inner set of pathways take over. From time to time, revisit the various descriptions and revise or add to them as further thoughts and insights come. As a new center of thinking begins to emerge, explore again the various paths that this may have. Rarely will the paths be connected at this point. Depending on the anticipated outcome or deadline, with the inadequacies of our own thinking and experience, this broadening process may go on for some time. Each time we revisit the various paths, based on the newer, higher center, we should discard or unite the end products of the original beginnings and clarify the new position.

When finally a solution or decision is produced, it may not be anywhere near the original thought that may have started the process, or it may be on a level much higher than the one we initiated or expected. This process should describe a series of widening loops, joined only by a common set of related cores. The indications of linear, non-linear (meandering) thought processing do not appear to be present. To be linear, we have to go from point to point along a straight line. To be non-linear (even meandering) we go from interesting point to interesting point, connected only by our interests at the time of conception of the new point. What we are doing more of is numerical processing.

Nine Numerical Questions to Keep the Information Flowing with Width

There are nine basic numerical processing questions we may use. Two questions request information about symbol attributes and two ask for location information. There are two questions that reference the past and two that reference the future (from our employee's perceptual present). This leaves the odd one out, which offers employees the opportunity to make a lateral shift in perception. The nine basic numerical questions are:

- *And is there anything else about ...?*
- *And what kind of ... is that ...?*
- *And where is ...?*
- *And where about ...?*
- *And what happens next ...?*
- *And then what happens ...?*
- *And what happens just before ...?*
- *And where does/could ...come from?*
- *And that's ... like what?*

We believe it is important here to capture some of the exact words of employees to facilitate problem-solving participation and involvement in the thinking-through process. Capturing the information is to our teams what gasoline is to a car's engine. If we choke off the flow, we'll stall.

Main Street U.S.A.: a Deviation from Disney's Standard

One of those working-my-way-through-college summers at Disneyland, I (Graham) was a supervisor on Main Street U.S.A. Daily problem solving was required to sustain the *picture perfect* standard given by Walt himself. He was uncompromising on the highest quality of visual perfection—everything had to look like the day Disneyland first opened. Any deviation from that standard had to be quickly resolved.

Main Street workers always had the challenge of welcoming and directing incoming guests to where the restrooms were. We realized that most had traveled hours on freeways, and took another hour getting parked, taking the tram to the entrance, and securing tickets before coming in under our Disneyland Diorama Train. While looking down Main Street, they would realize they needed to get to a restroom. Disney University taught us the "recognition reflex"—visually reading the facial-body language of our guests and quickly directing guests between City Hall and the lockers to the left of the circle. However, if they made it down the street into Fantasyland, the restrooms were discreetly identified as "Prince" and "Princess."

By late June, a new problem surfaced when reports came from the janitors and employees that guests were relieving themselves behind the flowers, halfway down Main Street in back of our side-street Flower Mart—just yards from restrooms located behind a picket fence. We were completely perplexed as to why they were not using our restrooms close by, and we quickly sought understanding and a solution.

My analytically minded manager, Rachael, worked with me to investigate.

Rachael: "Morris, This has never happened before. Again, what specifically is happening and how much?"

Guests are going Number 1 and Number 2 on the flowers. It looks like kids!

"Where specifically is it happening?"

Only behind the *Flower Mart, on the flowers; nowhere else on Main Street.*

"When did it start happening, and is it happening this week?"

Beginning June 18 and consistently between 8 am and 4 pm Monday through Friday—not at night or on the weekends. It happened yesterday!

"Do we have a pattern?"

Yes, cyclical.

"What changes happened on Main Street before June 18?"

Disney University stopped training non-Disney personnel—like Carnation, Pepsi Cola, Frito-Lay, Yale Lock, etc. employees—in the Foundations: Communication Course.

"What else happened just before June 18?"

Two new waitresses were hired in the Carnation Snack Bar, our short-order restaurant next to the Flower Mart.

"Let's dress like guests tomorrow and sit in Carnation and inconspicuously watch our two new girls in action."

As we sat in the corner for only a few minutes, we observed a young adolescent come into Carnation and approach one of the girls busily waiting on tables. We heard his question loud and clear: "Where do you go to the bathroom?" He was hopping from one foot to another as if he couldn't hold it much longer.

Our girl's response: "Behind the flowers (pointing)." She quickly returned to busing a table, and our young guest had that "you must be kidding" look on his face, but he was in no condition to stay and question. He was out the side door and behind the flowers in seconds, out of sight of the public eye. We had several B2-widening insights we immediately shared: (1) When kids come in our entrance, they see our characters like Goofy, Captain Hook, Donald Duck, Winnie the Pooh, etc., and they get hyper-excited; it isn't until halfway down Main Street that they get in touch with their immediate biological needs. If we pull out Goofy and Captain Hook, it should mellow the front; (2) training in communication skills with Disney University has to be reinstituted for all employees immediately. The Disney approach is face-to-face, clear directions, like, "When you get behind the flowers, you will see a white picket fence; go behind the fence and you'll see the restrooms. Questions?" You then watch facial language to get a "recognition reflex," if there is none, you walk them there; and (3) the problem was solved through quantitative problem solving (B2). Oh yes, the two girls were coached that very day by Rachael.

For our purposes, we define a BRIGHT2 problem as a situation where a quantitative *change* must be made to the current process to bring it back to an acceptable level or standard. A problem occurs when the standard has deviated as compared to a previous high point/level or previously agreed standard. Problems are found where developments are needed within the *existing* situation in order to return to the original plan.

If we are trying to raise the standard above an existing or agreed level, then it should be considered an *opportunity*. An opportunity occurs when we would like to widen or improve the existing situation beyond that which currently exists or has existed before. Main Street U.S.A. had a similar problem in our darkened Silent Cinema. It was an opportunity to reevaluate the efficacy of the Silent Cinema and subsequently replace it with something better in that location.

B2 problem solving is a widening process by which a situation is analyzed and solutions are formed to *solve* a problem (and uncover opportunities) and when steps are taken to remove or reduce the problem. A current problem and situation is analyzed, potential solutions are generated, and a workable solution is determined and put into place. Problem solving is the process of analyzing situations of uncertainty to produce actual improvements or changes in the situation.

> *Our job is not to make up anybody's mind, but to open minds and to make the agony of the decision-making so intense you can escape only by thinking.*
>
> Author Unknown

B2 *widening* (two-dimensional) is not the same as *integrative decision making* (three-dimensional or B3). Decision making is a spatial process of problem solving and is concerned with weighing different existing ideas and formulating a new idea, integrating the best of the existing options. Problem solving includes the actual formation of those ideas. Problem solving can involve varying degrees of the problem analysis and solution generation elements compared to the decision-making part.

A key benefit of our B2 widening is an increased awareness of our own processing.

The benefits of using B2 widening can be quite astounding when as executives we understand our employee predicaments at a very deep symbolic level. Perhaps the most noticeable benefit of this type of B2 widening is that we get to increase awareness of our own processing. We become observers of our own repeating patterns. We make connections between the symbolic pattern and our everyday life. This separates us from our stuff and allows new perspectives and insights.

At a certain stage, the process "takes over" and both we and our employees are led by the information. When this occurs, insightful shifts take place. Our employees are taken by surprise at the turn of perceptual events as long-standing patterns transform themselves into more useful ways of being and doing.

From our executive point of view, this can verge on the incredible. When the most unwanted and fearful symbols transform organically into resources and our employees experience deep psychological changes—these are hallowed moments.

B1+2 Axioms of Height + Width:

Things that equal the same thing also equal one another.

If equals are added to equals, the wholes are equal.

If equals are subtracted from equals, the remainders are equal.

Things that coincide with one another equal one another.

B2+3 Axiom of Width + Space:

The integrated whole is much more powerful than the sum of the units.

Developments in the past century bearing on the foundations of mathematics are best summarized in a story by Morris Kline:

> *On the banks of the Rhine, a beautiful castle had been standing for centuries. In the cellar of the castle, an intricate network of webbing had been constructed by industrious spiders who lived there. One day a strong wind sprang up and destroyed the web. Frantically, the spiders worked to repair the damage. They thought it was their webbing that was holding up the castle.* (1980)

Can we still agree that $1 + 1 = 2$? Numbers inhabit a world of quintessential certainty. Thinking and managing by the numbers is a commodity for executives who seek out certainty. Managing by the numbers prospers on data, answers, and solutions, but fails to embrace uncertainty, chaos, and risk. Going quantitatively wide means having the capacity to seek out uncertainty and move though it with some risk. We believe that one way to learn to balance risk is to hold simultaneously verbal height, quantitative width, and visual-spatial depth with real world happenings.

The London Business School was established in 1965 and serves approximately 1,200 graduate students and more than 4,000 executives each year. Outside of the United States, it is ranked as the top business school in the world. According to Dean John A. Quelch, the school isn't in the education business—it's in the *transformation* business. That is an intrepid and innovative approach to higher-level thinking/learning at such a prestigious school.

To quantitatively measure their success in reaching their goal, the London Business School's administrators developed a tool called a Transformational-Benchmarking Questionnaire, which is given to students who have taken programs there. The survey asks certain questions: How much of the program that you took do you recall? Do you stay in touch with faculty? Do you stay in touch with fellow students? How big an impact has the program had on your career and on your quality of life?

Administrators of the school plan to have the survey given repeatedly as students' careers advance, including one year after they leave the school and then again every five years after that. Survey results provide detailed, measurable information about the performance of each student, and administrators will then evaluate the performance against the school's goals of creating a transformational experience for every student.

Measuring Inventiveness: Applied B2 Processing

> *Logic will get you from A to B. Imagination will take you everywhere.*
>
> Albert Einstein

Imagination/inventiveness is crucial to technological and other progressive organizations. Inventiveness is both easy and difficult to measure. It is easy to measure outcomes in areas such as patents, copyrights, and employee initiatives. It is more difficult to measure the inventive strength of our employees. A concrete measurement is tracking the patents and trademarks that are not only used internally but are licensed for others to use through a patent and license exchange Web site. IBM, for example, in 2000 was granted more patents than any other company in the world (about 2,800). For IBM, this was the eighth year in a row to be at the top. In total, IBM has captured 19,000 US patents and 34,000 worldwide. IBM's vice president for licensing and intellectual property noted that IBM licensing of patents and technology generated more than $1.5 billion in profits for 2000 (Steinberg, 2001). While IBM is at the top of the list, most organizations in the new economy have trademarks, patents, and copyrights that they monitor as an important measure of the innovative talent of their employees.

There is a constant need within almost any organization to show the value of specific projects or initiatives designed to improve human capital or intellectual capital. Efforts to reduce turnover, for example, are easily recognized to show a return on investment. The challenge comes with attempting to measure initiatives such as executive capacity, knowledge management, or organizational commitment and accumulate, monitor, and make available the knowledge of expertise in a company.

Banking with Width: Two-Dimensional Thinking (B2) Intellectual Capital

The Chartered Institute of Personnel and Development in the United Kingdom states that, "Intellectual capital is the skill, experience, and capacity to develop and innovate, that is owned by individuals" (2006, p.6). Human capital management concerns how capabilities/capacities are developed and productively applied to deliver business performance and long-term strategic goals. However, human capital measurement focuses on the analytics deployed to measure and report on how well intellectual capital management strategies and interventions are delivering these desired capabilities.

The prevalence of intellectual capital is bound to increase as organizations become more focused on managing intangible assets, as senior management becomes more interested in the impact of innovative outcomes, and as technology evolves and analysts and investors demand improved information relating to the development of intellectual capacity as a contributor to shareholder value. Standard Charter Bank employs almost 60,000 people in 1,500 branches and offices across 55 countries and territories in Asia, Africa, and the Middle East, with headquarters in London. It is considered one of the UK's leaders in the practice of intellectual capital and scorecard measurement with a strength-based philosophy rooted in positive psychology. The bank helps its employees understand their intellectual capacities and apply their talents to work so that they can be the best they can be. Part of its approach is to develop exceptional executives who two-dimensionally increase their intellectual capacities and practice strength-based management. Here, the bank anticipates and responds to the changing world in which it operates. Rigorous and robust intellectual assets, measurement, and quantifiable executive standards allows the bank to build its people's capacity and accountability to deliver on their aspirations.

B2 Widening to Help Create Flat Organizations and Tall Talent

Perhaps the most disciplined and sustainable means of capturing intellectual property, and also the most challenging, is *processing* innovation outcomes by return-on-intellectual-investments. To illustrate, I (Graham) share an experience during which I facilitated a company (Litton Guidance and Control Systems in Salt Lake City) in the mid 1980s through a transformational process of getting wide—or flat. The large-scale change design and rollout was to create a company-wide, self-directed work-team-based organization. Engineers and staff had to convert from being unilaterally directed to taking responsibility and initiative to work in autonomous groupings and together take full charge of their own productivity measures (scorekeeping), improve procedures, process innovation and time to implement, increase efficiency, quality, and profitability, reduce scrap rates and down time, and rework their products (e.g., inertial navigation systems to subsequently be put in F-16 fighter planes). They were also commissioned to do a reduction in force or right-size their own workforce, decreasing it 20–25%. After about 18 months, we lost some people. Those still standing shared some dramatic improvements in all the imperatives cited above. Some of the process innovation work that came out of the teams was phenomenal. The return on investment (ROI) was 700%. One million dollars invested in this large-scale intervention effort had a $7 million return within less than two years. The single saving factor was the presence of two-dimensional thinking. For example, all designs and team scorecards were created through the help of sophisticated computer programs, design databases, and carefully controlled processes. The design team became the clearinghouse for monitoring processes and improvements, discovering good practices and bad, finding useful shortcuts, and building on what was learned over time. The tools, processes, and performances were significantly measured, reported, and improved within months and over the ensuing years.

The intellectual knowledge possessed by the design team was shared and baked into the new emerging culture. By the end of that decade, the tried and tested processes, constraints, and standards were all measurable and manageable through self-directed work teams. Why is symbolic widening so powerful as a way of thinking and creating a new culture of greater profitability? Three reasons come to mind after over 20 years.

First, B2 widening and processing was a part of everyday work, making the intellectual knowledge available at all times to all key people. Executives and employees continually worked with process flow maps, process performance, and process improvement. As a result, they became more adept at managing process than at managing culture.

Second, process knowledge was perpetually measured, monitored, and controlled. There were assigned owners or teams responsible for the integrity, efficiency, and currency of each process. This or that team had a continual and formal interest in keeping the data, trends, etc. That interest and thinking extended to ensuring that the intelligence/knowledge captured was accurate, relevant, and used appropriately.

Third, B2 processing allowed units to be more easily trimmed and expanded than the knowledge contained within the culture itself. As the company's strategy, technology, and competitive environment changed, so did the processes and process interactions within the company. B2 processing in time became the new sustainable culture of thinking and acting from an array of process management tools that were reintroduced to the workforce every decade or so. Senior executives adopted and sustained a quantifiable process-driven culture. Executives understood and communicated openly their successful way of thinking and processing, empowering others to adopt a similar perspective. And over time, with the help of MIS, the company developed a process maturity that opened the door to more effectively manage intellectual knowledge.

Finally, B2 processing opened our minds to deeper levels of understanding. It helped facilitate the connection of the ambiguous to the more simplistic and, therefore, widen (width) our thinking.

Margaret Thatcher—a Case of Quantitative Width

In her book, *The Path to Power*, Margaret Thatcher aptly describes her extraordinary ability to understand the symbolism of economics and turn the United Kingdom's financial problem around:

> *I came to 10 Downing Street with an overall conception of how to put Britain's economy right, rather than a detailed plan: progress in different areas would depend on circumstances, both economic and political. For example, the priority in our first Budget was cuts in income tax—both because marginal rates, particularly on those with higher incomes, had become a deterrent to work and an incentive to migrate, and because we had made such a firm pledge in our manifesto. But when political and economic imperatives pointed in opposing directions it was the economic requirements which came first—as when we put up personal taxes in order to control the deficit and beat inflation in that unpopular but crucial 1981 Budget.*
>
> *The economic strategy had four complementary elements. First, in time and in importance, was the fight against inflation. Inflation had become deeply rooted in the British political and economic system and in British psychology. It had risen to successively higher peaks in the post-war years and had, as I have described, come perilously close to hyper-inflation in 1975. As a result, it was all the more difficult to eliminate. Only a sustained policy to reduce monetary growth and change expectations would suffice. So from 1980 onward, monetary*

policy, supported by a fiscal policy which reduced government borrowing, was conducted within the framework of a Medium Term Financial Strategy (MTFS). Like any strategy worth the name, it had to adapt to circumstances. When, for example, problems arose with one particular monetary aggregate as a measure of monetary policy, it was necessary to look to others as well. Again, like any strategy, it did not of itself remove the risk of error. But it limited the scope for such errors and, as it was adhered to in passing years and in spite of difficulties, it gained credibility which itself inspired wider economic confidence. Between 1981 and 1986, when the MTFS was most consistently at the heart of policy, inflation was brought down from a high point of 21.9 percent (May 1980) to a low of 2.4 percent (summer 1986). During the mid-1980s it averaged around 5 per cent, until the shadowing of the Deutschmark in 1987–88, to which I was opposed, set off a sharp increase. It rose rapidly until it peaked at 10.9 per cent in October 1990. It had begun to fall the month I left office, and it came down rapidly during 1991, by which time the high interest rates of 1988–90 had brought monetary growth under control once more. The assessment of domestic monetary conditions remained the final determinant of policy on inflation until I took office. (1995)

In summary: B2-widening processing involves non-linearly cogitating the facts and trying to see a pattern—and patterns are not always obvious because the patterns are not always linear. The two together (linear and non-linear) are an extremely powerful combination. Needed is an *analysis methodology* that will sharpen executive ability through all the width and breadth of the thinking process, situational assessment, problem solving, and decision making. Executives, faced with competing demands and increasing expectations, need bench strength in B2 processing to hone their issue identification skills, refine their questioning techniques, and maximize their decision-making outcomes.

Executives often want to skip the *analysis methodology* phases of a performance-improvement process and go straight to determining solutions. However, when business, performance, and cause analyses are eliminated, the organization's real problem is not uncovered, and the barriers to achieving success are not identified. Time, money, and other valuable resources are wasted on correcting symptoms instead of dealing with the root causes of the problem. Solutions identified without supporting data may require frequent revision as they are tweaked in an attempt to make them work. The cost in terms of lost opportunity, performance snags, and team member frustration is often incalculable.

B2 widening and processing through analysis strategies should never deviate from our goal to provide reliable, quality data that helps any executive team or organization make sound two-dimensional decisions and that support improved business outcomes.

The **transmogrifier** changes colors in a repeating pattern of red, then blue, and then green. It also adds the letter "E" to the end of a person's name. Thus Sam = Same, Don = Done, Slim = Slime, Sid = Side, Justin = Justine, and Mal = Male. Tom, therefore, will turn into a red book: Tom = Tome.

TARGET PRACTICE: Each region has the same area, so they are all equally alike.

BIG STORE SALES: It sold for $36. (36% of the original price of $100.

CHAPTER SUMMARY
Key Points

- BRIGHT2 or quantitative thinking, is about *width*. The emphasis on literacy in the schools at the end of the last century is a testament to the panic our society is experiencing as consciousness begins to shift from linear to quantitative (B2).

- B2 widening and processing is cogitation of the facts and trying to see a pattern, and patterns are not always obvious because the patterns are not always linear. The two together (linear and non-linear) are an extremely powerful combination. Needed is an *analysis methodology* that will sharpen executive ability through all the width and breadth of the thinking process, situational assessment, problem solving, and decision making.

- Mathematics uses numeric reasoning, which adds a unique dimension to the executive (i.e., the ability to solve story or word problems). Mathematics is an essential tool in the experimental sciences, such as physics, chemistry, and biology. It is also applied successfully to various technological branches, such as engineering, computer science, and architecture, and is of tremendous use in the social sciences, including economics, sociology, and psychology. It is even used in musical composition and the visual arts. *Executives appear much broader/weightier with good mathematics skills.*

- A mathematical model, like Six-Sigma, offers an executive a tool that he can manipulate in analysis of a system under examination, without unsettling the system itself. Unfortunately, this approach does not guarantee obtaining the optimal, best solution(s), because the possibilities are enormous.

- The benefits of using quantitative thinking (B2) can be quite astounding. Employees often report that executives understand their predicament at a very deep level, and that this in itself is valuable.

• B2 widening and processing allows units to be more easily trimmed and expanded than the knowledge contained within a culture itself. As a company's strategy, technology, and competitive environment change, so should the processes and process interactions within the company. Symbolic processing in time should become the new sustainable culture of thinking and acting from an array of process management tools that are reintroduced to the workforce every decade or so.

• B2 widening and processing through analysis strategies should never deviate from the goal to provide reliable, quality data that helps our high-capacity team or organization make sound decisions that support improved business outcomes.

CHAPTER 5

BRIGHT3—Spatial Depth
Solving Problems with Inventions

> *I want to get beyond the reef to deeper waters and fish off my kayak—but stay close to the reef for needed support. Out on the reef's ocean edge I can see all kinds of fish that I wouldn't see from inside the bay.*
>
> Morris Graham—a Hawaiian kayaker

PICTURE or VISUALIZE this:

You are driving along in your car on a blustery, stormy night. It is raining heavily, when suddenly you pass by a bus stop and see three individuals waiting for a bus:

1. An elderly woman who appears as if she is about to die.

2. A friend who once saved your life.

3. The perfect partner you have been dreaming about.

Which one would you choose to offer a ride to, knowing very well that there can only be one passenger in your car?

We use this moral/ethical dilemma as part of our executive selection process. The options are:

• Pick up the elderly woman because she is going to die, and thus save her.

• Take the friend because he once saved your life and this would be an ideal opportunity to help him. However, you may never be able to find your perfect mate again.

- Take your perfect mate and live with the guilt of abandoning the sick elderly woman and letting a friend down.

The candidate who was hired (out of numerous applicants) had no trouble coming up with his answer. He/she said: "I would give the car keys, with a hug, to my friend and let him/her take the elderly woman to the hospital. I would stay behind and wait for the bus with the partner of my dreams."

What ultimately won this candidate the executive position was his ability to think spatially, to think three-dimensionally *(depth)*. He displayed an aptitude in what we call BRIGHT3 thinking that requires openness to new ways of seeing the world and a willingness to explore. B3-thinking executives know that new ideas need nurturing and support. They also know that having an idea is good, but refining and acting on it is more important.

BRIGHT3 thinkers understand the use of space and how to get around in it. They enjoy patterns, flowcharts, graphs, mind-maps, graphic representations, jigsaw puzzles, and mazes. B3 thinkers like to imagine, visualize, doodle, draw, and design clear visual images/illustrations when thinking about something. And they like to solve, build, and create things.

The spatial mind is a sacred endowment and the rational mind is a faithful servant

Albert Einstein is the name most associated with the term "genius." He lived from 1879 to 1955. He did not speak until he was four years old and didn't read until he was seven. His teacher described him as "mentally slow, unsociable, and adrift forever in his foolish dreams." He was expelled and refused admittance to Zurich Polytechnic School. Einstein described his own thinking as "an associative play of more or less clear images." To Einstein, words did not seem to play a major role in his thinking. He thought more in pictures. He thought principally with the *visual-spatial* part of his brain. He stated that "The intuitive mind is a sacred gift and the rational mind is a faithful servant. We have created a society that honors the servant and has forgotten the gift." Although he has been dead for over 50 years, he stands alone as the quintessential "spatial" thinker of the twentieth century.

Strive not to be a success, but rather to be of value.

The world we have created is a product of our thinking; it cannot be changed without changing our thinking

Albert Einstein

Visual-spatial ability is the power to see and think in three dimensions, not just in words and numbers but with pictures and visualization. Spatial ability has long been associated with Albert Einstein's creative thought. B3 executive thinking at its most fundamental level is the ability to think and invent the way a physicist, chemist, or engineer does. The abilities that underlie this process require not only verbal and mathematical abilities but also spatial abilities. This type of thinking requires us to think in three dimensions, not just in words and numbers, but with pictures and visualization. Unlike traditional subjects in school, such as math and English that require only pencil-and-paper applications, science requires *spatial ability* applications through laboratory experience with hands-on physical (three-dimensional) construction of experiments that have previously been designed with diverse objects and science equipment.

A Spatial Breakthrough

Spatial may be the single word that best describes Albert Einstein's uniqueness. *Visual-spatial* cognition is mediated by the right and left posterior parietal regions of the brain. In 1999, Sandra F. Witelson, Debra L. Kigar, and Thomas Harvey published their research on Einstein's brain that has been preserved for science since 1955. They found that Einstein's brain was 15% thicker than the control group, resulting in a larger expanse of the interior parietal lobule. Previous research on the brain of mathematician Carl Gauss had also noted extensive development of the interior parietal regions.

One of the most significant longitudinal studies ever conducted in education (and surprisingly not well known by the average person) is the Study of Mathematically Precocious Youth (SMPY), begun in

1972. SMPY has meticulously tracked 5,311 of the most talented students in the United States. The study was broken down into five cohorts. The initial tracking began with the administration of SAT Math and Verbal tests to 12- and 13-year-olds who had been previously identified as being in the top 3% of achievement in the United States.

A particularly revealing part of the study was the administration of *spatial* tests to the Cohort 2 group, who represented the top 0.5% (1 in 200) in general intelligence. For this group, we have SAT math and SAT verbal and *spatial* scores. For the next 35 years, Daniel L. Shea, David Lubinski, and Camilla Persson Benbow tracked important measurable outcomes of education such as the undergraduate degrees obtained and what these children, who were now adults, were doing with their lives at age 33. They found that spatial *tests provided greater overall discriminative power for this group than quantitative ability or verbal ability. Specifically, they found that intellectually talented adolescents with stronger spatial ability relative to verbal ability were more likely to be found in engineering and computer science—mathematical fields, whereas those with the inverse ability pattern tended to gravitate toward humanities, social science, organic science, medical arts, and legal fields.*

The meticulous tracking of the Cohort 2 group also serendipitously uncovered results that are of great interest. For example, those students who received a degree in one of the "hard sciences"—physics and chemistry—had the highest overall global scores (verbal/mathematical/spatial) at the age of 12. Do we find this surprising? Although it is intuitively obvious, we have never read a study tracking this important piece of information before Shea, Lubinski, and Benbow.

Albert Einstein is the embodiment of intelligence and creativity. Is it any wonder that *Time Magazine*'s Person of the Twentieth Century had a PhD in "hard science"? It is reasonable to suppose that anyone could approach his level of accomplishment without walking down a similar path (e.g., getting a PhD in hard science or engineering—for starters). Surprisingly, many top executives have walked a similar path by getting a graduate degree in science and engineering, including executives like: Jack Welch, Andrew Grove, Bill Hewlett, and Lee Iacocca. But more importantly, nearly all individuals can improve their habits of thought by developing their visual-spatial ability. The National Science Foundation reports that only 10.7% of American undergraduates have a degree in hard science or mathematics or engineering. What can be done to develop the spatial ability of the other 89.3%—to enable them to think on higher levels?

Visual-spatial ability itself is not new. The construct was first identified as a separate thing from general intelligence in the twentieth century, and its implications for computer system design were identified in the 1980s. In 1987, Kim Vicente and colleagues ran a battery of cognitive tests on a set of participants, and then determined which cognitive abilities correlated with performance on a computerized information-search task. They found that the only significant predictors of performance were vocabulary and spatial visualization ability, and that those with high spatial visualization ability were more inventive and twice as *fast* to perform the task as those with lower levels of visual-spatial ability.

Visual-spatial ability refers to the ability to mentally *visualize, invent, construct*, deconstruct, and *manipulate* two- and three-dimensional figures holistically in depth.

Visual-spatial ability is typically measured with simple cognitive tests and is predictive of user performance such as engineering ability. What do engineers do? They invent. An invention is a three-dimensional product that is manufactured. Any item or good that can be purchased is an invention, although some are much more complex than others. What should BRIGHT2+3 executives do? Invent— through construction (I) and deconstruction (II)!

Visual-spatial I & II, two complementary abilities: Construction and Deconstruction

Visual-spatial I consists of the ability to combine individual elements in order to form a whole, a gestalt. This process known as *visual construction*, is responsible for most of the patents in the United

States. *Visual construction* is an act of creation in a three-dimensional setting. It is the spatial skill needed most in making a better car, a better airplane, or a better product. This skill requires visualization of many parts, simultaneously forming a whole.

Visual-spatial II is the ability to deconstruct—break something down into its component parts. Most of our education (i.e., verbal and mathematical) is analysis. But we get very little laboratory experience in deconstruction.

Visual-spatial I & II provides the executive with an entire new and different set of spatial tools to use against problems encountered in a business. For visual-spatial problem solving to have its greatest value, the skills of both construction and deconstruction must be developed. There are two sides to every currency, and both sides are required to authenticate the other. Deconstruction without construction has limited value to the leader's problem-solving arsenal.

It is extremely important to understand that spatial ability to construct and deconstruct has been neglected for so long in education. Talent searches reveal that many of our gifted students have a relative weakness in this area. Shea, Lubinski, and Benbow (2001), while examining data from Cohort 2, discovered that students from this group who at age 33 were professionals in law, medicine, and business had scored significantly below the average of the group in spatial ability at age 12. The idea that gifted children have asynchronous development of their verbal, mathematical, and spatial talents may be a new concept for many readers and educators alike. Nevertheless, asynchronous development is common, and has been supported in many other studies with gifted children and adults.

Individuals high in visual-spatial intelligence excel in fields dependent on their spatial abilities. Frequently, they create their own businesses or become chief executive officers in major corporations because of their *inventiveness* and ability to see the relationships of large numbers of variables. America more than ever needs individuals with highly developed visual-spatial abilities for advancement in technology and business. These are our creative leaders, who do and will make needed inventions in the field.

There are several reasons why visual-spatial thinking as *inventiveness* **should become the critical focus for every business:**

1. We are realizing that inventiveness isn't just about new products; it's about looking at what we do, how we do it, and how we can do it better.

2. We are realizing that inventiveness is simply a mindset that involves constant probing to see how we can fix things, find new things, or transform things, whether those things be business processes, customer service methods, new products, marketing and distribution channel concepts, or just about anything else.

3. We know that inventiveness is driven by extreme velocity. In every industry, the certain minimum expectations that have long existed are now constantly rising. Whether there are issues of cost/price, customer service/support, logistics/delivery, brand coolness or new products, the rule is simple: to compete today, we have to keep up with high-velocity change. If we don't innovate to maintain the same velocity as everyone else, we get left behind. It's that simple.

4. The most important thing: We should discover or rediscover that if we focus on inventiveness, we can break away from the dull, restrictive, boring, routine activities that shackle us to the past. Instead, by focusing our energies on ideas, creativity, challenging the status quo, constantly seeking how we can do things better, growing things, or transforming things, we end up having a lot more fun—and seeing a lot more benefits.

5. Smart processing—reasoning and inventiveness—come only after smart visual-spatial capacity. Information is no better than the processing that provides information on what is going on in real time and space. The mind of a quarterback must quickly gather information in real time and process it. Our mind really

has nothing to think with without the senses and the processing of the senses. Conversely, "thinking" is the essential ingredient of perception itself. Such operations as active exploration, selection, grasping of essentials, simplification, abstraction, analysis and synthesis, completion, correction, comparison, and problem solving, as well as combining, separating, and putting in context are a part of B3.

Visual-spatial ability should embrace all mental operations involved in the receiving, storing, and processing of information (e.g., sensory perception, memory, thinking, and learning with depth).

Sensory perception offers proof that all things are in a flux of constant modification. The capacity to obtain information about what is going on at a distance, or global processing, is a higher operation of reasoning and executive thinking. Global processing, specifically, involves the balance between the assimilation of more and more global realities to pertinent action and an accommodation of this action to those realities. To a quarterback and a B3 executive, all things are in a flux of constant modification. Visual-spatial ability—B3 thinking—has to be at an intelligent level to extricate the lasting from the changing and to perceive the immobile as a phase of mobility. Both quarterback and executive have to capture and analyze personal and team(s)-wide thinking patterns to provide new insights into strengths, gaps and specific areas for optimization.

Visual-Spatial Ability: Football at "The Big House"

Visual-spatial ability is the ability to see things *holistically* from multiple perspectives. Imagine for a moment that we are at the University of Michigan's football stadium, The Big House, that holds 107,501 people. Imagine the different perspectives of the game. We would have some sitting in the last row versus some sitting in the first row. How would the game look different if we were in the home team's end zone or the opponent's end zone? Imagine the perspective differences from the Michigan head coach's view. How would that differ from the opposing head coach's view? How would the perspective be different if we were in the Goodyear blimp overhead? What differences in perspective would be seen by a scout in the press box? How would the game be perceived by a security guard at the entrance? What kind of view do the players have on the field? What would the defense see? What would the offense see?

Every player has spent at least the last week learning about the opposing team's play book and what they anticipate their opponent will do. Can we visualize before the game begins the final outcome? What pivotal plays and moments that will decide the game? In this static state, can we imagine the more than 107,501 different perspectives of the game? Imagine now that the game has begun and all the players are in motion. Can we visualize the view of the game from the moving cameras on the sideline? Can we imagine what perspective we might have if the field were transparent or if we were under the field—immediately under the players—how would that change our perspective? Imagine now that we are the quarterback. What play would we want to call? What competitive advantage do we see on the field that maybe even the head coach can't see?

Teams do not go physically flat, they go mentally stale.

Vincent Lombardi

Visual-spatial processing is the ability to see many different perspectives simultaneously in our "mind's eye." It is the ability to remember previous visual images and to modify those images to achieve our own purposes. It is the ability to process an enormous amount of visual information at the same time. It is the ability to create the imagery needed to potentially see more than 107,501 different views of each player in the game, at rest and in motion. The amount of visual information one is capable of processing is enormous. Our brain has the ability to simultaneously categorize those images and select the most appropriate visual images and/or ideas to respond to. Most importantly, visual-spatial processing can be developed far beyond its present levels. We are all freshman high school, visual quarterbacks with the potential to get much better visually with practice. Many great NFL quarterbacks weren't starting quarterbacks during their freshman high school seasons. However, the ones that made it to the NFL continued to develop their physical and spatial talents.

Why are we just running the ball and not passing?

Visual-spatial ability is not as well understood by most executives as verbal and quantitative ability. The Educational Testing Service (ETS) falls short by producing standard achievement tests (SATs) that rely only on measures of verbal and quantitative abilities. In short, the SAT has produced an educational system in which 89% of our college graduates are funneled into degrees in subjects other than math, technology, physics, chemistry, and engineering. We know how hard these majors are. Any intelligent person knows our country needs these scientists, as China is currently graduating 600,000 engineers each year, India 350,000, and the United States only 70,000.

The importance of visual-spatial ability is beyond dispute for physical scientists, engineers, and architects. In addition, the military learned long ago that its most important asset was its pilot talent pool. They demonstrated in volumes of studies that visual-spatial ability is a must for anyone entering a highly technical career field like that of a pilot entrusted with equipment costing millions. Numerous research studies have validated the need for visual-spatial ability to be successful in undergraduate majors in physical science or engineering. Humphreys, Davey, and Kashima went through the Project Talent Data Bank with a sample of approximately 400,000 children and affirmed that skill in mathematics alone does not incline students toward engineering. In fact, math skills are not sufficient longitudinally in distinguishing between engineers and future humanists.

Finally, the 35-year Study of Mathematically Precocious Youth gave empirical evidence beyond question. When they looked at the most gifted children and tracked their educational outcomes, the physical science majors were the only students who scored positively above the average gifted child in verbal, math, and spatial ability. The physical science graduates in this study had the greatest global capacity and were using it to problem solve in hard science. The capacity of these students with problem-solving skills may represent our nation's greatest asset, and today we are producing significantly fewer graduates in hard science that we did in 1966. We are going the wrong way as a country, and we need to make an adjustment.

Three-Dimensional Thinking—Simultaneous Processing: Laboratories and Breakthroughs, Manufacturing and Inventions

Charles H. Duell, director of The United States Patent and Trademark Office, said, "Everything that can be invented has been invented." That was in 1899. The best executives know intuitively that inventiveness and innovation are the life blood of their organization. New ideas can lead to curricula that become best practice for those that are already going on or planned in the organization, and which would have been divested or never initiated had a better idea or program come along. So, the charge of every executive should be to search continually for ideas and programs that are better than the ones the organization is currently committed to.

Have we seen the ad from IBM Corporation, in which there was a long alphabetized list of sixteenth-century words? The ad caption read, "Anyone could have used these 4,178 words. In the hands of William Shakespeare, they became *King Lear*." *King Lear* epitomizes the essence of creativity: to take commonly used and understood ideas and recombine them in elegant new ways; clearly the combinations have to have value.

Three-dimensional processing efforts involve consciously searching for many alternatives. Inventiveness is much more likely to emerge when a person considers many options and invests the time and effort to keep searching rather than settling for mediocre solutions.

Three-dimensional processing begins with a clear notion of what the problem is and the ability to state it clearly. The effective thinker begins by first focusing on the structure of the problem, rather than its technical detail. Symbolically, we put the problem statement onto a clean sheet of paper, because the next series of mental operations occurs in the mind, the so-called working memory. Also brought into working memory from creative operations are the potential solutions.

These come from each person's capacity, or permanent memory store, his or her lifetime database of knowledge and experience. Other potential alternatives are brought in from such external sources of input as reading, ideas from co-workers, and databases. Next, these alternatives can be processed logically (by associating, sorting, and aligning into new or unusual categories and contexts) or more "illogically," by the use of images, abstractions, models, metaphors, and analogies.

Three-Dimensional Thinking—Simultaneous Processing

An individual uses three-dimensional or simultaneous processing to relate separate pieces of information into a group or to see how parts are related as a whole. Simultaneous processing is also used when an individual has to recognize patterns. For this reason, simultaneous processing is important for doing geometry, seeing patterns in numbers, seeing a group of letters as a word, seeing words as a whole, understanding a sentence as part of a paragraph, and seeing how a paragraph fits as part of a complete story. Simultaneous processing is involved in reading comprehension because it requires the integration and understanding of word relationships and how all of the elements of a text fit together. Seeing how an image should look from the various perspectives involves simultaneous processing. Individuals who are good at simultaneous processing easily understand how pieces of a whole fit together. Individuals who score low in this process do not understand how things are related, have trouble with spatial relationships, and often miss the overall idea.

With recent advances in adult neuroscience at the behavioral and neural levels, Witelson, Kigar, and Harvey (1999) reported that:

- The generation and manipulation of three-dimensional spatial images and the mathematical representation of concepts would appear to be essential cognitive processes in the development of Einstein's theory of relativity.

- Einstein's brain weight was no different from that of other people indicating that a large (heavy) brain is not a necessary condition for exceptional intellect.

- Visual-spatial cognition, mathematical thought, and imagery of movement are strongly dependent on the parietal lobule (Einstein's supra-marginal gyrus within the inferior parietal lobule may reflect an extraordinarily large expanse of highly integrated cortex within a functional network).

- Visual-spatial cognition, mathematical thought, and imagery of movement are strongly dependent on the parietal lobule region. Visual-spatial cognition and mathematical ideation imagery of movement are mediated predominantly by right and left posterior regions. In Einstein's brain, extensive development of the posterior parietal lobes occurred early.

- Increased expansion of the inferior parietal region was noted in other physicists and mathematicians.

- Einstein's own description of his scientific thinking explained that there is "associative play" of "more or less clear images" of a "visual and muscular type."

- Adults (executives) that excel at three-dimensional thinking have the individual capacity to cope with complexity, amorphousness, and uncertainty. We do not have to have everything laid out for us. We have the resiliency and ingenuity to adapt to new and different circumstances.

The most important phase in the exercise of simultaneous three-dimensional thinking is the front-end work. The in-depth, serious thinking by leaders and their teams results in the creation of a visual framework for the future. Imagining the future first takes place in the mind of the leader and then must be communicated throughout the organization. Three-dimensional thinking and planning should guide people and the needed physical changes that manifest transformation. Without the tough up-front work of simultaneous thinking, physical and people changes will be unfocused, random, and unlikely to succeed.

What one-two-three do we know about three-dimensional thinkers?

1. Three-dimensional thinkers are inventive thinkers

Original thinking is not the same as simultaneous processing, but is obviously a prerequisite for creative thought. Originality requires an active search for the different. This may involve conscious attempts to invoke contrasts, opposites, bizarre associations, or symbolic thinking. Innovative thinking is sometimes no more than mere recognition that what is accepted by everybody else has flaws, is not adequate, or needs to be done differently. To complete the creative process, however, requires more than originality. Innovative thoughts that are not examined critically cannot be refined into useful and correct concepts; less creative people tend to be too quick to judge or reject ideas. Innovative people think out carefully what they are looking for and clarify the reasons for their reactions to emerging ideas. They tend to search more intensely for original thoughts that can improve upon or even replace the emerging ideas.

2. Three-dimensional thinkers ask provocative questions

A question provokes an answer; a problem, its solution. The skill is not only to ask questions, but to ask questions or pose problems in the most effective ways. A question can easily limit simultaneous processing if it restricts the space of potential answers. It therefore is important to pose questions in open-ended ways and ways that do not make too many assumptions about an acceptable answer. A major part of simultaneous processing is proper formulation of the problem itself.

3. Three-dimensional thinkers are wired for simultaneous processing

Inventive thinkers have a mind-set that enables simultaneous processing to happen, as if by chance. Fundamentally, inventive executives desire to be innovative; believe that there is an innovative solution; and expect that they will be the individuals to discover it. And, they are self-directed and self-starting, and follow the logic of identification:

- Identify and summarize the **problem/question** at issue (and/or the source's position).

- Identify and advocate their own **hypothesis, perspective, and position** as it is important to the analysis of the issue.

- Welcome and consider other salient **perspectives and positions** that are important to the analysis.

- Identify and assess the key **assumptions.**

- Identify and assess the quality of **supporting data/evidence** and provide additional data/evidence related to the issue.

- Identify and consider the influence of the **context** on the issue.

- Identify and assess informed conclusions, implications, and consequences.

Playing the Executive Game ... Simultaneously

A challenge for executives is to think and act on simultaneous variables while dealing with problems and dilemmas that they face constantly as leaders. We owe each other a suspension of judgment and a willingness to see our game of work in much higher, broader, deeper provisos than simple either-or, black-and-white, and right-and-wrong analysis. Unless we can do that, the breakthrough lessons will be lost in our organizations and in the wider, thicker world. We must help each other understand the complexities of our lives and help each other navigate the turbulent moral dilemmas of our times.

Scientific reasoning skills cannot be acquired sitting in a room studying textbooks. A future scientist must have hands-on practical experience in a three-dimensional laboratory. A future leader of greatness must have hands-on practical experience in a three-dimensional laboratory. The world is essentially a three-dimensional living laboratory, which should allow thinkers to self-regulate, be conscious of their own thoughts, be open to how they can be informed by others, and have the ability to adapt according to reality checks.

Imagine you have to visit Portland, San Diego, Chicago, and Edmonton in a week. What is the optimal route? Most executives will employ sequential thinking. They will pick the route of the closest cities. They may save money on their first choice, but by the last destination, it might cost an excessive amount.

Simultaneous thinking possesses the whole route at the same time. It considers all patterns, groupings, and possible solutions and identifies the best one. Executives don't handle simultaneous problems well—computers do. We tend to pluck the low-hanging fruit first, but often that leaves some higher valuable fruit to perish in time.

Switches and Light Bulbs: A Three-Dimensional Puzzle in Simultaneous Space

You have three light bulbs in a room and three switches outside the room on another floor. Each switch is connected to one and only one light bulb. Turning the switches on or off, you cannot see which bulb is going on or off. However, you know which position of the switches means "on" and which one means "off." You can exit the room and re-enter once. How can you match up the switches to the bulbs?

Did you answer, like most people, "It's impossible!" Let's look at the puzzle from a third-dimension. How many positions does a switch have? Only two (off and on). If we match a switch in a selected position with a bulb, we would be able to match two switches with two bulbs only. However, we have three bulbs. Still impossible to solve the task? Think again. We are trying to consider different states of the bulbs. Well, it is not just the two mentioned above. A bulb can be broken, that's another state; or can be removed, that's one more state. How can we break a bulb from outside the room?

After a number of attempts to think about different states of the switches and bulbs, one finds a state of bulbs that can be achieved using the switches. It is "recently turned off"!

If you turn a bulb on, then wait for a little while, and then turn it off and enter the room, the bulb will be off but still warm. That's the solution!

Assuming that all bulbs are off in the beginning, one can turn two switches on, wait a little, and then turn one of them off. One bulb will be off (and cold), one bulb will be on, and the third one will be off but warm. The task that seemed to have no solution is solved. To do it, we added one more dimension, in fact just a second one, into a one-dimensional (and discrete) system. In addition to the "on/off" dimension, we have added the "cold/warm" dimension.

The assumption was that the bulbs could be in only one of the two states: turned off or turned on. Once we decided that we could determine more than two states (such as recently turned off, for example), the puzzle was solved. (Kossoroukov, 2006).

The suitability of the problem representation to the problem structure is crucial.

How a problem is represented can affect how easy that problem is to solve, or whether it can be solved at all. The history of science is filled with examples of where scientists believe they solved difficult problems at least in part because they thought about them in spatial terms. The classic "Buddhist monk" problem is a good illustration of where a spatial representation can lead to a simple solution:

> One morning, a Buddhist monk sets out at sunrise to climb a path up the mountain to reach the temple at the summit. He arrives at the temple just before sunset. A few days later, he leaves the temple at sunrise to descend the mountain, traveling somewhat faster since it is downhill. The task here is to show that there is a spot along the path that the monk will occupy at precisely the same time of day on both trips.

The problem is difficult when people try to solve it quantitatively (B2) by focusing on issues such as relative speeds of travel. A spatial representation can make the answer apparent. If one imagines (B3) two monks, one ascending the mountain starting at sunrise, the other descending the mountain starting at sunrise, it is obvious that they must meet on the path, and when they do, they will be at the same point at the same time of day. One can do this imagining in different ways, ranging from generating perceptually rich images of monks and mountains to creating a simple schematic diagram to represent the problem's key spatial and temporal features. The suitability of the problem representation to the problem structure is crucial.

B3 processing bridges the gap between bewildering complexity of primary observation and the relative spatial simplicity of a problem.

Executive depth begins with mentally processing simultaneously images of qualities, objects, and events where visual perception lays the groundwork of concept formation. The minds of executives reach far beyond stimuli received by the eyes, directly and momentarily, and operate with the vast range of imagery available through learning and memory and organize a total lifetime's experience into a system of visual concepts. The thought mechanisms by which such executives manipulate these concepts operate in direct perception and stored experiences as well as their imagination. The thinking level is beyond conventional paradigms and examines traditional constraints using nontraditional thinking. The executives go outside their own frames of reference and find another way to look at a problem.

What do three-dimensional thinkers do so well that others don't?

- Come up with original awareness
- Recognize patterns
- Develop healthy memory capacity
- Detect anomalies
- Keep the big picture (situation awareness)
- Understand the way things work
- Observe opportunities and improvise
- Relate past, present, and future events
- Pick up on very subtle differences
- Address their own limitations

What do flat-dimensional experts do?

- Live in the moment, not recognizing complex relationships.

- Produce limited options—they are extremely reactive, not proactive.

- Manage routine—they are great at everyday stuff, strong procedural knowledge.

- Run into trouble when problems are ill-structured or novel.

B3 processing bridges the gap between bewildering complexity of primary observation and the relative simplicity of a problem. As long as leadership is based on being right, it will be difficult for us to entertain alternative world views. Official views will prevail. In uncertain times, such as we are living in now, it has become increasingly clear that a different kind of thinking (i.e., B3) is required.

Out of three-dimensional flowing come bright ideas.

The three-dimensional thinker flows through all reasonable alternatives, including many that may not seem "obvious." Each alternative needs to be examined, not only in isolation, but in relation to other alternatives-and in relation to the initial problem expressed in different ways. The practical problem then becomes one of reducing the size of the problem and alternative solution space to workable dimensions. That may well be why we have to be immersed in the problem for intensive thinking experiences, with subconscious "incubation" operating to help sort through various alternatives and combinations thereof.

The final flow of three-dimensional thinking is more straightforward. It involves critical, logical analysis, which typically forces a refinement of the emerging ideas. Deconstruction should force the rejection of premature ideas and reinstatement of the search and selection processes. Sometimes, construction will force the realization that the wrong problem is being worked, or that it needs to be reformulated. Eventually, out of these iterative processes will emerge bright ideas.

We know that discovery and inventive thought cannot be planned by an executive; it is the result of intensive thinking experiments—often during the course of ongoing activity that may have nothing to do with the new ideas—except that a third dimension is activated in the process of thinking about thinking.

Working with hundreds of effective leaders through volumes of their decisions over the past 30 years, we have clearly profiled how the best think. Our single question, especially over the past ten years, has been this: How do strong visual-spatial thinkers uniquely *process* their decision-making options in a way that promotes new, creative possibilities and not fall back on conventional options that are on the table?

B3 thinkers should be able to creatively flow through five related but discrete stages.

We discovered a defining characteristic common with our B3 thinkers. They would creatively flow through five related but discrete stages. Their spatial capacity apparently allowed these executives to approach their decision process from a higher, wider, thicker, and *deeper* perspective when considering short-term or long-term objectives, routine objectives, emergency objectives, or vast operational objectives that could affect the entire direction of their organization over a course of years or decades. The five stages are:

> 1. Gather all relevant information and possibilities/options upon which a creative decision will be based in verbal, numerical, and spatial dimensions. A decision is, ultimately, a choice between two, with the creation of a third possible way to achieve a goal. For this reason, the goal itself *must* be clearly defined.

> 2. All options for a course of activity in every dimension—verbal, numerical, spatial—to achieve the stated goals *must* be put forth and evaluated.

> 3. Based on previous decisions within the organization and the urgency of the decision at hand, the best options are advanced.

> 4. *A new option is creatively constructed that most likely contains elements from the best options.*

5. Specific plans for carrying out the new option are then made and implemented.

Most of their decisions involved a balance between inventiveness and practicality.

Balance is determined, to a large extent, by the overall culture of the organization. Some organizations are adverse to risk; others are more experimental and willing to undertake some degree of risk. Depending on the type of culture within the company, our effective executives, when deciding on an issue, would platform their thinking around the likely acceptance by their existing corporate culture. They would also consider systems factors significant to those outside the immediate reach of their jobs and functional specialties. Finally, they were confident that they would find their way through the woods and come out into the light with a solid resolution.

Three-dimensional decisions generate new plans from elements of existing two-dimensional plans. The process considers a potentially endless list, and, thus, avoids the "listing problem." An artist who must decide what a painting will look like, for example, keeps adjusting it until it's adequate. In this way, the decision-making process leads the decision maker to discover possibilities that weren't listed at the beginning of the process.

Three-dimensional thinking has the capacity to create depth and be imaginative, inventive, and artistic, and is characterized by being original or inventive in the decision-making process. Decisions are usually formulated by a new process. Three-dimensional thinking has the capacity to create and stimulate the imaginations of all engaged members and take the organization to a higher level of thinking and doing. No amount of energy will take the place of thought.

Finding Space and Maximizing Capacity in Edinburgh— "On the Fringe"

By mid-August to early September each year, Edinburgh, Scotland goes off the BRIGHT3 charts, swelling with tourists and guests from all quarters of the planet. The main event is the annual International

Festival and the Military Tattoo held daily in displays and parades, and nightly in Edinburgh Castle. During the same three weeks, an extraordinary "maverick" happening consumes every available space and *capacity*, every nook and cranny and stage in Edinburgh, from dust to dawn, some of the most creative, innovative, artistic talent ever assembled or gathered in any one place. Since 1947 when a few gate-crashers decided to incubate on **the fringe** of the world-famous Edinburgh International Festival, "The Fringe" evolved to become the largest artistic gathering in the world with over 250 venues. At the heart and soul of this festival is the *capacity* to amaze and confound with the daring, experimentally creative, innovative, avant-garde forms of theatre and comedy. Never have we been exposed to such high-level, visual-spatial creativity and innovation in the arts. The experience literally changed our understanding of the impact of intense spatial-ability.

We have learned and confirmed recently that "The Fringe" has no distinguished CEO, no committee, no guiding body of any kind to bring together this world-class, self-organizing system of fierce, precocious competition. The performers compete yearly to get in, get discovered, and move their entrepreneurship to new heights, direction, and sponsors. Many of the performers in these groups are stars in their own right, and if anyone tried to get in front of them and lead, they probably wouldn't follow. These highly innovative, self-directed, and engaging slices of genius are leveraged only from a sideline leadership that appreciates rare talents, is comfortable sharing power, and is generous in doing so. Their coordinating genius is based on communities of interest: tight-knit performing groups that pull together people from various functions, talents, and locations. Each community yearly comes up with creative, innovative ideas and competes with the other groups. As these performing communities of interest evolve, decision making is broadly distributed. The Fringe community requires collaboration even among support groups outside of Edinburgh.

Once a group makes it in, the thinking becomes: How can we differentiate ourselves from the competition to persuade visitors to attend our show as opposed to one of the hundreds of others taking place at the same time? And, how do we persuade the critics that ours is a show worth reviewing? Each unit in The Fringe appears to reinforce the other parts of the system to form an integrated whole that is much more powerful than the sum of the units. In a sense, the participants are thinking spatially and acting with insight and speed to capture social-networking audiences that make rapid choices from multiple options. These audiences spend time queuing in lines, waiting to get tickets, and talking to one another about what they've seen and what they like. If a performance excites imagination and provokes conversation, it's a success. No amount of energy will take the place of thought.

Deeper questions: How does the entire Fringe happen and not only work but get bigger and more impressive every year? Why are so many top-flight performers motivated to present their best work in Edinburgh? We think the answers come with a three-dimensional thinking that is found in "extreme sports," but also here with the pursuit of the Perrier Award for Comedy. It's like competing in the Olympics. The high stakes, the brutally intense competitive arena, and a unique endowment to think and create at elevated levels of their profession bring them and a crowd to Edinburgh year after year.

The Skill of Processing with Depth and Thickness

BRIGHT3 thinkers are able to juggle several alternative futures simultaneously without prejudice to any one view. We call this *depth and thickness* and recognize it as a skill that can be learned through visual-spatial processing.

Although most of us find this kind of thinking difficult, there is evidence that our brain does it naturally, for example, when considering whether to walk home or take the bus, to wear a coat or risk traveling light. Generating a set of solutions brings this thinking dimension into awareness and extends it so that a group of people can share the same set of alternate views of the future in considering what to do next. The overly analytical mind can find this especially challenging because it requires deliberately letting go of any single apparent solution. It's deliberately allowing one's mind to change its habitual perspective so that something new can come in and a creative reframe can take place.

To engage in B3 future thinking means acquiring the ability to suspend judgment and work inside several distinct worldviews, of which the default scenario is only one, with equal plausibility. From this perspective, the task for practitioners of scenario work is not simply to pick up methods and apply them, but rather *to develop a new set of mental skills* along with the ability to transmit them to the decision makers so that they can navigate confidently into the future. The development of these skills delivers the real value that scenario work is capable of giving. The absence of these skills can discourage people from taking alternative-futures work seriously.

The absence of three-dimensional thinking can elicit unforeseen outcomes. A state governor determined that his governmental expenses were too high in the current economic downturn. He ordered all his departments to reduce their operating budgets by 10%. The Department of Health looked at their operation and determined that by eliminating three steps they could reduce their costs by $7.5 million (a 12% reduction). The director of this department was pleased that they were able to meet the goal without adversely affecting the department's services.

However, the elimination of the three steps in the Department of Health had unforeseen, detrimental effects on the Department of Human Services. The removal of these steps in the Department of Health eliminated the ability of the Department of Human Services to fully maintain their family services program, which resulted in a 9% increase in the number Child Protective Services claims.

This action rendered an increase in cost of over $9 million annually for the state. Even though the Department of Health and the Department of Human Services met the Governor's goal of a 10% reduction in their operating expenses, the lost income of $11.2 million more than offset the expense savings and resulted in an increased expense ratio.

Unfortunately, this scenario plays out far too often in multifaceted organizations. The management of the Department of Health understood they were to solve the problem as quickly and efficiently as possible. They perceived the problem two-dimensionally from the context of their immediate system and created a workable response for a systemic decrease. The administration of the Department of Health failed to identify, let alone evaluate, an inter-agency dimension with other governmental departments. Using a simplistic two-dimensional view and not taking into consideration the interplay between two departments (three-dimensional), they inadvertently created a solution within limited space and with no regard for its "external" impact. Unfortunately, this occurrence is not all that uncommon in business today. The two-dimensional approach is myopic and serves as an incubator for unexpected, counterproductive, disruptive, and costly outcomes.

This governor possesses excellent verbal skills that may have stymied or crippled simultaneous processing at the highest levels by imposing an examination of self and ideas that were too strict, too logical, too sequential. Knowledge of a financial problem area was needed in order to understand the limits of current practices and to identify those areas where simultaneous processing would have been most fruitful. However, too much knowledge may have impeded creative progression, producing that thinking-process disease known as "hardening of the categories." This becomes a problem when the knowledge is focused in a small administrative circle because the breadth of alternative information that could be used in creative synthesis is missing.

Simultaneous processing is affected by ways in which we classify things.

The sensory or cognitive world of Sir Isaac Newton caused him by some means to see the similarity between an apple and the moon in a new way; of course they were both round, solid bodies. But it is not clear what caused him to perceive what is now obvious, namely that both are subject to the effects of gravity. Even seeing the apple fall from a tree would not be a meaningful mental stimulus to most people because they are not used to thinking of the moon as falling. Simultaneous processing is affected by the ways in which we classify things. We put apples and moons into categories, but by insisting on describing and naming them, we restrict the categories to which they belong. Apples are supposed to be round, red, and sweet, while moons are large, yellow, rocky, and far away. The names themselves get in the way of thinking of either as a classless object that is subject to gravity. A lesser order of simultaneous processing is commonly seen in the simple realization of the significance of obvious associations. The associations may even be negative.

Create Simultaneous Three-Dimensional Processing in Cross-Functional Teams

With visual-spatial aids, it is possible to devise explicit methods for taking cross-functional teams through generative processes that bring both alternative worldviews into being and help to develop the skill of possibility thinking. The starting point is usually a combination of

- A crucial strategic question (which must be owned by the decision maker) and
- A set of perceived uncertainties surrounding the question.

In order to ensure a broad and rich perspective, interviewing a variety of perceptive people (particularly those who do not share the corporate mindset but whose field or specialty may have some bearing on the strategic question) can extend the boundaries of uncertainty.

The next step is for a cross-functional team, which includes the decision makers, to work these uncertainties through a process of discussion, evaluation, and prioritization. The priority of uncertainties can then be imaginatively studied to elicit intuitions of alternate worldviews based on how each uncertainty might be resolved. It is possible to use analytical methods for this stage, but this would be at the expense of the engagement of decision makers due to the need for backroom software support.

These vague worldviews can then be focused on the decision question and further supportive work may then be done. A new B3 picture is available as a tool for further workshops in which the decision makers can be challenged to see how to achieve their goals in each distinct scenario. Fresh options and new ideas for robustness, resilience, and contingency/risk management emerge from this process.

On the one hand, the complexity of B3 processing requires in-depth research, the gathering and perusal of great amounts of information, and the distillation of critical factors. This is a lot for the decision makers to digest and requires intensity and effort that may not be readily available. On the other hand, if decision makers are not involved in the process, the impact of the tackling set may be lost on them as the process itself is integral to understanding. The resulting tackling set will tend to be reduced in their minds to variations on their known world.

In other words, to ensure real impact on decision making, responsible people must be involved in the project. If innovative activity is encapsulated in a staff function, the material may be excellent but not affect action. Decision makers are usually busy people. They are not interested in reading piles of data and will tend to short-cut the process because of time constraints and simply challenge themselves, tending thereby to fall prey to habits of mind, "groupthink," and self-promotion and inevitably arrive at sketchy outcomes. B3-thinking executives want the critical thinking needed for informed outcomes, but

- won't connect to too much analysis, and
- are not often available to work together.

A solution to this dilemma is

- to speed up the research input by crafting and locking into a network of extraordinary people. This guarantees that quality research underlies all the factors being considered, and
- to accelerate executive B3 thinking and involvement through interviews on strategic issues as well as with facilitated team events.

If a selected B3-level team can be thus engaged in the inventive process along with the decision makers, the quality of strategic conversation will be raised and resulting decisions will be more likely to generate significant competitive advantage.

Create a Three-Dimensional Culture: Four Critical Components

Over the years, we have rediscovered that the ability of executives and teams to create and sustain spatial-capacity cultures is the most critical step in ensuring their ability to consistently achieve superior results.

A *spatial-capacity culture* is a *healthy* values mind-set with accompanying and reinforcing B3 thinking, habits, practices, and routines—about how to optimize long-term organizational performance. Four components are needed to *align* a BRIGHT3 culture:

1. An Integrative, Three-Dimensional Milieu

• An integrative, three-dimensional environment (construction and deconstruction, decision making/problem solving together at all levels) is the most fundamental component, the very foundation of a B3-capacity culture.

• All members should feel that their points of view/ideas are welcome and of value and feel *obligated* to consistently participate fully and candidly.

• Members have full access to all of the ideas and suggestions of all and are characterized by extraordinary levels of both engagement and commitment.

• Exceptional members of B3-capacity come together and develop collaborative networks to produce better processes and better results.

Obstacles

1. A *lack* of skill in the art/science of tackling and integrating conflicting ideas.

2. A *tendency* to want to do things "one's own way" with the belief the "my ways (or thoughts/ideas) are best."

2. Inquisitive Questioning, Accountability, and Healthy Attitudes

A questioning culture respects the Einstein Formula: "Question! Question!" Be inquisitive; ask questions. Ask ourselves, "Why?" and "What if …" continuously to broaden our perspective, stimulate spatial thoughts, and generate new insights. This requires different attributes that include

- Willingness to take new perspectives to day-to-day work.
- Openness to do different things and to do things differently.
- A focus on the value of finding new ideas and acting on them.
- Striving to create value in new ways.
- Listening to others.
- Supporting and respecting others when they come up with new ideas.

Expectations around accountability and healthy attitudes/behaviors are:

- Three-dimensional thinking is recognized, reinforced, and appropriately rewarded.
- Performance problems, including the failure to meet one's commitments and close performance gaps, are quickly and fairly addressed (performance reviews).
- Attitudes and behaviors are supportive of a "one for all, and all for one" mind-set of holding self and everyone accountable.

Obstacles:

- *Failure* to hold members accountable for not challenging the status quo around key issues because of a mistaken belief that we are doing them a favor or because personal discomfort causes the desire to avoid confrontation.

- A "weak" human resource function unable or unwilling to provide training in creative/innovative thinking practices throughout the organization.

3. Visual-Spatial Focusing

- Ability to select those few goals in space and time that allow concentration of limited resources in order to establish clear, focused priorities and accomplish something of significance.

- The "focus" both facilitates and is facilitated by a collaborative climate, a culture of accountability, and robust processes.

- The focus does not allow the good to be enemy of the great because leadership practices clear priorities and concentration.

- The focus also is on what not to do and what to stop doing.

Obstacles:

- The human *tendency* to want to do too many things.

- The *difficulty* of walking away from a "good" opportunity in order to focus on a great one.

4. Simultaneous Processing

- Simultaneous processing allows for cross-pollination and three-dimensional thinking to integrate multiple contributions with a collective emphasis on effectively delivering services and/or products of the most *critical importance* to customers.

- Sustainable success comes through: (1) the ability to explicitly *focus* on the needs of the customer, and (2) the ability to *execute*.

- The ability to demonstrate savings and efficiency is achieved through simple process improvement.

- The ability to rethink structures, incentive systems and accountabilities is needed to create an environment in which people feel that not only is it safe to have conflicting ideas, but it is required. Changes in perspectives allow for alternative insights and create the preconditions for fresh and more creative approaches.

Obstacles:

- Traditional departments and linear functions instead of dynamic "processes" will tend to cut across *artificial* linear boundaries, cutting off potential vibrant linkages and healthy clusters.

- The *tendency* of most departmental or B1 or 2 executives to fiercely manage within their own silo, defending their boundaries and prerogatives, typically driven by an incentive system that only holds them accountable for their own departmental or functional goals, to the detriment of cross-functional "processes."

Stimulating Deeper, Deeper Thoughts

Great discoveries may emerge from our primal unconscious imagery—intuition. Words and language, according to Einstein, had no role in his creative thought. Some famous scientists claim that their best thinking occurs in the form of visual-spatial images, even at the level of fantasy. Einstein, for example, in one of his fantasies visualized himself riding on a beam of light, holding a mirror in front of him. Since the light and the mirror were traveling at the same speed in the same direction, and since the mirror was a little ahead of the light's front, the light could never catch up to the mirror to reflect an image. Thus Einstein could not see himself. He *thought* experiments first and he later created the physical experiments that led to his Nobel Prize. Although fantasy, such thinking is not the product of a hallucinating mind; there is clear logic and order imbedded in the fantasy.

Neuroscientists know that humans have a split brain, wherein the left half controls analytical thought involved in speech and mathematics, while the right brain deals more holistically with imagery, music, art, and assorted nonverbal thought. The creative process seems to depend on freeing our right brain from the domineering control of our left brain. Managers tend to reward people for left-brain thinking, which is rigorous and precise. Are we thereby stifling inventiveness?

Intuitive Processing: Where our Implicit and Explicit Minds Interact

As studies over the past decade have confirmed, our brain operates with a vast unconscious mind. Much of our informational processing occurs below the radar of our awareness—off stage, out of sight. Our unconscious processes pervade all aspects of mental and social life. Our consciousness naturally assumes that its own intentions and choices rule our life. But consciousness overrates its control. In reality, we fly through life and work mostly on autopilot. As Galileo "removed the earth from its privileged position at the center of the universe," so research is now removing consciousness from its privileged place. By studying the forces that shape our intuitions, scientists have revealed how this hidden mind feeds our insight and inventiveness.

Our intuitive mind is fast as a blink, automatic, effortless, associative, implicit (not available to introspection) and often emotionally charged. Our conscious mind is familiar, explicit, deliberate, sequential, and rational, and it requires effort to employ. We intuitively assume that fuzzy-looking objects are further away than clear ones, and usually they are. But on a foggy morning, that car ahead may be closer than it looks. Through life experiences, we gain expertise and we learn connections/associations that surface as intuitive feelings—like slowing down with the sight of that fuzzy-looking object ahead.

Intuition—fast, automatic, unreasoned thought and feeling—harvests our experience and guides our lives. Intuition is powerful and often wise. Research in cognitive science augments our appreciation for intuition but also reminds us to check it against reality. Smart, critical thinking often begins as we listen to the creative whispers of our vast unseen mind and builds as we evaluate evidence, test assumptions and conclusions, and plan for the future.

If we want to tap more intuitive powers in our leadership, then we should look at the object of inquiry from every conceivable perspective, without any prejudice, be unscrupulously objective, not care about what others may say, and pursue our interests with great interest and intensity—and then stop and listen to whisperings within. But this is impossible unless we have highly developed spatial abilities. *All perception begins with cognition.* We must have original awareness. Our brain can only recognize images and sounds that were initially "cognized." We cannot recognize something that we did not fully perceive in the first place. We can only see choices within the limits of our own perception. If we increase our spatial ability, we will have many more solutions available to select from.

We have to see the problem from many perspectives to cognize what the problem really is. Then, significant intuition/insights will emerge, putting us far ahead of the game, far ahead of our peers or rivals or associates, unseated by the herd mentality, enabling us to be a greater leader in our field, enabling us to accomplish beyond our wildest expectations and dreams. Intuition in life enables greatness in our leadership practices. It is the inspired leader who brings forth what the society subconsciously yearns for. We lead first by becoming a true, honest individual self.

Going to the Deepest Depth through Intuition

The deep oceans surrounding the islands of Hawaii are a pure and clean source of water. Drinking water is harvested from the uncontaminated depths of the ocean and desalinated. This deep ocean water is an ancient, inexhaustible, and mineral-rich source of drinkable water with multiple applications. Over a thousand years ago, water at the earth's poles froze, leaving denser colder water to sink to the depths of the ocean. This deep ocean water travels at the bottom of the ocean toward the equator to replace water being evaporated from the surface; a process referred to as the "deep ocean water conveyor." The deep ocean water conveyor passes through Hawaii, where it is harvested off the coast from a depth of over 2,000 feet. Too deep and too cold to be contaminated by mankind, this water stands alone in its flawless purity and richness of minerals and nutrients. The ocean's currents have carried this mineral- and nutrient-rich water to the deep sea channels of the Pacific Ocean, where it is harvested using smart technology and a state-of-the-art process.

Intuitive insight coming from our "deeper mental oceans" has a capacity that allows for inspirational input as well as learned wisdom to form whole ideas and directions that can be applied in our workplace and everyday life. It is a spiritual state of awareness needed to wipe clean the busy day planners of our executive lives and receive fresh, "mineral-rich" impressions. We can learn from this deepest source of wisdom to understand and create refreshment that otherwise would never occur to us. It welcomes us to approach a deeper-level understanding of a problem, if given ample time and reflection. It welcomes us to understand our current dilemmas and course of events in a specific subject area, and by application of thought and meditation, allows us to alter or influence events in another direction. This is perhaps the greatest use of mental-spiritual foresight: to see what is coming in these troubling times and avoid it skillfully to our benefit.

In preparing for a lunar flight, Astronaut Edgar Mitchell (the sixth man on the moon) explains, "We spent 10% of our time studying plans for the mission and 90% learning how to react intuitively to all the what-ifs." Mitchell claims that reliance on the intuitive response was the most important part of his astronaut training.

Intuition is always a friend to any of the four dimensions of thinking and should have a seat at the table in the following settings:

- In entrepreneurial and innovative organizations with a flat management structure;

- Where there are many different alternatives and a lack of adequate information;

- When time pressure exists;

- By managers who think holistically, have a positive attitude to intuition, and have a high tolerance for ambiguity.

Activating Intuitive Insight—be still and listen from within!

The thoughts that come often unsought, and, as it were, drop into the mind, are commonly the most valuable of any we have.

John Locke

The only really valuable thing is intuition.

Albert Einstein

Intuitive insight is a BRIGHT3+4 processing that allows for inspirational input as well as learned wisdom, to form whole ideas and directions that can be applied in the workplace and everyday life. It is a visual-inspirational state of awareness.

The best vision is insight.

Malcolm Forbes

We use this type of deep insight to make significant personal strides in many facets of our life, our family, portending problems, and business in particular. We have experienced that when we meditatively ponder issues in this markedly different "be still" or quiet fashion, it is probable to encounter situations in which our actions seem so different that to some they seem strange until our actions bring about the desired results.

Intuitive thinkers need to have space and time for quiet meditation.

If we think of space and time, we may think of sound, motion, and get-up-and-go. But there is another kind of space and time we need just as much—the power of silence.

Here we refer to the power of silence, as well as freedom from external constraints, to let emerging ideas take us where they will, even if they violate common wisdom or the constraints of time, money, and facilities. The quiet insights and breakthroughs we all experience should encourage us to have faith that the bigger moments will happen. Our brains bestow moments of illumination almost as a matter of course, as long as there has been adequate preparation and incubation. Because neural processes that take place during creativity and B3 activity remain hidden from consciousness, we cannot actively influence or accelerate them. It therefore behooves us to take time for meditation and practice patience.

Creative executives must have time when they do nothing. Turn off the computer and cell phone, pause the iPod, and take ten minutes of silence for ourselves. Find a quiet place. Even an empty office at work will do if it's the only place we can get away. Close our eyes and focus on our breathing. Inhale for three seconds; exhale for three seconds. Let ourselves get into a rhythm. Count our breaths, visualize our favorite place, or pray. Or just be still and don't think, but listen. The more we practice silence, the more natural it will feel. Make time to savor silence and stillness daily. We'll reduce stress, strengthen our immune system, and have more focus and mental clarity.

Every company could benefit from an on-site spatial laboratory where executives could go a couple of hours per week for quiet "thought experiments." They could be working on building and improving their spatial capacity/B3 thinking and have the opportunity for uninterrupted reflection on their work. A case can be made for being too productive in the usual sense. Creative thought usually involves a period of quiet meditation and aloneness. Aloneness is akin to sensory deprivation, a state in which subjects are less distracted by conventional stimuli or modes of thinking and are free to tap their inner capacity.

Provide opportunities for teams to be intuitive together.

A continued pursuit of a problem is often required before the inventive solution emerges. Executives should give themselves time to pursue unresolved problems and not discipline themselves as long as they are earnestly trying. Psychiatrist Carl Jung is quoted as saying that to get creative thought to emerge from its incubation stage, one must have a "special training for switching off consciousness, at least to a relative extent, thus giving the unconscious contents a chance to develop."

It is important to provide opportunities for executive teams to be intuitive in their processes to be inventive. We should expect an increase in productivity in executives and their teams when they can call upon their intuitive thinking together and be free to discuss possibilities openly. This approach is explicitly embodied in the champion programs of the Fortune 500 high-tech companies that Peters and Waterman studied and wrote about in *In Search of Excellence*.

Create an intuitive climate for discussion, disagreement, and invention.

Intuitive and inventive executives are more likely to be nonconformist, not only in their thinking, but sometimes in their attitudes and behavior. If such people are valued in an organization for what their ideas can do for the group, then a certain amount of tolerance for unconventional behavior is the price that has to be paid.

Sometimes intuitive, inventive executives are uncomfortably aggressive. They may be driven by ambition and not very tolerant of obstacles, be they material or managerial. "The best workers gripe the most," was the conclusion drawn by one analyst of a survey of industrial productivity. Clearly, malcontents and chronic complainers are not much of an asset to an organization. But it is axiomatic that the best producers and self-starters are assertive, sometimes "pushy," and even obnoxious. However, they should be responsive to input and direction, both from management and from colleagues.

Successful executives never cease their inquisitive probing. They are ingenious and inventive developers who can transcend old practices. They make enduring commitments to creativity, always setting aside the time and resources to cultivate it. Such a climate stimulates executives to come forth with their thinking and ideas, giving others a chance to use those inputs to generate even better, more workable ideas. Creativity feeds upon creativity, producing more and more creative ideas.

The inventiveness of executives is directly proportional to the extent to which they can communicate with both supervisors and other employees. Leaders should openly solicit the ideas of workers and then listen to what they say. This not only affirms the positive motivational purpose of making employees feel like they are important, but it also gives the leadership access to information and ideas they might otherwise not obtain. This principle lies at the hub of Deming's quality control philosophy which has been so successfully employed by Japanese industry.

Employees need good, clear avenues of communication with leadership, particularly those executives who operate at the policymaking levels. Among the reasons this is important is that in this climate, employees have some expectation that they have access to policymakers when they get a good idea. They need not fear that somebody else will steal their ideas and get the credit. Leadership needs to encourage the surfacing of novel ideas by openly valuing them and providing positive reinforcement to those who advance new ideas, even ideas that are not feasible.

In the case of peer communication, Pelz and Andrews found that increased productivity was directly correlated with the number of peers whom a given worker contacted as well as the total number of contacts.

It is one thing for workers to have a good idea. It is another to get them to "surface it." Some work environments discourage innovation, if not actively, at least unwittingly. Younger workers need extra encouragement. The need helps in verbalizing their ideas about how to improve the organization. Paradoxically, those with spatial giftedness are often verbally challenged. This is why B3-thinking managers are needed to lift their subordinates toward the goals. High verbal communication skills are needed to bring out the spatial ideas of employees who may not feel adequate with their verbal ability. Executives should not assign young "spatially strong" workers to a narrow piece of the problem, but rather see that they read and talk about it from many levels and angles.

The 3M Company, noting the large numbers of diverse product innovations, has a slogan: "Thou Shall Not Kill a New Product Idea." They do not implement all of their employees' ideas, but they make it company policy to encourage all the ideas they can get. They don't intimidate their employees with criticism, but rather promote and help them to develop their ideas into marketable products.

Over the years, we have been endeared to the psychological work of Robert Epstein, one of the world's leading experts on creativity and inventiveness. He has shown in laboratory experiments that novel behavior in people emerges in an orderly and predictable way, and that such behavior can be precisely engineered. Dr. Epstein believes that everyone has roughly equal creative, inventive potential, no matter how much creativity they currently express. He articulates four different skill sets, or competencies, essential for creative, inventive expression.

The first and most important competency is **"capturing"**—preserving new ideas as they occur to us and doing so without judging them. There are many ways to capture new ideas. Otto Loewi won a Nobel Prize for work based on an idea about cell biology that he almost failed to capture. He had the idea in his sleep, woke up and scribbled the idea on a pad, but found the next morning that he couldn't read his notes or remember the idea. When the idea turned up in his dreams the following night, he used a better capturing technique: he put on his pants and went straight to his lab!

From his research, Epstein has concluded that four competencies are essential:

- **Capturing**—the most important competency. "Capturing" means "preserving new ideas as they occur to us and doing so without judging them"—while countering negative thoughts and habits that block novel thinking.

- **Challenging**—giving ourselves tough problems to solve. In tough situations, multiple behaviors compete with one another, and their interconnections create new behaviors and ideas.

- **Broadening**—The more diverse our knowledge, the more interesting the interconnections—so we can boost our creativity simply by learning interesting new things.

- **Surrounding**—has to do with how we manage our physical and social environments. The more interesting and diverse the things and the people around us, the more interesting our own ideas become.

Encouraging open-ended problem solving and unleashing creativity and three-dimensional thinking within our executive circles is something anyone can cultivate using a variety of "spatial" techniques.

OUR BEST SEVEN ORGANIZATIONAL VISUAL-SPATIAL TECHNIQUES

1. "On-the-Fringe" Technique

On-the-Fringe technique calls for the wildest, most outrageous and preposterous things any of us can imagine and generate. We use true fringe thinking, where there are no rules, etiquette, laws, or standards. We escape the physical limitations of the world to see what our ultimate solution would be. We should not limit ourselves by anything except our own imagination, and even this we should push.

Our approach here is to write down the wildest, most ridiculous, stupid, wacky ideas we can come up with to solve our problem/opportunity. They do not have to be practical, possible, or even sensible.

Once we have done this, and only when we have finished, we should look back at the ideas we have generated. Then we should look for ways in which all or part of these ideas could be made practical. This is the part that requires spatial abilities to look for patterns and connections between unrelated parts. Think of the benefits we could gain by using the idea and work out how we can achieve the same thing in reality. How could we modify the suggested solution to make it work? How could we get the same effect? What changes in the world would we need to make the idea possible and how would we make those changes happen?

2. Challenge Facts Technique

The Challenge Facts technique asks us to consider what we think are facts and investigate what differences and advantages it would make if they were not facts. We could try to imagine what would be the case if the fact were totally wrong. Or we could try to modify the fact and see whether the modified fact fits into the current situation better than the original one. Or is the world likely to change so that the modified fact will fit in better in the future? If so, what new ideas does this future world suggest? If we find that our new consideration blatantly doesn't fit, then consider what advantages this hypothetical situation might have and how we might be able to incorporate them into our current solution. We are using the challenge of a fact as a stimulus for new ideas, nothing more.

First list the facts; then write a statement that challenges that fact, and then use that challenge to develop new ideas. The following example should demonstrate the process:

Fact: Companies pay employees for their time.

Challenge of the fact: Employees pay their company for the use of its facilities.

New idea based on challenging the fact:

Each employee receives a percentage of the profits based on their position within the company and the amount of time and contributions spent on its products or services. Out of this amount is taken the amount of money related to that employee's use of the facilities. In this way, the employee is directly affected by the quality of the product or service and is more motivated to improve it. Also, employees are directly affected by the amount of money they use in the course of their work. It could also mean that employees are free to live their own life and work the way they want to work.

3. Wishful Thinking Technique

The Wishful Thinking technique is a very useful tool for coming up with new ideas. By dreaming of our ideal situation or solution, we can often come up with something that can have a similar effect but in a more practical, realistic way. It can also be useful because we have something to aim for and we can then consider how far we want your solution to meet our ideal.

We use our ideal solution to come up with ideas for how it can be obtained, or how part of it can be obtained.

Some wishful questions you might ask yourself might be:

- What would my perfect solution be?
- What effect would my ideal solution have?
- What if money/morals/laws did not matter at all?
- What would I do if I had unlimited power and resources?
- What would my ideal solution look like?

Once we have dreamed of our perfect solution, we must then look at how much of it can be put into practice and how we can achieve it. See what practical benefits we can get from the perfect solution.

4. Role-Play Technique

This technique allows us to change our perspective by getting us to role-play a different person and see how they would approach the problem/opportunity. Different people use different bits of information and knowledge to approach the same problem, and it's extremely helpful to view a task from different angles. Have you ever noticed that an artist and a mathematician will approach a subject from different angles and different ways of thinking? Imagine the ideas we will have as we take the role of both occupations and play around with the displacements of thought!

Begin by simply selecting another occupation to role-play. The easiest way to get this is to use a computer to select from a list of occupations. A randomly selected list is best so that we don't select easy or less challenging ones.

Next, when we have our occupation to role-play, then we try to approach our problem/opportunity in the way this person would.

- How would they think?
- What objects and items would they be using?
- Where would they be doing it?
- How would they see the problem?
- What action would they take?
- How would they explain the problem?
- How would they solve the problem?

See how many different ways we can approach the problem and its solutions using our new assumed personality.

5. Imagineering Technique

To clarify how spatial thinking works, imagine a real-life "invention" situation, for example, the invention of the light bulb. We can digress from history and give undue credit to one individual, in short romanticizing the whole thing and creating a bit of a fictitious story. Let's assume that Thomas Edison was the only person responsible for inventing the incandescent bulb, as is commonly believed. Further, we will assume that no other supporting work by any other individual in any supporting field had ever been done. Try to create a work picture. Edison is sitting in the flickering light of a candle reading a book. He is getting annoyed at the fitful illumination it is providing. Ultimately, he lays his book aside and stares malevolently at the candle. He finally comes to the conclusion that he will find a better way. Are we getting visual and spatial?

Now, visually put ourselves in the picture. What would we do? We may want to begin improving the wick and the wax, then using additives in the wax—the whole gamut. And with each prototype built, we are as dissatisfied as ever. Nothing is working. We are operating in the known and thinking of ways of improving the candle. No solution, no go.

The moment of transition comes when we go into spatial thinking. Look at the result we want and separate it from the means. The result we want is strong, steady illumination, right? OK. The transition comes the moment we start considering the possibility of something else solving the problem. The moment we stop thinking candles and start thinking hot metals is the moment of truth. Once that transition takes place, the paradigm shifts to imagination. It is not only imagination; there is vision there, and genius and passion. We then can more easily move into the higher levels of thinking on other problems yet to be solved. The thing that enables this process to take place with any similar innovation is our willingness to let go of the traditional way of thinking.

6. Envisioning, Imaging, Pictures Technique

"Envisioning, Imaging, and Pictures" is a form of concentrated focus that is a movie-style use of imagination in teams—turning mental thoughts, emotions, or expectations into *visual* forms or images on paper. "Envisioning, Imaging, and Pictures" develops the team's ability to construct, manipulate and interpret extraordinary images/patterns in the minds of its members. We believe that the best of creative problem solving is shown by competent executives who can process together in higher levels of visualization.

One of the best uses of "Envisioning, Imaging, and Pictures" is to picture something that the team is about to do and take themselves through the steps, anticipating the problems before they occur, and testing out what they can do. For example: *Imagine the executive group is a football team headed for the big game, and the main task is to defend themselves against the other team's quarterback and pass receiver. We've watched endless videotapes to learn how their key players act and react. We also know the way we play. By focusing our imagination on it, we can do the brain's version of a computer simulation game, picturing how we'd play in order to succeed. We might even do it while we're asleep, while dreaming, if our focus is strong. The result is that we'll know and anticipate the opponent's moves, and be ready to make our own moves, making us a more effective executive team.*

"Envisioning, Imaging, and Pictures" builds and sustains self-efficacy because it requires team members to focus on a specific leadership practice in a particular context and with a particular successful outcome. "Envisioning, Imaging, and Pictures" has a threefold effect. It builds the team's positive thinking, their self-belief, and a sense of self-efficacy. Through these three benefits, executive processing helps to develop the inner game of extraordinary leadership.

7. Improvisational (Improv) Theatre Technique

Will Ferrell comedies, such as Talladega Nights, are hits in part because planned scenes are jumping-off points for improvisation between the actors, leading to the funniest moments. In our fringe teams, we have seen improv and brainstorming-manipulations between multiple members—multiple minds—bring together wholes that otherwise would stay in the detail camps.

One of the most creative spatial thinking techniques we employ with executive groups in corporate events is *improvisational theatre*, which uses audience suggestions to shape the action that unfolds on stage. Unlike conventional scripted theatre, there is an element of spontaneity and unpredictability that makes *improvisational theatre*, or *improv*, a unique and exciting experience for the employee-performers as well as the employee-audience to tackle some of their difficult challenges. Every performance is completely different, and there's an element of risk involved, since there's no guarantee that any given scene will "work."

The performers (employees) must accept each other's ideas, and build on them—that's the fundamental process of improvisation needed to stimulate innovative thinking—on stage and in the audience. The basic skills of listening, clarity, confidence, and performing instinctively and spontaneously are considered important skills for employee-actors to develop. Improvisational theatre allows an interactive relationship with the audience. Improv groups frequently solicit suggestions from the audience as a source of inspiration, a way of getting the audience involved, and a means of proving that the performance is not scripted.

There are lots of different styles of improvisation, but the one that's currently our favorite is "spot" improve, which we experienced at the *Fringe* in Edinburgh, Scotland. "Spot" improv involves taking audience suggestions (in a problem-solving setting) and using them immediately ("on the spot") to create scenes around possible solutions. The scenes usually wind up being very funny, but that's not a requirement. Good scenes can be serious and touching instead of (or in addition to) being comedic. A key is to identify your thinker-actors in the organization and put them "on stage."

There are several different ways to structure an improv show. Most groups simply present a series of improvised scenes, possibly tied together by a common theme. Perhaps the single most important thing that improvisers learn is the value of *creativity and agreement*. Since nothing exists until the actors create it, a scene will only be "real" (for both the performers and the audience) if everyone agrees with each other about things like where they are, who they are, what's going on, and how are they getting "on the fringe" in their thinking.

In order for an improvised scene to be successful, the employee-actors involved must work together responsively to define the parameters and action of the scene, in a process of co-creation of solutions to a problem. With each spoken word or action in the scene, an actor makes an *offer*, meaning that he or she defines some element of the reality of the scene. This might include giving another character a name, identifying a relationship or location, or using mime to define the physical environment. It is the responsibility of the other actors to accept the offers/solutions that their fellow employee-performers make; to not do so is known as blocking, or negation, which usually prevents the scene from developing. Some performers may deliberately block (or otherwise break out of character) for comedic effect—but this generally prevents the scene from advancing. Accepting an offer is usually accompanied by adding a new offer, often building on the earlier one; this is a process improvisers refer to as *"Yes, and ..., "* and is considered the cornerstone of improvisational creativity. Every new piece of information added helps the actors to refine their characters and progress the action of the scene and gain fresh insights into the problem.

Our experiences affirm that executives/employees/staff will recall their corporate event a great deal longer than their typical stuffy organizational meetings. In fact, many of our clients have already asked if we can do it again sometime.

Five Personal Tips to Become Better at Visual-Spatial Thinking and Intuition

We have collected tips from many of our best executives who personify spatial thinking and inventiveness.

1. Keep a notebook and pen on hand at all times.

Keeping a notebook around, we will always be able to capture our ideas at any time of the day.

Leonardo da Vinci was well known for keeping a journal of his ideas. His notebooks are now prized possessions that hold the many creative and genius thoughts of this master thinker, painter, and inventor. His notebooks were filled with plans for flying machines, a parachute, a helicopter, the extendable ladder, the bicycle, folding furniture, and a number of automated tools for increasing productivity.

A blank page is an open invitation for the creative and curious mind. The simple act of writing gets us into a creative flow that can last for hours. The free-flowing, exploratory practice of keeping a journal encourages freedom of thought and expanded perspectives.

2. Ask questions.

Questions are the root of all knowledge and creativity. By continually asking questions about the world around us, we fuel our creative fire. Great minds are those that have asked the greatest questions. Leonardo da Vinci asked such questions as, *"Why does the thunder last a longer time than that which causes it?"* and *"Why is the sky blue?"*

Socrates asked such questions as:

- *"What is wisdom?"*

- *"What is piety?"*
- *"What is beauty?"*

As a young boy, Albert Einstein asked himself, *"What would it be like to run beside a light beam at the speed of light?"*

A number of inventions have been created by asking one simple question: *"What if ...?"*

By asking questions, we increase our level of consciousness and our perspective of the world.

3. Gather information

Intuitive leadership is a complicated combination of *thinking, acting, and influencing*—and each of these three processes is complex in and of itself. Spatial thinking involves gathering information, making connections among the various pieces of information, and filtering the information to form ideas and strategies that are focused, relevant, and sound. We recommend to executives:

- Constantly scan the internal and external environments for factors, trends, and patterns that may have an impact on the organization's business.

- Pay attention to whether the organization is fulfilling its mission and values. Does the culture support the employees' capabilities and talents, or budgetary issues? Do units and systems function and interrelate?

- Build networks that foster trusting relationships up and down the organization to encourage and accept employee input and feedback.

- Manage by wandering around—spending time among and genuinely communicating with employees throughout the organization to see the business through their eyes.

- Pay attention to external market conditions, global economies, changing technology, industry innovations, and shifting supplies of resources.

Seek out new experiences and new vistas. Our minds are much like a garden. Without proper care, the weeds will take over. Nothing sparks the mind like learning something new. If we want to expand our spatial thinking, then we should learn a new skill. It can be anything we choose. Learn a new language. Learn to water ski. Learn to play an instrument. Pick up photography or even try a new sport. All of these activities get our mind working outside of its regular patterns.

4. Develop an imaginary dialogue.

This technique was first introduced in the best-selling book by Napoleon Hill, *Think and Grow Rich*. Before achieving his success, Hill was first meeting with an imaginary mastermind each night. He would close his eyes and visualize a table occupied by such great men as Abraham Lincoln, George Washington, Napoleon Bonaparte, Ralph Waldo Emerson, and Elbert Hubbard. Napoleon Hill would then speak to the members of his imaginary mastermind table in the following manner:

"Mr. Lincoln: I desire to build in my own character those qualities of patience and fairness toward all mankind and the keen sense of humor which were your outstanding characteristics."

"Mr. Washington: I desire to build in my own character those qualities of patriotism and self-sacrifice and leadership which were your outstanding characteristics."

"Mr. Hubbard: I desire to develop the ability to equal and even to excel the ability that you possessed with which to express yourself in clear, concise and forceful language."

After meeting with his mastermind group for several months, he found that he had developed each of their desired characteristics into his own personality. Hill also went to his imaginary mastermind group to help solve any problem he was facing. The imaginary mastermind is a master tool for finding new perspectives and looking at your problem from a different angle.

For example, let's say that you own a business. Why not develop an imaginary mastermind group of the greatest business minds in history? You can call to your table such names as Henry Ford, Andrew Carnegie, Walt Disney, Bill Gates, Ray Kroc, and Sam Walton. Call on them daily for advice and you will begin to see your problems in a new light. As Albert Einstein said, "You can't solve a problem with the same mind that created it." You can have even more creative fun by imagining a discussion between two different well-known people. Some examples to get you started include:

Bill Gates vs. Steve Jobs

Leonardo da Vinci vs. Albert Einstein

William Shakespeare vs. Maya Angelou

Let our mind wander and we will be surprised at all of the connections we begin to make.

5. Create a healthy lifestyle that is enriched, complex, and fresh

- Regular physical activity/exercise that is enjoyable

- Service to others with uplifting, inspiring friendships

- Spirituality—striving for betterment and happiness through righteous living

- Mental stimulation (e.g., reading, puzzles, chess, Scrabble, Sudoku, second language, etc.)

- Good nutrition that promotes health and longevity

A closing observation is that productivity is usually better with healthy, inventive executives who can work within multiple levels and conflicting ideas, including both basic and applied research, and plot it all in visual space. Those who can focus on either basic research or applied research only (two-dimensional surface) are usually much less productive. This may indicate that executives are more productive because they are capable enough to work spatially at several different levels with multiple perspectives and initiatives.

CHAPTER SUMMARY
Key Points

• Visual Spatial Ability (BRIGHT3) is the ability to see things from many different perspectives. It is the capacity to construct and deconstruct three-dimensional, physical, solutions to real world problems.

• Over the years, we have rediscovered that the ability of executives and teams to create and sustain high-capacity cultures is the most critical step in ensuring their ability to consistently achieve superior results.

• The third dimension is simultaneous processing, which individuals use to relate separate pieces of information into a group or to see how parts are related as a whole. Simultaneous processing is also used when individuals have to recognize patterns. For this reason, simultaneous processing is important for doing geometry, seeing patterns in numbers, seeing a group of letters as a word, seeing words as a whole, understanding a sentence as part of a paragraph, and seeing how a paragraph fits as part of a complete story. Simultaneous processing is involved in reading comprehension because it requires the integration and understanding of word relationships and how all of the elements of a text fit together.

• The most important phase in the exercise of simultaneous/three-dimensional thinking is the front-end work. The in-depth, serious thinking by leaders and their teams results in the creation of an intellectual framework for the future.

• Executive depth begins with mentally processing simultaneously images of qualities, objects, and events where visual perception lays the groundwork of concept formation. The minds of executives reach far beyond stimuli received by the eyes directly and momentarily. They operate with the vast range of imagery available through learning and memory and organize a total lifetime's experience into a system of visual concepts.

• Our Visual-Spatial Processing Program creates more capacity for the working memory and makes it more efficient. The most collaborative factor would seem to be the mechanics of supplying information input from external sources. One example of a technique we already use to increase the efficiency of external source input is the use of brainstorming.

• Companies need help to overcome the dual challenges of dealing with complex and alternate worldviews, at the same time dealing with the dynamics of cross-functional teams. The inherent potential of the individual brain to entertain several alternate scenes must be tapped.

• Successful executives never cease their inquisitive probing. They are ingenious and innovative developers who can transcend old practices.

• Spatial I and II are fundamental problem-solving skills for an executive. I and II are the two attack strategies (construction and deconstruction) in a visual spatial world—attack from the front with construction and in the rear with deconstruction. Spatial I and II are the two sides of executive currency desperately needed by executive teams.

CHAPTER 6

BRIGHT4—Global Insight
Executing Decisiveness, Direction, and Speed

> *The quarterback must be a very quick and decisive thinker ... must be a bright guy, but the emphasis must be on quick thinking*
>
> Mark Lawrence, Football 101: Tight Ends & Quarterbacks

> *The one word that makes a good manager—decisiveness.*
>
> Lee Iacocca

> *Sure, luck means a lot in football. Not having a good quarterback is bad luck.*
>
> Don Shula

Imagine being a freshman quarterback coming off the bench with a pass receiver. Your team just got possession of the ball and is three points behind with 30 seconds of play remaining in a bowl game. Fans are going wild. Your team's lead quarterback was with the medics as you received the last instructions from your coach, and you are on your way to the huddle.

You finally reach the huddle. All eyes are on you. Your heart is racing. It is so loud in that stadium you can barely hear yourself. How many times have you practiced 30-second drill plays just for a situation like this? *Is this really happening? Am I ready?*

You feel the roar of the crowd as you approach the line of scrimmage. *This is it. The fans are counting on me. Have I done what is necessary to win? What have I done to be the best quarterback I can be? Did I mentally rehearse the best football passing-receiving drills, option drills, exchange drills, ball drills, time/speed and agility-conditioning drills, and make sure I had the best quarterback knowledge available?*

My speed of decision-execution in the backfield must be under 3.8 seconds! Will the pass reception of over 30 yards be off? I have trained well to mentally process through all viable options and execute with timing, speed, and quickness. Thank goodness, my confidence is there. I know I have the arm strength and agility to pass to the receiver 30–40 yards down field.

Wait, a defensive lineman just grabbed my non-throwing arm. Don't worry, my strength and confidence are there to shrug him off. A reception opening is happening. Throw the bomb, NOW!

Execution through space with direction, speed, and precision is the cut that makes a great quarterback and leader. When a quarterback or executive fails, it's usually not because of a flaw in his or her vision of the field/organization. Rather, the fatal error generally lies in an inability to take action with speed, direction, and precision.

The construction of "BRIGHT4" as our highest dimension must sustain a thinking needed for bar-raising and leaping above BRIGHT1+2+3 assumptions to setting a course for speed, direction, and precision. B3 thinkers without B4 ability will be highly aware of space but pay little attention to time, speed, direction, and precision. Since the rate of change in our business environment is increasing along with occasional discontinuous or disruptive changes, the amount of time for a given set of strategic assumptions to remain valid is inevitably reducing. This condition demands a conscious initiative to challenge the mental models behind current thinking to generate new, better-matched ones, and to do this *faster and faster*. This has spurred the innovation of fast processes to gain the benefits of simultaneous and *decisive thinking* in pressured and timed settings.

Decision Making: Pressured and Timed

In football as well as in business and organizational life, two fundamental decision processes must be navigated: (1) untimed, unpressured decision making; and (2) timed, often pressured decision making. Success in any given game or season will be determined by a combination of both timed and untimed decisions.

Untimed decision making is the development of the team's strategic long term plan. This is represented by the playbook and game plans that are developed before and during the season. It includes player and coaching acquisitions and player and coaching long-term development when time is more abundant for reflection, goal setting, and creativity. Untimed decision making taps into the potential of human beings. It shows what is possible under potentially ideal thinking conditions, when no-trade off is necessary between maximum speed and maximum accuracy. Nevertheless, potential must be actualized on the field and on the scoreboard. Professional football rosters are loaded with so many individuals of great potential (physical endowments, incredible credentials, work ethics, etc.) who are unable to achieve individual greatness on the field or play with time ticking and decisiveness at a premium.

> *In short, in life, as in a football game, the principle to follow is: Hit the line hard; don't foul and don't shirk, but hit the line hard!*
>
> Theodore Roosevelt, *The Strenuous Life* (1900)

Super Bowl XLII (2008): New York Giants 17, New England Patriots 14— "Timed"

New York Giants quarterback Eli Manning quickly rallied his team from trailing the Patriots with two historic fourth-quarter touchdowns to engineer one of the most stunning comeback upsets in Super Bowl history. The New England Patriots, with an undefeated season, led into the fourth quarter with less than three minutes left. The Giants team, offense and defense, played extraordinarily well, with journalists reporting: "It's all but ordained the greatest team ever." Eli Manning's decisive 13-yard touchdown pass to wide receiver Plaxico Burress was executed with 35 seconds remaining to win the game. Manning explained later that he went back to work with no sense of panic and was confident that all the pieces were coming together. "I said [to the team], 'This is where you want to be.' I've talked to the coach [Tom Coughlin] before and its kind of a situation you want to be in. You want to be down by four at the end of the game, where your kind of have to score a touchdown."

Team decisiveness is a characteristic trait of a Super or Pro Bowl champion. The Pro Bowl is filled with players who have demonstrated individual decisiveness, but Super Bowl rings are only given to the team that is most decisive. The Super Bowl champion team—the New York Giants—only placed one player in the 2008 Pro Bowl, but through team decisiveness they toppled the Goliath New England Patriots. Although Eli Manning was given the most valuable player award for the game, he was the first to exclaim that every Giant player made great decisive plays that resulted in the victory. Every catch, run, rush, sack collectively produced a result greater than the sum of the individual abilities they possessed. The New York Giants had synergy, and their thinking was fixed on decisive plays leading to an end in mind—Super Bowl rings.

Timed spatial judgment making is the actual decision making that occurs during the playing of the game. This process occurs on every play, but is intensified in the hurry-up offense (no-huddle offense and the two-minute drill) and diminishes in intensity during half time or a time out. The essence of timed decision making is the ability as a team to be decisive, making decisions quickly, firmly, and clearly. For a football team, decisive is the operational word of effective timed decision making. Every successful play requires decisive action by each member of the team. If a decisive action is produced by ten players and an indecisive action by only one player (e.g., a running back fumbles the ball), the team registers an indecisive action and moves away from their objective.

Visual-spatial ability supports and sustains a quality of creative problem solving that originates in perceptual-information processing and is characteristic of higher-level executive thinking. Visual-spatial thinking has a holistic logic and life of its own that, as usable potential, can be brought to bear creatively and analytically to solve various kinds and levels of problems. Visual-spatial thinking operates on every level of awareness, from subliminal perceptual process to holistic, high level creative thinking.

Four-dimensional thinking is the ability to insightfully think quickly and confidently, and be decisive with direction.

In our turbulent, fast-flowing business environment, do we have the luxury of time when making decisions? Executives have to make sense out of a tremendous volume of complexity, simplify this complexity, make good decisions that are simultaneously long- and short-term in nature, and then influence their associates in a direction that supports the goals of the organization. It is the ability to distill an essence from a large amount of data and it is also about the ability to foresee emerging scenarios and be prepared for them. Rather than be sacked in the backfield, are we able to quickly size up the situation, identify the most workable and expedient course of action, and then execute—often without having all the data or the time to consider every possible option? B4 quarterbacks and thinkers do not necessarily think harder, longer, or more exactly; they have simply learned to think in directions that are more likely to be productive.

Do we face any of these issues?

- Approach every decision in the same way, regardless of the time, risk, and resources involved?

- Struggle to make quality decisions when pressed for time?

- Lose opportunities because we don't make timely executions with direction?

Does our executive team use "fancy footwork" for the annual strategy-planning marathon—making strategic decisions on the fly? Does it idle away precious hours wrestling with strategically irrelevant issues? If so, we're not alone. Most of us abhor formal strategic planning because it doesn't help us respond swiftly to threats and opportunities that arise unexpectedly. But lacking fourth-dimensional capacity to conceptualize multiple variables quickly, we avoid debating strategy and don't gather the data we need to make informed decisions. When we do discuss strategy, we wrangle over alternatives. Result? Wasted time, poor decisions, and lost opportunities.

Ways we can avoid indecisiveness could include establishing a rigorous discipline for addressing strategic issues as they crop up. We could conduct separate meetings for operational and strategic questions, and concentrate strategy discussions on issues driving our organization's long-term value. Put real choices on the table before approving any strategy. And, transform squabbling into constructive "fights" that expose smart solutions. Finally, we should clarify who's accountable for carrying out each decision—and when the work must be done.

Many of the facts of life themselves are not as important as what we think about them. The ability to think quickly and confidently, to be decisive, is at a premium. It means visualizing the relationship between objects (ideas) in space, both in dynamic and static environments, and developing and communicating relevant and meaningful integrations. This level of processing is the art and science of increasing the height, breadth, and depth of visual perception along with the accompanying visual speed components. Visual-processing speed, or decisiveness and velocity, is at the highest levels of cognition.

Sherlock Holmes: BRIGHT4—Global and Decisive with Timely Solutions

Perhaps Sherlock Holmes's greatest genius was his ability to observe a situation, see it from its myriad of dimensions and subtleties (global), and draw this cornucopia of details together into a series of insights, from which he could come up with an integral analysis and thereby a decisive, timely solution to the situation at hand (BRIGHT1+2+3+4). Arthur Conan Doyle's brilliant creation, Sherlock Holmes, said:

- "I have already explained to you that what is out of the common is usually a guide rather than a hindrance. In solving a problem of this sort, the grand thing is to be able to reason backward. That is a very useful accomplishment, and a very easy one, but people do not practice it much. In the everyday affairs of life it is more useful to reason forward, and so the other comes to be neglected. There are 50 who can reason synthetically for one who can reason analytically" (*A Study in Scarlet,* 1887).

- "How often have I said to you that when you have eliminated the impossible, whatever remains, *however improbable*, must be the truth?" (*The Sign of Four,* 1890).

- "That process, said I, starts upon the supposition that when you have eliminated all which is impossible, then whatever remains, however improbable, must be the truth. It may well be that several explanations remain, in which case one tries test after test until one or other of them has a convincing amount of support" (*The Case Book of Sherlock Holmes,* 1927).

- "It is a capital mistake to theorize before one has data. Insensibly one begins to twist facts to suit theories, instead of theories to suit facts" (*The Adventures of Sherlock Holmes,* 1892).

- "I ought to know by this time that when a fact appears to be opposed to a long train of deductions, it invariably proves to be capable of bearing some other interpretation" (*A Study in Scarlet,* 1887).

As with Mr. Holmes, who obviously never paid any income tax because he had "brilliant deductions" (ha ha), we cannot think or deduce without facts. But the reverse does not hold true. Putting the accent on facts and recall does not in turn spontaneously generate high-level thinking. The single most significant fact of current research is that it is incorrect to think that there is a sequence from lower-level linear activities that do not require much independent thinking or judgment to higher-level ones that do. The single overarching message emerging from the twenty-first century and the economy of the Web is that higher level thought is not just central to its future, but is its present and our future.

Is the modern "Sherlock" being stuck in a default scenario?

Our observation with multiple businesses and governments has confirmed that the assumptions behind strategic decisions, however accurate at the time of their making, invalidate quickly—especially since 9/11. This has the effect of bringing the long-range future closer and closer. The future, in the spatial sense of change, is crashing into the present at an unprecedented rate. Where the "crash" occurs is where confusion and chaos meets order. Here, the edge or cliff of chaos is where people think they are thinking globally with direction when they are merely rearranging their biases and prejudices on their organizational "decks."

Holding to one worldview of the future and basing current judgments and decisions upon it is like assuming a lottery win through a single set of numbers. This state of affairs has been called "being stuck in a default scenario," which is a depiction of the future extrapolated from the present. As the Irishman said when being asked the way to a certain pub, "Well, now, if I was you, I wouldn't start from here."

Insight & Velocity

Insight and velocity facilitates high-level spatial speed processing that energizes executives to truly understand the forces that affect their organization and make better business decisions. Here, executives visualize, predict, and compare the impacts of potential business scenarios and strategic decisions. Spatial speed processing helps to make decisions quickly and efficiently through questioning:

- When should I introduce new services to my customers?
- Where should I allocate my resources?
- How should I segment my market?

Developing new business ideas and setting goals can be easy compared to the challenge of effectively implementing a strategy to achieve the desired results.

We accelerate implementation by putting sophisticated analytical technology in the hands of business users and decision makers.

Intuitive ease of use, and speed of processing and viewing information help make location-sensitive decisions accurately and efficiently.

Keeping B4-dimensional thinking alive around the table will ultimately:

- Save time and money
- Generate and increase revenue
- Meet and exceed performance measurements
- Efficiently manage resources
- Accurately build business cases and budgets
- Effectively communicate performance and strategy
- Quickly and efficiently make the quality decisions customers and stakeholders expect

You have to pretend you're 100% sure. You have to take action; you can't hesitate or hedge. Anything less will condemn your efforts to failure.

Andrew Grove

Robert Kail, distinguished psychology professor at Purdue University, has published extensively on processing speed, mental capacity, and intelligence. His research has shown that global processing speed is a fundamental element of intelligence. Dr. Kail states, "As children develop, they process information more rapidly, apparently reflecting age-related change in the Central Nervous System. This more rapid processing results in more effective use of working memory, which enhances performance on many reasoning tasks." This dynamic view of global information processing helps us to understand how an increase in global processing can have spillover effects to many different areas of intellectual ability.

We have firsthand experience on the effect of Visual Information Processing (VIP) on global processing speed. The intense visual stimulation that accompanies VIP development provides an incredible opportunity for students to use large amounts of visual attention in order to complete the tasks. Global processing speed is one of the first abilities to improve with normal students and has been demonstrated in Dr. Baize's laboratory to continue to improve over time. Executives/students have demonstrated sustained improvements five years later.

One common question asked by our quarterbacks, executives, and senior managers alike is: *"Is a quarterback or a manager who is more decisive than another quarterback or manager actually brighter? Are they actually smarter than quarterbacks or managers who take more time to do the same exact task?"* The answer is yes! However, remember that time is relative. What our capacity is today need not be our capacity for the rest of our lives. Research confirms that quickness of information processing is directly related to our developed thinking capacity. But remember, each of us has so much room for greater thinking capacity.

Let's start from a 30-second backfield exercise.

Take out some paper. You have 30 seconds to write down 15 ways in which a football is like a church sermon. Are you having problems being creative? Sort yourselves into teams of three, and try it again. Answers should quickly flow from right brain responses: "They both … They can be either … They … They are hard to …"

Why do we need an exercise like this for executives? Basically, because 80% of all new products fail in the marketplace. The definition of innovation is commercial success. It's not just about creativity—it's about risk thinking in the new marketplace.

Faced with chaos and emergence, companies need to reorient themselves to welcome their uncertainties as a catalyst for innovative thinking and problem solving. If we try to eliminate rather than manage chaos, we will surely be surprised and caught outside of the thinking and action needed to move our system forward.

BRIGHT4—Insight and velocity occur at the higher levels of thinking and activity.

The art and practice of visualizing/imaging an athletic movement in order to perfect it became popular in the 1970s. A sports psychologist would work with a quarterback by having him stand quietly on the field with his eyes closed and imagine himself throwing the ball to a pass receiver. He would be thinking something like, *The football is an extension of my throwing arm. My entire body is tingling with excitement, but I am utterly relaxed. I am enjoying every opportunity to pass that comes to me. I am absolutely sure that with my next pass I can place the ball into the arms of my pass receiver in any place on the field. The field is enormously wide.* For our quarterback to put himself into such an ideal performance state, he seeks a healthy balance of strain and relaxation. He must become completely immersed in his own movements—confident in his own actions, blocking his distractions, reveling in the experience. By repeatedly visualizing the movement, he strengthens or adds synaptic connections among relevant neurons.

Golfer Tiger Woods reports that it is easier for him to sink putts when he imagines the rattle of the ball in the cup. As the massive impact of images on the quality of our lives becomes clearer, the necessity to educate ourselves to the implications of an image-driven society becomes more critical. In this age of massive discontinuities, distractions, disconnects, and accelerating change, savvy backfield executives desperately need new ways of thinking and new ways of "seeing" (visualization) challenges and opportunities to help them develop a steady stream of new ideas and innovations. Visual-spatial thinking meets these needs by visualizing and manipulating possibilities, and offering a collection of simple, elegant, and vivid ways to represent problems and solutions.

We need to learn to move fast with *insight and velocity* before our markets and publics move past us. Insightful, fast-acting leadership is increasingly essential for us to stay ahead of the curve. Our challenge is to build leaders within and smartly recruit them from without. Use the score card for selection criteria: the candidate should have capacity to know how to make fast and accurate decisions with insight, implement strategies and create change at the speed of sound if not light. Our capacity to drive a fast-moving organization and to be a quick and nimble mover is an essential skill.

BRIGHT1+2+3+4 = Insight and Velocity—occurs at the higher levels of thinking and activity. At lower levels, our brain accepts input, processes it, and produces output without any feedback. At the 4-D level, feedback from a lower level is accepted with the capacity for both rewriting the rules used at the lower level and providing feedback to the lower level. The "lower" action process simply executes, resets, and executes again. The 4-D executive thinker can edit or adjust the action process after considering feedback. Unless we master 4-D thinking, we will not be able to manage our personal development as a high-level thinker and executive.

Thinking skills, in the current literature, are viewed in both general and specific terms, but generally categorized into three broad thinking processes that are: critical thinking, creative thinking, and problem solving. *Critical thinking* (B1+2) is the process of determining the authenticity, accuracy, or value of something which is characterized by the ability to seek reasons and alternatives, perceive the total situation, and change our view based on evidence. *Problem solving (B2)*, however, is the basic thinking processes used to resolve a defined or unknown problem, assemble facts about the problem, determine additional information needed, or suggest alternative solutions and test for appropriateness, revision, and evaluation as necessary. *Creative thinking (B2+3)* is inventive thinking that explores novel situations, reaches new solutions to old problems, or results in thoughts original with the thinker.

Decision makers naturally crave to make their decisions quickly with as much certainty as possible regarding the outcome. In scientific management, this has fueled the development of ever more sophisticated forecasting methods. The rapid change and unpredictability of the modern global environment is showing up severe limitations in this way of making decisions. The science behind forecasting and extrapolation needs to be augmented with the science of complexity or three- and four-dimensional thinking. The world has emergent properties that, by their very nature, are unpredictable. We need to consider not just, for example, oil prices and stock market movements, but also software developments, discoveries in genetics, climate change, and above all, people behavior.

Decisiveness is a way of conceptualizing, acting, and motivating others that enables effective executive leadership. In decision situations, decisiveness enables us to look at an entire situation with all of its interdependencies and complexities. We'll learn to simplify the complex so that the essence of the decision situation can be understood in its proper context. And we'll learn to design new, innovative strategies for action and lead their implementation.

Skills Needed for Executing Decisiveness, Direction, and Speed

Being able to globally visualize the "field" and execute with decisiveness, direction, and speed are essential cognitive skills for B4 processing.

A. **Spatializing Skills** are the essence of B4 processing. It is the ability to take everything that is available to us and create or construct a mental picture of different possible options/solutions. It is seeing beyond current knowledge, producing new information, meaning or ideas through vision, intuition, and inspiration.

> 1. Inferring: seeing beyond available information to visualizing what might be.

> 2. Predicting: visually anticipating future events, or the outcome of a situation—visualizing possible scenarios and using analogies.

> 3. Elaborating: expanding visions by adding details, examples, or other relevant information; responding to hunches and gut feelings.

B. **Integrating Skills**—connecting and combining information.

> 4. Summarizing: simultaneously combining information efficiently into a holistic, cohesive statement.

5. Restructuring: changing existing knowledge structures to incorporate new information.

C. **Positioning Skills**—assessing and validating the reasonableness and decisiveness of the statement needed for direction and velocity.

6. Launching criteria: setting standards for making judgments, direction, and launch.

7. Verifying: confirming the accuracy of a launch and then responding to any course correction with speed.

We should ask ourselves: *Do I do better in jobs where I'm expected to think things out for myself? Do I try to see the value of another person's opinion, even though I may reject it later? Do I invite significant others to inquire into my logic, reasoning, and assumptions?* Making intelligently informed, decisive decisions is more important than winning arguments.

The Essential Role of Facilitating B4 Spatial Decisiveness and Judgment

To make this workable within the constraints of corporate life, good facilitation is essential. The role of the executive facilitator (or team leader) is to:

- Lead the process that begins: "What is the world asking us to do, to be?"
- Introduce and guide the application of verbal, quantitative, and spatial techniques
- Exploit the feedback of the visual media
- Ensure capture of outputs
- Stimulate the exchange of ideas
- Help articulate and test assumptions
- Challenge fixed mindsets
- Share from previous experience the creation of scenarios

- Ensure the scenarios relate to the original question but in a stretching way.

Tackling complex tasks, developing and articulating inventive solutions, can be quite daunting for the facilitator. However, time and practice allows the facilitator to develop a remarkable combination of skills, including group dynamics, creative thinking, visual-spatial (picture) thinking, and novel content appreciation. The value to an organization in cultivating such facilitation is that inventive work can be brought into the mainstream of decision-making. Too often such work is carried out as an odd project done by a project group that barely influences decision power. But to make this work well, the facilitator's tight spots need to be understood.

Decisiveness and Memory Capacity

Quick thinking that is accompanied by a well-developed visual and auditory memory capacity provides executives with a sense of confidence of what they have seen or heard or touched or smelled or tasted. All of us are not alike in quick thinking or memory capacity. Most of us can be spatially super-charged.

We have found that the development of visual memory concurrently with visual quickness provides much more rapid growth than addressing each component individually. Our brains have the capacity to shift through enormous amounts of visual information in a manageable way. Remember, auditory memory is a sequential process. We can only remember one word at a time. Visual memory, on the other hand, is a simultaneous process, and many images can be stored in the same instant it takes to store one word.

Visual memory is an important area that responds to Visual Information Processing Technology (VIPT). Most importantly, visual and auditory capacities are integrated in a much more effective manner in the learning process. By developing visual memory, we provide executives with the ability to make more confident decisions. By increasing both the quickness of processing and visual memory executives can process much more information in the same amount of time. This means that under pressure and time constraints, executives can consider more possible solutions to the problem at hand. The greater the number of workable solutions, the easier it becomes to find the best solution or to compare the significant from the insignificant aspects of two competing solutions. In short, VIPT helps executives to be decisive: think quicker with firm and clear solutions.

Visual-spatial methods can help cross-functional teams process multiple perspectives.

Companies need help to overcome the dual challenges of dealing with complex and alternate worldviews and dealing with the dynamics of cross-functional teams. The inherent potential of the individual brain to entertain several alternate scenes must be tapped. This psychological process must be bridged into the group effort. Visual methods are extremely helpful here, providing they are both flexible and disciplined at the same time.

These visual-spatial methods facilitate shared work within the group:

- Visibility—Members can see and remember each other's contributions.
- Flexibility—As patterns of relationships change, they can be tracked and recorded in real time.
- Inclusiveness—Views from many perspectives can be included, ensuring richness of texture.
- Interactivity—Members respond to the emerging pattern and deeper conversations are stimulated. Good communication is defined as "the picture is the same."
- Efficacious—Members more easily avoid antagonistic debate and instead build on each other's ideas.

The optimum environment for working this way is not the traditional training room, presentation room, or boardroom, but a specially configured space with plenty of whiteboards, newsprint, large Post-its, and appropriate visual and technological aids to support the thinking tasks at hand. Companies that have gone this route have found considerable benefit in customizing space for working in this way, creating strategy centers or decision centers where work is easily displayed and manipulated by project teams, cross-functional, and executive teams.

The Speed of Opportunity

Teresa Roche, Vice President and Chief Learning Officer of Agilent Technologies with headquarters in Santa Clara, California, revealed in an interview with *Training and Development* (August 2009) how they build inventive and intuitive leadership capacity at Agilent to create worldwide leadership in their field. The firm was part of Hewlett Packard until 1999 when it became an independent company with a strategic intent to be the world's premier measurement company. It is a top supplier of electronic test and measurement products that assist engineers, scientists, and researchers, and help solve crimes (CSI activity). Agilent tests more than half of the world's 1.3 billion cell phones. In 2008, the revenue was $5.7 billion. CEO Bill Sullivan, a 33-year veteran of HP and Agilent, outlined the company's focus on customers, employees, and shareholders, with specific measures of success. Participating senior managers committed to "best-in-the-class" leadership create a follow-up action plan to accelerate their business results, which they then report on three months following the program.

Bill Sullivan believes that general managers should be the heart of the company's ability to innovate and execute. It is the general manager's thinking role to deepen their financial acumen and operational excellence. Inspired by Dave Ulrich and Norm Smallwood's construct of *leadership brand*— "uncompromising integrity with speed of opportunity"—that creates an advantage for Agilent and differentiates them in the eyes of their customers. A leadership development program (Agilent Leadership Core) places participants in diverse teams that compete in a dynamic business simulation. Each team creates a strategic intent and competes for six quarters to win market share, spur growth, and achieve the highest return on invested capital. This development initiative continues the cascading of leadership capabilities defined for every level of leadership throughout the company. Participants apply their learning and inventiveness in "pods," using a wiki to keep connected following the program, and a Webinar is held with the cohort group to discuss their results 10 to 15 weeks after the session. The goal is to focus on the critical few customer opportunities in their challenging market environment and act with **speed and decisiveness**. It is moving from best-in-company versus internal peers, to best-in-class versus external benchmarks.

Piloting Outside our Cockpits

An analogy we often use is the successful helicopter pilot who needs exceptional situational awareness. What distinguishes the best from the merely good is the ability not just to know their position from instruments and maps, and from looking outside, but to be able to visualize their position as if standing away from their aircraft—to be able to understand their position in the normal physical dimensions as well as that of time and the dimensions of numerous alternatives.

Successful pilots are able to communicate simply and effectively in such a way that others are able to see and understand the same picture and turn it into action. And of course, the picture needs to be constantly updated and re-evaluated as the context changes. Too many struggling organizations have lost even the ability to look outside their cockpit. Their instruments are telling them only what they want to know as they fly into the side of the mountain in front of them.

We can learn from an "outside our cockpits" approach to understand and create processes that otherwise would never occur to us. It welcomes us to approach a higher-level understanding of a problem, if given ample time and reflection. It welcomes us to understand the current dilemmas and course of events in a specific subject area, and by application of thought and meditation, allows us to alter or influence events in another direction and speed. This is perhaps the greatest use of mental-spiritual foresight, to see what is coming in these troubling times and avoid crashing into the sides of mountains.

We commend this type of higher insight to make significant personal strides in many facets of our life, our family, portending problems, and business in particular. We have experienced that when we prayerfully ponder issues in this markedly different fashion, it is probable we will encounter situations in which our actions seem so different that to some they seem strange—until our actions bring about the desired results. The following steps should sequence the approach:

1. Initiate with an idea of the topic, subject, or issue we are going to address. We will need this idea or issue as a starting point.

2. Fall into a sequestered, prayerful, quiet, reflective mood. We will recognize it either by the meditative feeling, the clarity, and lack of verbalized thought, or we may notice clear picture like images in our mind.

3. Once we are in a quiet, clear, peaceful mind state, present the idea we are going to work on. Hold it in our thoughts, getting a sense of an "inner voice" of each portion of thought.

4. We will begin to feel as if we are thinking from the centers of our mind and heart. This is a sign that we are entering a state of reverence and receptivity.

5. Now, we should be able to focus on each critical part of an idea and allow the intuition and inspirational powers to direct us from one part of the idea to the next. What is of interest here is that we will often move from information we already know to information that is true, but that we had no awareness of before.

6. We should employ this form of thought and meditation in daily life to draw upon higher powers. This takes great practice and control, but will allow us to live as an intuitive being, rather than simply as a self-made thinker. This is also a learning process. It will take time for our mind to learn how to listen to an inner voice and react to the world differently while in this integrated state.

Remember, we are not just in a meditative state, but a logical one, that uses intuition and inspirational information as part of its base. We will also find ourselves understanding not only what will happen, but often why and how to change it to a different, hopefully better, outcome, if needed.

Velocity: Go for Direction and Speed—with Wisdom and Caution

Strategic decisions made too fast may kill brands and products because there isn't sufficient time to develop the new way. Charging straight ahead like a teenage dragster, fueled with alcohol, is a death wish. Though our organization needs to move faster than ever, speed can win, but speed can also kill us if we don't do the thinking and things that allow us to be fast. If we think that we can occasionally step on the accelerator, that shouldn't mean that we can keep it floored indefinitely.

One of the best examples of Executive BRIGHT1+2+3+4 *velocity* is what happens in the pits at an Indy car race (Byrne, 2005). Pit crews say these rules are important if we are going to more quickly:

> 1. *The faster we go, the more we need to talk.* Everyone needs to be clear about what is going to be done by whom and when. Constant communication is vital.
>
> 2. *Don't panic when someone overtakes us early on.* Stick with what got us here.
>
> 3. *Whatever it takes, stay in the race.* Keep moving and fix problems on the fly whenever possible.
>
> 4. *Make the most of downtime.* It is inevitable that there will be some downtime. Make the necessary repairs and reenergize.

Information Technology (IT), which played a minimal role in the first generation of speed, is now absolutely essential to stay in any competitive game. The new executive "playbook" reads as such:

> 1. Move velocity into our executive think tanks—constantly stimulate our understanding of the competitive perspective, test, and redefine direction and boundaries in real time.
>
> 2. Shift from stock car velocity to Formula 1. Develop our organization's ability to brake and shift direction as rapidly as it accelerates.
>
> 3. Use IT, particularly Intranet/Internet, to reduce information float and increase decision/execution velocity.

4. Use IT to hard- and soft-wire our firm to critical partners—redesign business processes across organizations; move from multi-functional to global-organizational thinking.

5. Develop quarterback flexibility within the ranks to define/redefine and design/redesign globally as well.

Taking fast action can be difficult if we spend too much time thinking about it. Instead of imagining all the potential problems the action, or the lack of it, could cause, we should focus instead on the capacity we already have as executives to affect the energy of every employee. They want to make a personal contribution and belong to a worthwhile team. Executives are the catalysts that unleash the unlimited reserves of energy currently lying dormant in our organization.

Velocity: The Highest Level of Cognition

BRIGHT4 insight is the highest level of thinking that can be developed as a thinking process and decision-making-velocity approach. This process simplifies and elevates the complex nature of decision making and cognition. BRIGHT4 thinking gives leaders and Fringe Team members the ability to analyze future decisions from multiple perspectives and prepare to respond to the rapid changes predicted by the advent of the information age and globalization. The *concept of velocity*, a means of accomplishing rapid decision making, increases the speed both of decision making and of measurable effects. Velocity means acquiring data quickly, converting it rapidly to usable information, quickly synthesizing information into knowledge, and then acting expeditiously to change and shape the environment to one's advantage. The action must measurably create a new direction beneficial to the decision maker. Decision theory and cognitive theory show that higher-order thinking such as BRIGHT4 thinking and velocity can be taught through visual-informational processing.

Our Capacity Team training includes Velocity as the crowning jewel of thinking and practice.

The past isn't always prologue—think future, think speed and velocity.

Many of us take a tactical or flavor-of-the-month rather than a *velocity* approach to our leadership competence. When we do, our leadership development reacts to shortcomings in current practices rather than to developing leaders to meet our future needs. Training alone will not lead to sustained change as will an executive velocity to continually think through the gaps between current state and desired future state or future needs. Our leadership development model needs to focus on sustaining capacities to smartly, quickly assess, align, apply, and achieve the future now.

Also, when thinking about our potential risks, think ahead to the future with velocity. We all get comfortable and smug basing our strategies for the future on the past. That's why risks that we didn't foresee can be a bolt from the blue. And, that is why it's so difficult to think about portending events for which there is no precedent for quick movement.

Problems will never stop popping up, and a problem will remain an issue if it is not properly solved or thoroughly thought through. While we're committing our full focus to some issues, other issues get neglected or escalate.

As executives involved in multi-functional issues, we need to be able to apply insight and velocity thinking to important business and organizational goals. Spatial speed and decision making is a culmination of intelligent direction and skillful execution. We need to raise the quality of our decisions and learn to lead rather than going around in circles with what may seem like an endless line of issues and/or tough problems under pressure.

Maximize High-Capacity People within High-Capacity Teams

Two distinctions that make great quarterbacks and executives are: (1) the ability to maximize exceptional people around them and (2) the ability to empower these key players to respond to any of the options with **decisiveness** on a fast-paced playing field. These "distinctions" are enhanced by communication that quickly advocates play options and welcomes others on the team to inquire into the quarterback's or executive's assumptions and reasoning. Executives and members of high-capacity teams should be skilled in advocacy-inquiry with each other to do that very thing.

The way to set up the play/work is to assign specific responsibilities to specific individuals within the executive team and correlate the individuals' activities so that their contributions smartly coalesce into a team outcome. This is the way most football coaches build their teams. Once in place, shared priorities and initiatives can be launched and sustained in the practice of high-capacity teamwork. A high-capacity team, prepared and empowered with the appropriate thinking sets and skills, will need some autonomy to go about the business relatively unencumbered. Leadership support that does not impair the work will provide ongoing regular maintenance and investments. Not only will the context and culture likely change, *decisiveness* and the organizational systems that interface with the team should change over time.

Teaming should be about building the *capacity* to take the thinking and the game to the higher levels. The *capacity* to apply new knowledge to new situations is the most valued currency on any team. More than ever, *capacity to perform* should be encouraged and recognized. Curiosity about *capacity* should be primed everywhere through individuals' questioning accepted views and being open to consider contradictory ones. Such an appreciation for paradox further defines persons of high thinking *capacity*. The implications of this asynchrony are obvious to see: BRIGHT4 dimensional thinking is an essential ingredient of being creative and decisive. High-capacity thinking groups produce higher levels of activity and outcomes. This reasoning applies to organizations, research teams, think tanks, and other groups of creators and doers. Those CEOs and executives who rely on high-capacity teams are more likely to innovate than those who rely on other hybrid combinations.

BRIGHT4 leadership involves a process of motivating others to think smartly and work together collaboratively to accomplish great things quickly.

Here is what Lee Iacocca learned as a CEO:

> You succeed or fail based on your team. If you want to succeed, you've got to have a group of people that know what they're doing. Vince Lombardi was a friend of mine, and he used to tell me, "Teamwork is what makes the Green Bay Packers great. People who work together will win—period! And that applies to companies and governments." But he also stressed that the raw material has to be there first. You have to start with talent. (Iacocca, 2007, p. 16)

Much of the innovative work can be accomplished in high-capacity project teams, or what we have branded "Fringe Teams"—because they don't think and act in the "common way." High-capacity Fringe Teams have a mandate and priority to complete project tasks faster, deliver results more quickly, and reduce schedule time. These Fringe Teams achieve results all out of proportion to their numbers. They create solutions where others see problems. In our experience of 25 years of building teams, Fringe Teams can show initiative when faced with unanticipated challenges. However, without full management support and appropriate training, resources, and autonomy—Fringe Teams can sputter, loose altitude, and crash and burn.

A project manager, for example, builds his Fringe Team by organizing a critically needed project with thorough planning; recruiting the best people possible; selecting more effective strategies; challenging team members with shared vision; recruiting best resources; stimulating members to challenge status quo; encouraging them to think "on the fringe"; making project work exciting; assessing skills more accurately; and ensuring knowledge transfer between team members. Fusion and cohesion between individuals is essential.

An effective project manager will not probe or interrogate his/her people to find weaknesses or question how a direct report is doing in their work. The exception is to question how his/her leadership can help, ask what needs to happen, or understand what's being done to offer assistance. The only evaluation is employees holding themselves accountable, and in turn, leaders asking, "Am I holding myself accountable in supporting them?"

Mass Rapid Transit (Singapore), the Speed of Global Insight

The Mass Rapid Transit or MRT is a rapid transit system that forms the backbone of the railway system in Singapore, Southeast Asia, with a network spanning the entire city-state. The origins of the MRT were derived from a forecast by city planners in 1967 that identified the need for a rail-based, urban transport system by 1992. Following a debate on whether a bus-only system would be more cost-effective, the parliament came to the conclusion that an all-bus system would be inadequate, since it would have to compete for road space in a land-scarce country. The initial $5 billion construction of the Mass Rapid Transit network was Singapore's largest public works project at the time, starting on October 22, 1983 at Shan Road.

The majority of the initial fleet of rail cars was built between 1986 and 1989 by Kawasaki Heavy Industries in consortium with Nippon Sharyo, Tokyo Car Corporation, and Kinki Sharyo. Price negotiations between the Singapore Chinese MRT Corporation leaders and the Kawasaki group were conducted in Singapore in 1985 while I (Graham) was employed as a consultant with the Singapore Productivity Board (NPB). I had the privilege of working alongside one of my former students, Dean Williams from Australia (now a professor at Harvard University). Dean had a reputation for being NPB's most outstanding organizational trainer and consultant. Blue-eyed, blond Dean was asked to join the all-Chinese Singapore bargaining group to work out the cost agreements with Japanese negotiators from Kawasaki.

The story is told and retold that these two cultural groups represented some of the shrewdest and cleverest negotiators on the planet. A translator from Japan was provided to assist both parties through intense discussions and help them come to a clear agreement of terms and costs. In the final hours, the Japanese were apparently making out like bandits on the deal before the signing, and commenting among themselves, made pejorative remarks about the fools across the table. The Tokyo translator went mute. Unknown to all was the fact that Dean Williams had served a two-year church mission in Japan as young man and could speak and understand Japanese fluently. He requested a short respite with his Chinese colleagues in another room before the signing, and it was in that setting Dean informed his group of the rude and condescending remarks of their visitors. The group asked Dean to return to the table with them, be their spokesman, speak only Japanese, and express how offended the Singapore community was by the Japanese pejorative remarks. Before the Singapore group could proceed, this offense had to be resolved. This is where the story line is savored throughout Singapore. Having lost face, the embarrassed Japanese team bowed low, apologized, and conceded the deal at a significantly lower price.

Mastering others is strength. Mastering yourself is true power.

Tao Te Ching

Kindness in words creates confidence. Kindness in thinking creates profoundness. Kindness in giving creates love.

Lao Tzu

BRIGHT4 thinking executives are expected to have a high level of integrity, plasticity, and conceptual capacity to stand a better chance of understanding and articulating new insights on issues and problems at a global level with speed.

Ability to Think and Execute Faster through Thinking-Capacity Teams

We may argue about exactly what makes a 50-mile stretch of northern California so successful, but certainly no one can argue that Silicon Valley is a high-capacity culture. It has become the poster child for talent coming uniquely together in cyberspace. Mixing and schmoozing is essential to its success. "If you subtracted that," says Anne Eschoo, a member of Congress who represents the area, "the valley would collapse." The idea of success is that Silicon companies recruit the best people, build on capacity, and make history happen.

As the pace of change renders many traditional solutions obsolete and organizational challenges become more multifaceted and complex, many executives find it hard to clearly visualize this maelstrom of elements, factors, and influences in their minds. Also, words are often imprecise and open to interpretation by team members, further clouding the problem definition and solution-finding processes. Transferring all the "stuff" to paper in a more symbolic form helps to make these pieces—and the relationships between them—more understandable. As a result, high-capacity teams can pick up on these notes and often develop better and *faster* solutions using their visual-spatial thinking techniques.

The benefits of thinking-capacity teams can be extraordinary, but conversion and practice take finesse. It isn't easy for a mature organization, with run-of-the-mill practices and few national champions, to go high-capacity quickly. We may strive to raise the level of capacity, but without a supportive culture that values skunk works and supports talent, the exercise is fraught with resistance.

Successful executives and analysts at Dell Computer Company (Byrne, 2005) will testify that *speed* is their ultimate competitive weapon. Here is Dell's five-point plan for building thinking-capacity into a *fast company culture*:

> 1. **The supply chain starts with the customer.** By cutting out retailers and selling directly to customers, Dell is in a far better position to forecast real consumer demand. If we have to use middlemen, as retailers such as Walmart do, we can obtain this sort of information by monitoring every sale in real time.
>
> 2. **Replace inventory with information.** To operate with close to zero inventory, Dell communicates constantly with its suppliers—several times a day.
>
> 3. **If we can't measure it, we can't improve it.** Dell knows what works because it measures everything—inventory, cash,

time to build a computer. Once they have the numbers, they concentrate on improving them.

4. **Complexity slows us down.** Dell cut the number of its core suppliers from several hundred to about 25 and standardized everything it could.

5. **Work to become radically faster.** Dell sets out to obtain massive improvement, not incremental change. For example, the goal is not 3% faster production, but 30%.

By drawing upon both the visual and logical/linear capabilities of the brain, we can think flexibly and faster, think more clearly, develop more creative solutions, present our ideas more persuasively, and achieve better results from our teams. These teams will need clear goals and priorities in order to think and work fast. Flexibility allows us to see problems from more than one perspective, allows us to reframe complex problems so that solutions become clearer, and allows us to accommodate seemingly ambiguous solutions. And, being flexible allows us to question or test underlying assumptions about a problem and facilitates the generation of an array of possible solutions.

The following outlines will help high-capacity teams chart their level of maturity in thinking, communicating and questioning on different dimensions.

In Review: Four-Level Capacities of BRIGHT1+2+3+4 Thinking and Communicating

B1: An Executive's Height—*Sequential (step-by-step) Processing*

BRIGHT1 thinking and language is linear, step-by-step, and is what we do when we put our facts in flat-line order. Verbal height is using concepts framed in words. It aims at using logic and reasoning to think constructively, rather than at simple fluency or vocabulary recognition. Thoughts and words are immediately tied to a specific tangible, known, observable designation of the things thought about and referred to. Although objects and things are not physically present, our verbal height will construct pictures in our mind to assume they are there. Verbal height is sustained with strong reading and writing, listening and speaking capabilities.

B2: An Executive's Width—*Quantitative Processing*

BRIGHT2 thinking uses symbolic/quantitative reasoning (i.e., the ability to digest large amounts of information to solve problems via symbolic assistance). We appear much *broader* with good math skills. Thoughts and words no longer have to refer to specific tangible, known, observable entities, but are used as true symbols. They can be construed and symbolically worked with as though they themselves were things. Like Sherlock Holmes, we can look for quantitative clues and can verbalize possibilities that we have in mind even though we have not yet found them. This second dimension uses symbolic/quantitative/numeric information and reasoning to digest, tackle, and solve problems and make informed decisions, and verbalizes possibilities by means of symbols/numbers that come to mind through quantitative investigation/analysis/trending/evaluation.

B3: An Executive's Depth—*Spatial Judgment Processing*

BRIGHT3 thinking uses abstract operations for integrative work. As three-dimensional thinkers, we mentally question the validity and merits of two contending options and formulate a new alternative integrating the best from the options. Our thoughts and words can seem abstract in the sense that they refer to other thoughts and words rather than to things. That is, abstract thoughts and words put ideas together, but they must be able to move above conflicting ideas and be related to tangible things more than once removed (three-dimensional processing). Scientific reasoning skills are intangible thoughts and words that can be used for coming up with solutions to problems only if they reach through/beyond their symbol-word content to real things. If they don't, they are merely hollow abstract word concepts. To be truly three-dimensional in thought and words, we must be able to use those thoughts and words to form coherent propositions, but also to illustrate them concretely in terms of observable examples, by way of intermediate one- and two-dimensional concepts. The world is essentially a three-dimensional living laboratory that should allow the thinker to be self-regulating, most creative, and inventive.

B4: An Executive's Insight, Decisiveness and Direction, Speed and Velocity

BRIGHT4 thinking is insightfully creating new theories, global/complex systems, and decisive directions. The fourth-dimension abstraction of thoughts and words is about spatial speed in the sense that at this level there is a lot of reformulation of contemporary thought and language. In a global economy, we need thinking flexibility with rapid micro- and macro-plasticity and decision-making ability. Being flexible allows us to see challenges from multiple perspectives, allows others to question and test our underlying formulations about problems/issues, and facilitates the generation of an array of possible solutions. Four-dimensionally-thinking executives are expected to have a high-level of conceptual/plasticity capacity to stand a better chance of understanding and articulating new insights on issues and problems at a systemic level. Making sound decisions and execution in an atmosphere of increasing time pressures, uncertainty, and conflicting advice, and in crisis situations creates the highest challenges for any executive, but it's where a four-dimensional thinker will rise-up to the challenge.

In Review: Four-Dimensional Communication Levels of BRIGHT4

Executive Questioning

B1: An Executive's Height—*Sequential (step-by-step) Processing*

What's the problem, event, or issue? "Help me understand what happened. Where did it happen, when did it happen, who was involved, who saw it, what happened before, has this happened before, how often ...?" *Look for a pattern.* How do we know what the people we're communicating with feel and think? (e.g., "On a scale of 1 to 10, with 10 being your happiest/most reassuring feelings, and 1 being when you're most upset/confused, how did that make you feel?") How are we going to change the way we communicate? What skills do we need to develop to improve our communication? How do we know we're communicating effectively? What associated behaviors do we need to improve? When will we begin this process? How will we know when we are communicating effectively?

B2: An Executive's Width—*Quantitative Processing*

What's possible? What is the person, business, or network trying to accomplish through the communication? What are the outcomes and results required for us, the business, and the system? What has to happen for communication to work effectively? What does the person intend through communication? Do we understand what the other person wants and needs? Are we able to put ourselves in someone else's position? What are the barriers that are in place to cause ineffective communication?

B3: An Executive's Depth—*Spatial Judgment Processing*

Why is effective communication important to me/us? Why might effective communication be important to others? How are we able to identify the issues and perspectives that are core to a conflict? What are the less obvious but potentially relevant factors? What are the multi-directional and nonlinear relationships among the variables? How can I help others recognize underlying agendas, assumptions, and motivations that are involved in a situation? How can I pursue and encourage feedback that may reveal an error in my own thinking or judgment, and then make informed and appropriate adjustments? How can I recognize my own biases, flaws, and limitations in my ideas and actions? What is needed to appropriately articulate the essential flaws in the arguments of others and restate the merits of one's own position? How are we to consider the probable effects and likely unintended consequences that may result from taking a particular course of action? What is needed to appropriately resist the objections of others and remain committed to a sound course of action? What do we need to communicate to address and balance the different needs of all relevant stakeholders?

B4: An Executive's Inventiveness, Decisiveness and Direction, Speed and Velocity

How can we articulate all the perspectives together into a synthesized whole? How do the parts fit together? How do our decisions affect one another? How are we able to creatively resolve tensions among opposing ideas? How are we able to generate inventive outcomes? Questions here need to have a degree of insight, learning, plasticity, and directionality to be able to hold objectively the multidimensional streams of consciousness required in the 4-D level of complexity. Here, a deepening ability is needed to view more perspectives or parallel systems and more variables simultaneously before execution. To the extent that we can take a backfield vantage point, where personal, business, and network systems are perceived together on the playing field, we can enter the fourth dimension with a communication level that few can understand and respond to. Very seldom is it a single answer or component of content that provides the learning and questioning necessary to help others move beyond their current limiting levels of capacity.

Global Decisiveness Average

Global Decisiveness Average (GDA) is the new twenty-first-century equation that formulates the summation of one's problem-solving capacity and is a best-predictor for excelling throughout one's professional career. Global Decisiveness is one's ability to quickly solve problems with words, numbers, and three-dimensional solutions. The GDA equation is *Verbal Problem Solving Quickness* + *Quantitative Problem Solving* Quickness + *Spatial Problem Solving Quickness*. Executive teams should know their Global Decisiveness strength. High-performance executive teams have a strong Global Decisiveness percentile number, which represents their single greatest asset to their organization. Executive teams with Global Decisiveness of 98% have a far different destiny from that of executive teams at the 90th or 80th percentile. Most CEOs are like parents when it comes to objectively assessing their talent pool. Most parents overlook many of their children's obvious shortcomings or are quick to put a premium on the things they do well. Unfortunately, most parents postpone their most critical evaluation of their child until it's virtually too late to change their child's destiny—or, in the case of the executive, the destiny of their company.

Global Decisiveness is an objective, highly reliable assessment for executive bench-strength. More importantly, Global Decisiveness responds to Global Processing Technologies. A 5–10% elevated change in Global Decisiveness for an executive team, through training, can represent a huge change in the organization's ability for greater competitive advantage.

Global Insight/Decisiveness—Sir Winston Churchill: Tough Decisions

At first blush, insight seems effortless: understand the problem or situation and then make a decision. In reality, things are rarely that simple—and in war time millions of lives are at stake! Effective decision making combines elements of Winston Churchill's leadership traits (courage, drive to take action, communication, creativity, vision), but historians would include decisiveness as a separate Churchill Leadership Trait because they see it as critical to Sir Winston's leadership approach.

However, according to his wife Clementine (Combs & Churchill, 2004), Churchill could be terribly indecisive about trivial matters. When it came to making the most serious and tough decisions, which he would rehearse in his mind, he could be ruthless. The most often quoted example of his ruthless decision making is the July 1940 order to open fire on French warships at anchor in Oran. This came about after the French-German armistice, in which it was decreed that French warships would be handed over to the Nazis. Britain was desperate that these vessels should not make up part of a German invasion fleet and offered their French commanders a choice: either scuttle (sink) the boats, hand them over to the British Royal Navy, or sail them to a neutral port for the duration of the war. If none of these options were taken, then it was clearly communicated that the Royal Navy would attack and attempt to sink or disable them. Tragically for the 1,250 French sailors who died, the French commanders refused the British terms and their warships were attacked. Churchill, who loved France and the French, is on record as having found the decision horrendous and he wept after announcing the decision and its consequences to the House of Commons. The (somewhat unexpected) benefit of this tragedy was that it cemented in the minds of the American leadership (in particular Franklin Roosevelt) that Britain was prepared to fight on and tough it out. Another example of taking (the right) tough decision was Churchill's order that the wounded should be the last to be evacuated from the beaches of Dunkirk. At the time, the prevailing belief was that fewer than 50,000 could be safely evacuated and Britain desperately needed able-bodied soldiers for her defense. It therefore was undoubtedly the correct decision, but a horrid one to make nevertheless.

Compassion

Churchill could and did make tough decisions, but they were always tempered with his sensitive and humane nature. Don't forget, this was a man who had experienced first-hand the horrific (and often unnecessary) slaughter of the trenches of the First World War, and he tried as hard as he could not to make the same mistakes. He would never shirk from making the tough decisions, but he was never reckless in his treatment of human life.

Hire and Fire

A good leader hires the right people to do the job. A good leader is equally good at making the decision to sack people who are not up to the job. This is another area where Winston Churchill time and again showed his mettle. Even with friends such as Bob Boothby and Alfred Duff Cooper, Churchill had no hesitation in "moving" them out of posts that they were clearly not suited for into other roles. With less-close friends, he had even fewer qualms.

Global Insight—Decisive Teamwork

"Houston, we've had a problem" were the now legendary words that announced a crisis onboard Apollo 13. Halfway through Apollo's mission to the moon, one of the spacecraft's oxygen tanks exploded, putting the lives of the crew in grave jeopardy. A group of engineers from NASA was speedily assembled. Their mission: invent a way for the crew to survive and to pilot their damaged vessel back to Earth safely. The engineers were successful, transforming a potential disaster into a legend of decisive and effective teamwork.

One of most vital things a team brings to any task is its members' capacity to think, using relevant, collective information to accomplish goals and tasks together. Building teamwork should employ the following conditions to promote informed decisions:

> 1. Designed well from the outset, bringing together people who can contribute to the right mix of knowledge, skills, tools, and other resources necessary to succeed.
>
> 2. Vis-à-vis meetings and social interaction among members, a decisive leader who establishes a good relationship with every team member, a climate that promotes the best use of expertise, and creates a cohesive mission.
>
> 3. Imbedded teamwork skills, such as setting goals, adapting to change, resolving conflict, and providing feedback to allow the team to learn from each challenge, and resources to continually improve their performance.

BRIGHT4: The Global Insightful Leadership of Abraham Lincoln

That Lincoln, after winning the presidency, Doris Kearns Goodwin writes in her landmark study on Lincoln, *made the unprecedented decision to incorporate his eminent rivals into his political family, the cabinet, was evident of a profound self-confidence and first indication of what would prove to others a most unexpected greatness.* (2005, p. XVI))

His success in dealing with strong egos of the men in his cabinet suggests that in the hands of a truly great politician the qualities we generally associate with decency and morality—kindness, sensitivity, compassion, honesty, and empathy—can be impressive political resources.

This form of greatness is one that should be studied with the keenest attention, not only for the purpose of Lincoln studies but for the purpose of understanding crucial aspects of leadership and dimensions of executive thinking. It is greatness in person that draws upon the challenging diversity of others, creates activities that are interconnected, and involves the subject himself in situations that are context-sensitive and cognitively non-transparent. Even while lacking clear precedents or codes to rely upon, Lincoln was able to act constructively and productively within an emerging whole as it unfolded to him.

What was inherent with Lincoln was a thinking capacity of the highest order, involving cultivation and care, insight and intuition, effort and trial, emotional and social intelligence, command of the symbolic order, sensitivities for other people and for the possibilities of the moment as well as for the complexities involved, a sense for the most relevant factors and an ability to integrate conflicting forces, and a fierce resolve toward a desired state of affairs.

An Executive Power and Light Building—*Building a Thinking-Capacity Culture*

BRIGHT1+2+3+4 create a thinking-capacity culture that requires the exercise of multiple capacities. To describe these capacities, we use the metaphor of an *executive power and light building* with four floors and a solid foundation. The first two floors (verbal and quantitative) are easily accessible. The latter two floors (spatial and global decisiveness) and an attached workout room (speed, direction, and precision) are more obscure, with varying degrees of habitation. The mastery of integrated decisiveness requires BRIGHT1+2+3+4 being facile, with all four levels interconnected to deep investments in the foundation.

The first two floors

(verbal and quantitative capacities) address current business literacy with such things as financial flows, strategic research and planning, and competitive scanning. They also involve understanding the value of things, such as people's time, and internal and external relationships as well as the assets. Many are directly attending to these capacities, ensuring they are distributed throughout the office building.

Social capacity is found more on the second floor and is beyond "soft, touchy-feely stuff." It is evident here that the quality of relationships directly impacts productivity. Maximizing this capacity means choosing the appropriate social form for the organization—committed, self-directed work teams/fringe teams, virtual work groups, and executive coaching to bring out the best in others. Social capacity also senses what is going on with employees and constituencies and addresses their issues before they become big problems.

The third floor

is spacious, with capacity to perform simultaneous/integrative activity. Here the focus is on the capability for holding multiple ideas at once and doing integrative thinking. It's the "human software" of the organization—a true competitive advantage. A problem comes with people's impatience with thinking about thinking. Roger Martin (2007) detailed these integrative thinkers in the Harvard Business Review:

- Seek less obvious but potentially relevant factors.

- Consider multidirectional and nonlinear relationships among variables.

- See problems as a whole, examining how the parts fit together and how decisions affect one another.

- Creatively settle for best available among old and new options.

After tending to the fiscal, social, and simultaneous capacities of the organization, emotional capacity is also on the third floor (and other floors) with strong undergirding in the foundation. This spatial judgment ability pays attention to sensing and surfacing emotions in real time and identifying the message they are conveying. Integrative decisiveness depends on leaders who can sense the emotional health of the community so that the community will not be blocked or sabotaged by unarticulated, suppressed, or misaligned emotions. Emotional strength is rare in organizational structures because they have endorsed the discouragement of the experience and expression of emotions, especially by those in executive positions.

The fourth floor

is global capacity, representing attention to spatial speed, memory, insight, direction, and velocity. Executives here are about evaluating time and pressure demands—creating new types of society, new systems of ethics and morality, new values and cultures, sweeping new theories and innovations. The fourth floor reflects an abstraction of thoughts and words in a global sense and can reformulate all current thought and language. Leaders on this floor have flexibility for rapid micro-macro-decision-making ability. Macro thinking focuses on the whole through a process of synthesis. Micro thinking looks into things while macro thinking looks out at things. The four-dimensional thinker pragmatically focuses continuous assessment on determining what is actually happening to the whole building, thereby preventing self-delusional wishful thinking.

The mind of a BRIGHT4 executive has to be spacious, with ample capacity to process, think, deal with ambiguities and multiple factors, conflicting polarities, contentious emotions, and contradictory ideas—and daily make tough choices. Four-dimensional thinking is required of executives on the fourth floor, who:

- Think in terms of synthesis over analysis, the whole over the parts that need to fit together. Patterns over time and feedback loops are a better way to think about the dynamics of complex systems.

- See what is actually happening over what they want to see happen. The focus is on the purpose for which a system was created over the processes and procedures of the system.

- Think about whether there are any patterns that appear over weeks or months and attempt to depict what is actually occurring. Recognizing the pattern of a system over time is a high-order level of thinking.

- Think how decisions affect one another.

- Think about systems and their dynamics—suggesting resolving tension among opposing ideas.

- Think about alternative approaches and generating innovative outcomes and the important aspects of organizational behavior.

Being flexible, or "plastic," allows executives to see challenges from more than one perspective, allows them to reframe complex problems so that solutions become clearer, and allows them to question and test underlying assumptions about a problem. These executives can facilitate a generation of an array of possible solutions. Capacity leadership on the fourth floor is thinking in four dimensions. Successful executives here know how to focus in on the ambiguities and multiple perspectives around them and be insightful and decisive with direction and velocity. Creativity and inventiveness are not mysterious forces over which these capacity leaders have no control. BRIGHT1+2+3+4 leadership can and does create a climate that stimulates problem solving, creativity, and inventiveness with effective implementation.

The Power & Light Building's *foundation and basement*

sustain the spiritual footings and value-based generators that ignite and sustain capacity and character throughout the building. The basement represents a deep sense of purpose, character, conscientiousness, and commitment to create light and regulate appropriate temperature.

CHAPTER 7

Character Capacity - Integrity and Authenticity (CC)

Character

isn't a superficial feature in the building. The word comes from the ancient Greek verb meaning "to engrave" and its related noun, meaning mark or distinctive quality. Character is who we essentially are as growing and developing people. The process of *becoming* a leader is much the same process as becoming an integrated, healthy human beings. We believe that the connection between what it takes to be a capacity leader and the process of character growth is similar.

> *People, especially people in positions of power, have invested a tremendous amount of effort and time to get to where they are. They really don't want to hear that we're on the wrong path, that we've got to shift gears and start thinking differently.*
>
> David Suzuki

Leadership

is character in action with achievement markers along the way. Achievement is reflected through satisfaction or accolades received by the building for supporting its leadership. Achievement acts as feedback to the building and the people that its faith in supporting the leader's vision and character has not been in vain.

> *I know that love is ultimately the only answer to mankind's problems. And I'm going to talk about it everywhere I go. I know it isn't popular to talk about it in some circles today. I'm not talking about emotional bosh when I talk about love. I'm talking about a strong, demanding love.*

Martin Luther King, Jr.

Character capacity is about the space, freedom, and safety to bring our whole beings to work. Without attention to this dimension, people complain of work being tiring, fractured, and dissatisfying. People feel invalidated and used. The spirit of any organization is palpable—just walk around and notice. We can sense if people are hassled or supported, trampled and victimized or developed and valued. A vibrant, nurturing spirit retains talent. It is not about what's in it for me, but about what I can contribute.

> *I sought my God and my God I could not find.*
>
> *I sought my soul and my soul eluded me.*
>
> *I sought my brother to serve him in his need,*
>
> *And I found all three—my God, my soul and thee.*

Anonymous

Life is much about our choices to strengthen others. Choices are much about authenticity, consequences, and character. Our character is much about the wise use of experience, competence, and integrity. Integrity is much about keeping our promises, being true to self, and strengthening others.

Integrity and pride cannot coexist. Pride is an illusion and is a prime factor in preventing the realization of our greater potential to contribute. Pride distorts the truth about things as they are, as they have been, and as they will be. The central feature of pride is enmity—enmity toward the divine and enmity toward others. Enmity means dislike toward or hostility to others, or a state of competitive self-interest. It is a major obstacle to our advancement. Whereas:

> *The man who has become a thinking being feels a compulsion to give every will to live the same reverence for life that he gives to his own. He experiences that other life in his own.*

Albert Schweitzer

Dr. Stephen R. Covey, who addressed the need for restoring the character ethic and who successfully published *The Seven Habits of Highly Effective People: Powerful Lessons in Personal Change*, and who wrote the foreword of our last book (*Horizontal Revolution*) was asked what the one thing was that he would do differently as a business person. "I would do more strategic, proactive recruitment and selecting ... you really have to look deeply into both character and competence, because eventually downstream flaws in either area will manifest themselves in both areas. I am convinced that although training and development is important, recruiting and selection are much more important."

Character and competence are about our capacity, skill, and knowledge to execute higher principles and purposes. Principles should guide us to respect all people, to celebrate their differences, and to realize service above self.

> *If your thinking is sloppy, your business will be sloppy. If you are disorganized, your business will be disorganized. If you are greedy, your employees will be greedy, giving you less and less of themselves and always asking for more.*
>
> Michael Gerber

When we build strong character *and* competence, we develop greater portable capacity for wisdom, judgment, and trustworthiness—the foundation of all great and lasting achievements. Life becomes a festival for us if we have a solid base for our character and competence.

The process of becoming a BRIGHT1+2+3+4+Character Capacity executive, whose ideas have never been expressed thusly before, is to review, categorize, and *integrate* our own unique thoughts gathered along the way in our work with ethical principles. This process should be the most telling and should energize our mind to continuously experience a newfound pleasure in thought and wisdom. The result of processing higher levels of thinking, we will see things in never-ending new light, understood and expressed as insight. If we then choose the spiritual path, we can open the portals to *infinite* insight, through silence, prayer, meditation, intuition, and revelation. Then, we become inspiring thinkers (i.e., we think what few have expressed before). If pursued to the end, we can then go on to become a BRIGHT1+2+3+4+Character Capacity executive and spiritual "light" in our field.

Confidence

in our character is not enough to justify trust. We believe the trust factor involves the conviction that executives will successfully do what is expected to strengthen the well-being of others and the organization. Trust embraces faith in ability, knowledge, integrity, and judgment as well as a belief that one's leadership must be reliable and responsive. Indifference, indolence, and indulgence do reflect character flaws and do immobilize leadership, so as to diminish contribution in any organization. Reliability is established through integrity, diligence, and follow-through, while responsiveness involves respectful communication and a genuine concern for others.

> *Nurture your mind with great thoughts; to believe in the heroic makes heroes.*
>
> Benjamin Disraeli

Leaders with character capacity are of sound thinking, judgment, and integrity, capable of generating and sustaining vision, purpose, and love. No leader can be fully effective without the capacity of love—needed to encourage openness, empathic listening, candidness, accountability, and trustworthiness in their communication and actions. Through the power of love, there is awareness, foresight, caring, persuasion, healing, stewardship, commitment to the growth of people, and building community. In most of their communication, their people feel that they're being heard and understood. Listening doesn't mean agreeing, but it does mean having the empathic reach to understand, trust, and have confidence in one another.

Ho'oponopono

The building is blessed by a Hawaiian Kapuna with **Ho'oponopono**—our ancient Hawaiian practice of reconciliation, forgiveness, and mental cleansing, in which relationships are set right through prayer, discussion, confession, and mutual restitution and forgiveness. The blessing:

Life is full of change.

The good passes ... but so does the bad.

Nothing remains the same in this unstable world.

Not a single element of anything ... physical or mental

is the same today as it was yesterday.

When we are down at the pit of despair ... the only way to go is up.

If we only wait a little ... the cycle ... the endless unfailing tide of

things will sweep us up again.

"Without darkness," said the old ones, "we would not appreciate

the light when it comes."

Kristin Zambucka, Ano Ano:The Seed

Literally, **ho'o** is defined as goodness, uprightness, morality, moral qualities, correct or proper procedure, excellence, well-being, prosperity, welfare, benefit, true condition or nature, duty, fitness, righteous, right, upright, just, virtuous, fair, beneficial, successful, in perfect order, accurate, correct, eased, relieved, could, ought, must, and necessary.

What people want most from their leaders in this building is what many organizations in Hawaii have embraced: a culture of **Ho'oponopono**—direction and meaning, trust, and hope, and a willful determination to achieve a set of goals, a set of convictions about what they want the organization to achieve. Leaders here have a bias toward action and a capacity to convert purpose and vision into action—manifested in products and services. Even when it means making mistakes, they learn from those mistakes and act with integrity. They actively help their followers to reach their fuller potential. All together, our *executive high-capacity building* represents a distinguished architecture illuminated by the light of wisdom gleaned from the useable processing of BRIGHT1+2+3+4+Character thinking—not merely its collection and storage.

Impressive are leaders who exemplify strong core values and commendable practices.

As cited earlier, I (Graham) was living in the United Kingdom during the early 1980s. The country was going through an economic downturn of the worse kind that dimmed the lights of most industries struggling to stay afloat. There were massive layoffs, early retirements given, and double-digit unemployment throughout the country. Quite visible were those few organizations that were still thriving, even under the most challenging circumstances. I had the privilege of visiting many, only to discover that most of them were faith-based, with shared ownership practices. More impressive were their leaders, who believed in and exemplified strong core values and commendable practices. Thoughtfulness for others, generosity, modesty and self-respect were standard qualities of their leadership. Their employees gave their very best efforts and loyalties to a "higher purpose" for surviving in those hard times.

> *I don't claim anything of the work. It is His work. I am like a little pencil in His hand. That is all. He does the thinking. He does the writing. The pencil has nothing to do with it.*
>
> Mother Teresa

Your authors believe that there is a greater urgency in the twenty-first century to have more leaders of "sound understanding"—men and women of character, faith, and courage. The present state of the world is like no other in the history of mankind. Shameful practices, unspeakable organizational corruption, and organized violence are manifest in nearly every corner of our globe. The fact that great leaders will need to be more prepared to surmount every challenge and every condition with great faith, character, and competence is abundantly clear.

The thought process itself is the key to exercising greater faith.

As we grasp the process of faith, we will realize that we can change our circumstances by changing our attitude and exercising faith. Our thoughts inform our circumstances because thoughts preside over habits and habits govern circumstances. If we drastically change our thoughts, we will be amazed at how quickly the temporal conditions of our life will be renovated. In time, we will begin to experience the power of faith in our life when we have been triumphant in maintaining the needed mental discipline coupled with righteous living. If we constantly labor at using faith as a principle of power, we will discover the process becomes easier until finally it becomes almost spontaneous.

Our childlike metaphor for BRIGHT1+2+3+4+Character Capacity is a battery-powered toy car making its way around the room. It goes forward as far as it can; when it meets an obstacle, it doesn't beat against it but tries to get around it. It backs up, adjusts its direction, and tries to move forward again. Over and over it stops when its way is blocked, backs up, and tries again until it finds a clear *space* where it can make progress.

Similarly, our value/faith-based leaders in the United Kingdom, United States, and Asia were persistent in exercising their faith to overcome or "get around" their obstacles. As with them, we should never stop trying or exercising our faith until we reach our worthy goals.

An Ultimate Challenge

Developing BRIGHT1+2+3+4+Character Capacity means breaking away from the effects of years of convergent thinking, or educational backgrounds that stifle creative/inventive potential. It also means viewing the brain as a creature of habit that uses well-established neural pathways as the more comfortable processes, rather than elaborating new or unusual processes. For any of us, the failure to develop our creative faculties permits key neural connections to skew and diminish. Over time it becomes more challenging for us to overcome our thought barriers—making sense of the maxim "If we always think the way we always thought, we'll always get what we always got—the same old ideas."

BRIGHT1+2+3+4+Character Capacity is not a total mental-rework prescription for what leadership can be or should be all about. Rather, it speaks to how we, as executives, can think higher, wider, deeper, thicker, and faster with wisdom and integrity. It is how we can with new eyes better consider our options in an insightful, creative, and decisive way that leads to new possibilities and not merely back to the same old inadequate alternatives. What's distinctive about BRIGHT1+2+3+4+Character Capacity is how we will process information differently and actively seek the less obvious but potentially relevant factors of those perplexing problems we deal with.

BRIGHT1+2+3+4+Character Capacity, simply stated, is our icon for four dimensions of executive thinking (e.g., (1) Verbal Thinking, (2) Quantitative (symbolic) Thinking, (3) Spatial Thinking (simultaneous), and (4) Decisive Thinking—Insight with Velocity). Our highest endorsement comes with the third and fourth dimensions, which combine to create extraordinary depth, direction, and speed in creative problem solving and inventive decision making. Dimensions three and four can only be realized on the fringe of verbal, quantitative capacities, and through strong visual-spatial ability. When responding to our critical challenges or dilemmas, we can visualize and process in higher levels of thinking and thereby rise above a flat-line mentality that often forces us and our team to make less desirable trade-offs.

Such was the field of Lincoln's leadership in the 1860s, and such is the field for us as BRIGHT1+2+3+4+Character Capacity executives in the humanly dramatic, impenetrable complexity of the twenty-first century. It will take our global decisiveness as a starting point. It will take seeking to highlight what we do right even when we do not know exactly why it is right or know for sure if it will be right. In other words, to paraphrase Dr. Goodwin's tribute to Lincoln, we should seek to connect two distinct intellectual and life-directional paradigms: the tradition of rationally thinking about, controlling, engineering, and commanding complex structures, and the tradition of sensing, experiencing, and sharing the subtleties of our environment through human connectivity and our subjective fourth dimension.

As a nation, it's not too late; we still have a porthole of opportunity. We have become complacent with our "progressive" educational and political systems and the notion that our competitive advantage—inventive energy and executive intelligence—cannot be topped or outsourced. That is not true! We traveled through Asian markets and workplaces and witnessed talented, dedicated, and extremely hardworking individuals who want the same things we Americans want. Engineers and scientists are being produced in numbers unheard of by China, India, Singapore, Japan, and Korea. China and India together are producing almost a million engineering graduates each year. When we consider that the United States is producing only 70,000 each year, we wonder how long our country can remain competitive. No matter how smart our top students are, they may be outflanked by ten times more engineers from China and India working on the same problem. It is analogous to playing basketball one-on-ten. No matter how our one person plays during the first quarter, we know we will lose unless we play at a BRIGHT4 level of global decisiveness. The Chinese are loading heavily on quantitative and spatial dimensions but not doing what it takes for a championship team—BRIGHT4. America is at a critical time. We desperately need to ramp up our pool of talented scientists, engineers, and executives to solve the world's problems in energy, environment, manufacturing, etc.

Imagine being a young Shanghai Chinese engineer working for a Chinese technology company that is successfully starting to challenge some of the most established service providers on the planet. Decidedly, you would want to make good money and purchase a home. But just as likely, your work isn't exclusively about personal achievement or even your employer's market cap: it's a statement of national identity. There was/is in China and India the same passion, pride, and loyalty that we found in Japan in the late 1970s, which could be channeled to create an indomitable engineering and manufacturing force. Most likely, the company in Shanghai will be a partner with a US firm and will be a part of an outsourced arrangement that in time will take a local leadership role in launching innovative initiatives in dramatically less time.

Our recent Asian interface with successful Chinese leaders was gripping, to say the least. When they talked about their values and desires to be smart, thinking leaders in the international marketplace, they would cite their mission. It goes like this: "First—I want my own sharpness of thinking; then—far-sighted thinking; next—I want to directly and accurately analyze problems around an exciting vision and goals; followed by—developing my people in line with enterprise development strategies; and finally—lead and manage my entire team to promote the constant development of enterprises." They believe that Chinese entrepreneurs will begin leading in innovation in the world marketplace with nationalistic pride: "Invented here in China."

In Summary

This new century is really a global marketplace vying for a competitive lead assembled on *plasticity, speed, and adaptability*. Leaders of the past relied on the lens of rational analysis to peer into the future, only to discover, too late, that the urgent and vital task of understanding how their world—their business and their personal lives—would unfold requires a different kind of thinking power. Situations in which accepted rules and norms supply all the answers are now an endangered species.

Constant inventiveness and global decisiveness is America's only hope and means to sustain competitive advantage in the world marketplace. That will require selecting our best people, best minds, best thinking, and best resources to continually create new products, services, business systems, and practices. We will need to use them to stay ahead of our off-shore competition through successful and sustainable innovation. Our success ultimately rests in the hands of executives who possess exceptional potential, BRIGHT1+2+3+4+Character Capacity thinking, inventive problem solving *capacity*, and a moral compass that inspires and sets a direction that others can both trust and admire. It's not too late to rev up to the challenge and ramp up our national reserve of competent executive capacity. We firmly believe that the development of B1+2+3+4+CC with any leader or executive will create greater capacity for Americans to globally compete.

CHAPTER SUMMARY
Key Points

- Capacity, in addition to our abilities and knowledge, is about how much we can spatially process combinations of height, width, and depth simultaneously with insight, decisiveness, direction, and speed.

- What our present capacity is today need not be our capacity for the rest of our lives. Each of us has so much room for expanded thinking capacity.

- Global insight (BRIGHT4) is a way of conceptualizing, acting, and motivating others that enables effective executive leadership. In decision situations, decisiveness enables us to look at an entire situation with all of its interdependencies and complexities.

- Visualization is a program we employ to help us learn how to think and communicate better using the visual part of our brain. Visual thinking is a way to organize our thoughts and improve our ability to think and communicate. It's a way to expand our range and capacity by going beyond the linear world of the written word, list, and spreadsheet, and entering the non-linear world of complex spatial relationships, networks, maps, and diagrams.

- BRIGHT4 insight is our highest level of thinking that can be developed as a thinking process and decision-making-velocity approach. This process simplifies and elevates the complex nature of decision making and cognition. The one word that makes a great executive is decisiveness. A second word of greatness is teaming.

- The benefits of high-capacity teams can be extraordinary, but conversion and practice takes finesse. It isn't easy for a mature organization, with run-of-the-mill practices and few national champions, to go high-capacity quickly. We may strive to raise our level of capacity, but without a supportive culture that values and supports talent, the exercise is fraught with resistance.

• Global Insight is an objective, highly reliable evaluation of the Executive Talent Pool. A 5–10% change in Global Insight for our executive team represents a enormous change in our organization's competitiveness.

• Constant inventiveness is America's only hope and means to sustain our competitive advantage in the world marketplace.

• Life is about our choices. Choices are about authenticity, consequences, and character. Our character is about the wise use of experience, competence, and integrity. Integrity is about keeping our promises, being true to self, and maturing wisely.

• We believe that much of our survival as Americans will ultimately rest in the heads and hearts of leaders who possess exceptional faith and thinking capacity—"BRIGHT1+2+3+4+Character Capacity".

REFERENCES

Adams, J. L. (1986). *Conceptual blockbusting: A guide to better ideas.* New York, NY: Penguin.

Alan (2010). "Haiku." *Sharpbrains: Brain fitness for all.* Retrieved from http://www.sharpbrains.com/teasers/top-15-puzzles-teasers-riddles/

Anllo-Vento, M. L. (1992). Visual-spatial selective attention and reading ability in children: A study using event-related potentials and behavioral measures. *Dissertation Abstracts International, 53 (2B),* 1100.

Banich, M. T. (1997). *Neuropsychology: The neural bases of mental function.* NewYork: Houghton Mifflin.

Bear, M. F., Connors, B.W. & Paradiso, M.A. (2006). *Neuroscience: Exploring the brain* (3rd ed.). Philadelphia, PA: Lippincott.

Baron, J. (2008) *Thinking and deciding.* Cambridge, UK: Cambridge University Press.

Benbow, C. (1990). Cognitive profiles of verbally and mathematically precocious students: implications for identification of the gifted. *Gifted Child Quarterly, 34,* (1), Winter.

Benbow, C. P. (1992). Academic achievement in math and science between ages 13 and 23: Are there differences in the top one percent of ability? *Journal of Educational Psychology, 84,* 51–61.

Bennett, G., Seashore, H. G., & Weisman, A. (1989). *Differential aptitude tests forms V and W (DAT).* U.S.A. Psychological Corporation, Inventory No. 2941.

Benton, A. (1994). Brigham, Carl C. (1890–1943). In R. J. Sternberg (Ed.). *Encyclopedia of human intelligence.* New York, NY: Macmillan.

Berkeley Optometry, University of California (2008). Retrieved from: http://spectacle.berkeley.edu/opt_txtpp/programs/clinical_prog/clin_curriculum_od.html

Black, H., Black, S. (1984). Figural classifications: changing characteristics. *Building thinking skills. Book 2,* 82. Pacific Grove: Midwest Publications Critical Thinking Press and Software.

Borden, M., Breen, B., Chu, J., Dean, J., Fannin, R., Feldman, A., Fishman, C., Hochman, P., Kushner, D., Lacter, M., Levine, R., Lidsky, D., McGirt, E., Sacks, D., Salter, C., Svoboda, E., & Tischler, L. (2008). The world's most innovative companies. *Fast Company, 123,* 62.

Bordogna, J.,Colwell, R., & Brighton J. (2003). Ensuring manufacturing strength through bold vision. National Science Foundation. Available at: http://www.ostp.gov/pdf/finalpcastitmanuf_reportpackage.pdf

Bowerman, M. & Levinson, S. (Eds.). (2001). *Language acquisition and conceptual development.* Cambridge, UK: Cambridge University Press.

Bricken, M. (1991) Virtual reality learning environments: potential and challenges. *Computer Graphics,* (25)3, 178–184.

Bricken, M. & Byrne, C. (1993). Summer students in virtual reality, a pilot study on educational applications of virtual technology. In A. Wexelblat (Ed.) *Virtual Reality, Applications and Explorations.* Cambridge, MA: Academic Press Professional.

Brill, L. (1993). Metaphors for the traveling cybernaut (virtual reality). *Virtual Reality World, 1(1),* Q–S.

Brodsky, S. L., Esquerre, J., & Jackson, R. R. (1990–91). Dream consciousness in problem solving. *Imagination, Cognition, and Personality, 10(4),* 353–360.

Brookfield, S. (1987). *Developing critical thinking: Challenging adults to explore alternative ways of thinking and acting.* San Francisco, CA: Jossey-Bass.

Bruner, J. S. (2001, December). Thriving in academe: A rationale for verbal communication. *National Education Association Advocate Online.*

Bruner, J. S. (1966). *Towards a theory of instruction.* New York, NY: W. W. Norton & Company, Inc.

Byrne, C. (1993). *Virtual reality in education.* Seattle, WA: Human Interface Technology Laboratory at the University of Washington, Technical Publications R-93-6.

Byrne, John A. (2005). *Fast Company: The Rules of Business.* New York: Broadway Business.

Calahan, J. (2008), The four c's of emotion: A framework for managing emotions in organizations, *Organization Development Journal, 26(2),* 33–37.

Case, R. (1984). The process of stage transition: a neo-Piagetian view. In R.J. Sternberg (Ed.), *Mechanisms of cognitive development* (20–44). New York, NY: Freeman.

Case, R. (1985). *Intellectual development: Birth to adulthood.* New York, NY: Academic Press.

Case, R. (1987). The structure and process of intellectual development. *International Journal of Psychology, 22,* 571–607.

Chartered Institute of Personnel and Development (2006, Spring). *Human capital evaluation: Getting started.* London, UK: CIPD.

Chauncey, H. & Hilton, T. (1965). Are aptitude tests valid for the highly able? *Science, 148,* 1297–1304.

Choi, S. & Gopnik, A. (1995). Early acquisition of verbs in Korean: a cross-linguistic study. *Journal of Child Language, 22*, 497–529.

Cohen, Robert (1985). *The development of spatial cognition.* Hillsdale, NJ: L. Erlbaum Associates.

College Board (2008). AP National Report. Retrieved from http://www.collegeboard.com/student/testing/ap/exgrd_sum/2008.html

Collins, J. *Good to great.* (2001). New York, NY: Harper Collins Publishers.

Combs, D. & Churchill, M. (2004) *Sir Winston Churchill: His life and his paintings.* Philadelphia, PA: Running Press Book Publisher.

Covey, S. (1989). *The seven habits of highly effective people.* New York, NY: Free Press.

Csikszentmihalyri, M. & Nakamura, J. (1986). Optimal experience and the uses of talent. Paper presented at the 94th Annual Meeting of the American Psychological Association. Washington DC.

De Bono, E. (1990). *I am right, you are wrong.* New York, NY: Viking.

De Bono, E. (1986). *Six thinking hats.* New York, NY: Viking.

Denis, M. (1991). Imagery and thinking. In Cornoldi, C. & McDaniel, M. A. (Eds.), *Imagery and cognition.* New York, NY: Springer-Verlag.

Diamond, M. C. (1988). *Enriching heredity*, New York, NY: Free Press.

Diamond, M. C., Weidner, J., Schow, P., Grell, S., & Everett, M. (2001). Mental stimulation increases circulating CD4-positive T lymphocytes: a preliminary study. *Cognitive Brain Research, 12*, 329–331.

Diamond, M. C. (2001). Enrichment response of the brain. *Encyclopedia of Neuroscience.* 3rd edition, London, UK: Elsevier Science.

Diamond, M. C. (2001). Response of the brain to enrichment. *Annals of the Brazilian Academy of Sciences, 73(2).*

Doidge, N. (2007). *The brain that changes itself.* New York, NY: Viking.

Domestic Policy Office of Science and Technology Policy (2006). *American competitiveness initiative: Leading the world in innovation.* Washington DC: Government Printing Office.

Dorans, N. J. (1999). Correspondence between ACT and SAT I Scores, *College Board Research Report, 99(1).* New York, NY: The College Board.

Dorans, N. J. (2002). The re-centering of the SAT scales and its effects on score distributions and score interpretations, *College Board Research Report, 11.* New York, NY: The College Board.

Dwyer, F. M. (1988). Examining the symbiotic relationship between verbal and visual literacy in terms of facilitating student achievement. *Reading Psychology, 9,* 365–380.

Epstein, R. (2006), *The big book of creativity games: Quick, fun activities for jumpstarting innovation,* New York: McGraw-Hill.

Exercise, Estrogen, and Mental Function (2008, February). *Harvard Mental Health Letter, 3.*

Feldhusen, J. F. (1994) Terman's giftedness study. In R. J. Sternberg (Ed.). *Encyclopedia of human intelligence.* New York, NY: Macmillan.

Frey, M. & Detterman, D. (2004). Scholastic assessment or g? The relationship between the scholastic assessment test and general cognitive ability. *Psychological Science. 15,* 373–378.

Friend, J. & Hickling, A. (1987). *Planning under pressure.* Oxford, UK: Pergamon Press.

Fry, A. F. & Hale, S. (1996). Processing speed, working memory, and fluid intelligence: Evidence for a developmental cascade. *Psychological Science. 7,* 237–241

Furth, H. (1970). *An inventory of Piaget's developmental tasks.* Washington DC: Catholic University, Department of Psychology, Center for Research in Thinking and Language.

Gagné, E. (1985). *Cognitive psychology of education.* Boston, MA: Little, Brown.

Galyean, B. C. (1982). The use of guided imagery in elementary and secondary schools. *Imagination, Cognition and Personality, 2(2)*, 145-151.

Gardner, H. (1984). *Frames of mind: The theory of multiple intelligences.* London, UK:Heinemann.

Gardner, H. (1993). *Multiple intelligences: The theory in practice, a reader.* New York: Basic Books.

Gates, B. (2005). Prepared remarks by Bill Gates, Co-founder. Washington DC: National Education Summit on High Schools.

Gazzaniga, M. S. (2005). Forty-five years of split-brain research and still going strong. [Review]. *Nature Reviews Neuroscience, 6(8)*, 653–U651.

General Accounting Office (2003). *Military education—DOD needs to align academy preparatory schools' mission statements with overall guidance and establish performance goals.* Retrieved from http://www.gao.gov/new.items/d031017.pdf

Gleick, J. (1987). *Chaos.* New York, NY: Penguin.

Gohm, C. L., Humphreys, L. G., & Yao, G. (1998). Underachievement among spatially gifted students. American EducationalResearch Journal, 35, 515–531.

Goldstein, E. (2005). *Cognitive psychology—Connecting, mind research, and everyday experience.* New York, NY: Thomson Wadsworth.

Goldberg, E. (2009). The new executive brain: Frontal lobes in a complex world, New York, NY: Oxford University Press.

Goodwin, D. K. (2005). *Team of rivals: The political genius of Abraham Lincoln.* New York, NY: Simon and Schuster.

Gopnik, A., Choi, S., & Baumberger, T. (1996). Cross-linguistic differences in early semantic and cognitive development. *Cognitive Development, 11*:197–227.

Graham, M. (1974*).* Cross-cultural variations of paradigmatic-syntagmatic dominance in organization of free-recall (*Dissertation*). Tucson, AZ: University of Arizona Archives.

Graham, M. A. (1994). *Horizontal revolution: Reengineering your organization through teams.* San Francisco, CA: Jossey-Bass.

Grauer, S. (1985). *Beyond the curriculum: Creating the conditions for learning.* Del Mar, CA. ERIC Document ED 166 181.

Greenleaf, R. K. (1991). *The servant as leader*, Indianapolis, IN: The Robert K. Greenleaf Center (Original essay published in 1970).

Griese, B. (2000). *Undefeated: How father and son triumphed over unbelievable odds both on and off the field.* Nashville, TN: Thomas Nelson Publishers.

Hammes,D. (2007). The contribution of the University of Hawaii to Hawaii's economy in 2006: As of September 28, 2008. Retrieved from http://www.hawaiiedu/offices/app/opp/econimpact/report2007.pdf

Hammond, J. S., Keeney, R. L., & Raiffa, H. (1998). The hidden traps in decision-making. *Harvard Business Review*, 17.

Hammonds, K. (2000, October 31). How do we break out of the box we're stuck in? *Fast Company 40.*Retrieved from http://www.fastcompany.com/magazine/40/wf_winkler.html.

Hampden-Turner, C. (1990). *Charting the corporate mind.* Oxford, UK: Blackwell.

Hartigan, J. & Wigdor, A. (1989). Fairness in employment testing: Validity generalization, minority issues, and the general aptitude test battery. Washington, DC: National Academy Press. Retrieved from http://www.nap.edu/openbook/0309040337/html/73.html

Heath, D. & Heath, C. (2007, December 1). Get back in the box. *Fast Company, 121*. Retrieved from http://www.fastcompany.com/magazine/121/get-back-in-the-box.html

Hill, B. (1993). The value of competitive debate as a vehicle for promoting development of critical thinking ability. In A. Gill (Ed.), *CEDA Yearbook 14* (pp. 1–22). Dubuque, IA: Kendall/Hunt Publishing Company.

Hilton, T. (1985). National changes in spatial-visual ability from 1960–1980. Educational Testing Service,RR-85-27. Retrieved from http://www.eric.ed.gov/ERICDocs/data/ericdocs2sql/content_storage_01/0000019b/80/2f/23/f9.pdf

Hirose, M., Hirota, K., & Kijima, R. (1992). Human behaviour in virtual environments. *Proceedings of the SPIE—The International Society for Optical Engineering, 1666* 548–59.

Holland, J. H., Holyoak, K. J., Nisbett, R. E., & Thagard, P. R. (1987). *Induction—Processes of inference, learning and discovery.* Cambridge, MA: MIT Press.

Humphreys, L. G., Davey, T. C., and Kashima, E. (1986). Experimental measures of cognitive privilege/deprivation and some of their correlates. *Intelligence, 10*, 355–370.

Humphreys, L. G., Lubinski, D., & Yao, G. (1993). Utility of predicting group membership and the role of spatial Visualization in becoming an engineer, physical scientist, or artist. *Journal of Applied Psychology, 78. (2)*, 230–261.

Hunter, J. E. (1994). General aptitude test battery. In R.J. Strernberg (Ed.). *Encyclopedia of human intelligence.* New York, NY: Macmillan.

Hunter, J. E. (1980). Test validation for 12000 jobs: An application of synthetic validity and validity generalization to the General Aptitude Test Battery (GATB). Washington DC: U.S Employment Service, US Department of Labor.

Hunter, J. E. (1983). The dimensionality of the General Aptitude Test battery (GATB) and the dominance of the general factors over specific factors in the prediction of job performance for the U.S Employment Service. *USES test research report no. 44*. Division of Counseling and Test Development, Employment and Training Administration. Washington DC: US Department of Labor.

Hunter, J. E., & Hunter, R. F. (1984). Validity and utility of alternative predictors of job performance. *Psychological Bulletin, 98 (1)*, 72–98.

Idon Ltd. Publications (1990). *Thinking with hexagons.* Company Publication, Idon Ltd.

Idons-for-Thinking (for Windows) (1996), Idon Software Ltd, (the successor to CK Modeller).

Isenberg, D. J. (1987). Inside the mind of the senior manager in: Perkins, Lochhead and Bishop (Eds.). *Thinking.* London, UK: Erlbaum.

Javidan, P.,Dorfman, W, Gupta, V, & Associates (Eds.), Culture, leadership, and organizations: The GLOBE study of 62 societies (pp. 9–28). Thousand Oaks, CA: Sage.

Johnson-Laird, P.N. (1983). *Mental models—Towards a cognitive science of language inference and consciousness.* Cambridge, UK: Cambridge University Press.

Kail, R. (2000) Speed of information processing: developmental change and links to intelligence. *Journal of School Psychology, 38(1)*, 51–61.

Kamenetz, Anya (2010, February 17). Most innovative companies: #6 First Solar. *Fast Company,* Retrieved from http://www.fastcompany.com/mic/2010/profile/first-solar .

Kennedy, J. M. (1983). What can we learn about pictures from the blind? *American Scientist, 71*, 19–23.

Kirby, J. R., Moore, P. J. & Schofield, N. J. (1988). Verbal and visual learning styles. *Contemporary Educational Psychology, 13*, 169–184.

Kline, M. (1980). *Mathematics, The loss of certainty.* New York, NY: Oxford Press.

Koob A. (2009). *The root of thought: Unlocking glia—the brain cell that will help us sharpen our wits, heal injury, and treat brain disease,* London, UK: FT Press.

Kosslyn, S. M. (1983). *Ghosts in the mind's machine: Creating & using images in the brain.* New York, NY: W. W. Norton.

Kossoroukov, Andrei (2006, July). Three-dimensional thinking and job problem. *TRIZ Journal,* Retrieved from http://www.triz-journal.com/archives/2006/07/.

Kotter, J. P. (1990). *A Force for change: How leadership differs from management.* New York, NY: The Free Press.

Kotter, R. (2004). Neuroscience databases: tools for exploring brain structure-function relationships. *Philos Trans R Soc Lond B Biol Sci, 356(1412),* 1111–1120.

Kouwenhoven, J. (1967). *The arts in modern American civilization.* New York, NY: W.W. Norton.

Kouzes, J. M. & Posner, B. Z. (2002). *The leadership challenge* (3rd ed.). San Francisco, CA: Jossey-Bass.

Kuenzi, J. (2008). CRS Report for Congress Science, Technology, Engineering, and Mathematics (STEM) Education: Background, federal policy, and legislative action.Congressional Research Service. Retrieved from http://assets.opencrs.com/rpts/RL33434_20080321.pdf

Lanier, J. (1992). Virtual reality: The promise of the future. *Interactive Learning International, 8,* 275–279.

Lanier, J. & Biocca, F. (1992). An insider's view of the future of virtual reality. *Journal of Communication, 42(4),* 150–172.

Laurel, B. (1991). *Computers as theatre.* Reading, MA: Addison-Wesley.

Lawler, R. W. (1985). *Computer experience and cognitive development: A child's learning in a computer culture.* Chichester: E. Horwood.

Lawrence, L., Rigol, G.W., Essen, T. V., & Jackson, C. A. (2002). A historical perspective on the SAT 1926–2001. *College Board Research Report,* No. 2002–7, New York, NY: The College Board.

Lawson, B. (2001). *The language of space.* Oxford, UK: Architectural Press.

Lohman, D. F.(1994). Spatial ability. In R.J. Sternberg (Ed.). *Encyclopedia of human intelligence.* New York, NY: Macmillan.

Lohman, D. F., & Korb, K. (2006). Gifted today but not tomorrow? Longitudinal changes in ITBS and CogAT scores during elementary school. *Journal for the Education of the Gifted, 29*, 451–484.

Lopez, A. M. (1992). Declarative thinking and the investigation of spatial relationships in a block microworld. *Journal of Computing in Childhood Education, 3,* 181–192.

Lubinski, D., Benbow, C. P., Webb, R. M., & Bleske-Rechek, A. (2006). Tracking exceptional human capital over two decades. *Psychological Science, 17,* 194–199.

Lubinski, D., & Benbow, C. P., (2006). Study of mathematically precocious youth after 35 years: Uncovering antecedents for the development of math-science expertise. *Perspectives on Psychological Science, 1,* 316–345.

Lucy, J. (1992a). *Language diversity and thought: A reformulation of the linguistic relativity hypothesis.* Cambridge, UK: Cambridge University Press.

Mackintosh, N. J., (1998). *IQ and human intelligence*, New York: Oxford University Press.

Manjoo, F. (July/August 2010). Apple nation. *Fast Company, 147.* Retrieved from http://www.fastcompany.com/magazine/147/apple-nation.html

Marburger, J. (2006). Statement of Dr. John Marburger, III Director, Office of Science and Technology Policy Executive office of the President to the Subcommittee on Technology, Innovation and Competitiveness Committee on Commerce, Science and Transportation United States Senate. Retrieved from http://www.ostp.gov/galleries/default-file/Marburger%20 testimoney%20FINAL%20Senate%20Commerce3-29-06,pdf.

Martin, R. (2007, June). How successful leaders think. *Harvard Business Review,* 60–67.

McClurg, P. A., & Chaillé, C. (1987). Computer games: Environments for developing spatial cognition? *Educational Computing Research, 3(11),* 95–111.

McClurg, P. A. (1992). Investigating the development of spatial cognition in problem-solving microworlds. *Journal of Computing in Childhood Education, 3,* 111–126.

McGregor, D. (1960). *The human side of enterprise.* New York, NY: McGraw Hill.

McKeough, T. (2007). The power of shape shifters. *Fast Company, 121.* Retrieved from http://www.fastcompany.com/magazine/121/the-power-of-shape-shifters.html

Menkes, J. *Executive intelligence: What all great leaders have.* New York, NY: Collins, 2005.

Merzenich, M. (2001). *Mechanisms in cognitive development: Behavioral and neural perspectives.* J McClelland and R Siegler (Eds.), (67–96). Mahwah, NJ: L. Ehrlbaum Assoc.

Merickel, M. (1992). The creative technologies project: A study of the relationship between virtual reality (perceived realism) and the ability of children to create, manipulate, and utilize mental images for spatially related problem solving. (*ERIC Document* ED 352 942).

Merzenich, M. (1989). Neural network simulation of somatosensory representational plasticity. Vancouver, CA: Neural Information Processing Systems, 52–59.

Merzenich, M. (2001). *Mechanisms in cognitive development: Behavioral and neural perspectives.* J McClelland & R Siegler, eds., L. Ehrlbaum Assoc., Mahwah NJ, pp. 67–96.

Merzenich, M. (2007). Neuroscience via computer: brain exercise for older adults. *Interactions,* 14(4): 42–45.

Meyer, K, & Damasio, A. (2009, July). Convergence and divergence in a neural architecture for recognition and memory. *Trends in Neuroscience, 32(7)*, 376–82.

Michels, W. (1958). The teaching of elementary physics. *Scientific American, 198*:57–62.

Middleton, T. (1992). Applications of virtual reality to learning. *Interactive Learning International,* 8, 253–257.

Milakofsky, L. & Patterson, H. O., (1979). The reliability and validity of an instrument to assess Piaget's tasks. *Journal of Chemical Education,* 56, 87–90.

Miller, G. A. (1956). The magical number seven, plus or minus two; Some limits on our capacity for processing information. *Psychological Review,* 63, 81–87.

Morecroft, J. (1992). Executive knowledge models and learning. *European Journal of Operational Research, 59,* 9–27.

NASA History Office (2002). Apollo 11 30th Anniversary Page. Retrieved from http://history.nasa.gov/ap11ann/introduction.htm

National Science Foundation (2007). *Science and engineering degrees: 1966–2004*. Retrieved from http://www.nsf.gov/statistics/nsf07307/pdf/nsf07307.pdf

Nelson, C. (1996). *Language in cognitive development*. Cambridge, UK: Cambridge University Press.

Newton, I. (1999). *The Principia: Mathematical principals of natural philosophy*. (I. B. Cohen & A. Whitman, Trans.). Berkeley, CA: University of California Press. (Original work published 1687).

Nonaka, I. (1988). Creating organizational order out of chaos: Self-renewal in Japanese firms. *California Management Review, Spring*, 51–53.

OECD (2008). *Education at a glance: OECD Indicators—2008 Edition*. Paris, France: OECD. Retrieved from http://www.oecd.org/dataoecd/23/46/41284038.pdf

Osberg, K. M. (2010). *Virtual reality and spatial cognition enhancement: A pilot study*. Seattle, WA: Human Interface Technology Laboratory at the University of Washington.

Osberg, K. M. (1992). *Virtual reality in education: A look at both sides of the sword*. Seattle, WA: Human Interface Technology Laboratory at the University of Washington, Technical Publications R-93-7.

Patterson, H. O. & Milakofsky, L. (1980). A paper-and-pencil inventory for the assessment of Piaget's tasks. *Applied Psychological Measurement, 4(3)*, 341–353.

Pelligrino, J. W., Alderton, D. L., & Shute, V. J. (1984). Understanding spatial ability. *Educational Psychologist, 19(3)*, 239–253.

Pfeffer, J. & Sutton, R. (2006, May).The half-truths of leadership, *Stanford Business*, 14–19.

Piaget, J. (1952). *The origins of intelligence in children*. New York, NY: International Universities Press.

Piaget, J. (1963). *The psychology of intelligence.* New York, NY: Routledge.

Pinaud, R., Tremere, L. A., & De Weerd, P., (Eds.). (2006). *Plasticity in the visual system: from genes to circuits.* New York, NY: Springer.

Plato (1993). Apology. *The last days of Socrates.* Harold Tannant (Ed.) New York, NY: Penguin, pp. 29–68. (Original work written 399 BCE).

Pope, K. S., & Singer, J. L. (1978). *The streams of consciousness.* New York, NY: Plenum.

Powell, C. & Persico, J. (1995). *My American journey,* New York, NY: Random House.

Proceedings of the National Academy of Sciences, November, 2004.

Rabinovitch, J. S. (1992). *What you see is what you get: Examining the critical link between visual processing, language, and learning.* Seattle, WA: Presentations 11/21 & 12/5.

Rasiel, E. M. (1999). *The McKinsey way.* New York, NY: McGraw-Hill.

Reagan, R. (1994). *Sunset and dawn.* Reprinted in Nation Review Online, 2004. Retrieved from http://old.nationalreview.com/document/reagan_sunset200406070915.asp.

Regian, J. W., Shebilske, W. L., & Monk, J. M. (1992). Virtual reality: an instructional medium for visual-spatial tasks. *Journal of Communication, (42)4,* 136–149.

Resnick, L. (1987). *Education and learning to think.* Washington DC: National Academy Press.

Robertson, I. H. (2002). *Opening the mind's eye: How images and languages teach us how to see.* New York, NY: St. Martin's Press.

Rocke, T. (2009, August). Building leadership and organizational capability of Agilent. *Training and Development*, 40–43.

Roe, A. (1952). *The making of a scientist*, New York, NY: Dodd, Mead.

Saarnio, D. A., & Bjorklund, D. F. (1984). Children's memory for objects in self-generated scenes. *Merrill-Palmer Quarterly*, 287–301.

Sadowsky, M. (1983). An exploratory study of the relationships between reported imagery and the comprehension and recall of a story. *Reading Research Quarterly, Fall*, 110–123.

Samuels, M., & Samuels, N. (1975). *Seeing with the mind's eye*. New York, NY: Random House.

Schmidt, F. & Hunter, J., (2004). General mental ability in the world of work: occupational attainment and job performance. *Journal of Personality and Social Psychology, 86(1)*, 161–173.

Schmidt, F. & Hunter, J., (1998). The validity and utility of selection methods in personnel psychology: practical and theoretical implementation of 85 years of research findings. *Psychological Bulletin, 124(2)*, 262–274.

Senge, P. (1990). *The fifth discipline: The art and practice of the learning organization*. New York, NY: Doubleday.

Shea, D., Lubinski, D., & Benbow (2001). Importance of assessing spatial ability in intellectually talented young adolescents: A 20-year longitudinal study. *Journal of Educational Psychology, 93(3)*, 604–614.

Shepard, R. & Metzler, J. (1971). Mental rotation of three-dimensional objects. *Science, 191*, 952–954.

Siegler, R. S. (1978). *Children's thinking: What develops?* Hillsdale, NJ: L. Erlbaum Associates.

Siegler, R. S. (1986). Unities across domains in children's strategy choices. In M. Perlmutter (Ed.) *Perspectives on intellectual* development: *The Minnesota Symposia on child psychology, 19*, 1–48, Hillsdale, NJ: Erlbaum.

Siegler, R. S. (1987). The perils of averaging data over strategies: An example from children's addition. *Journal of Experimental Psychology: General, 116*, 250–64.

Silverman, L. (2002). *Upside-down brilliance: The visual-spatial learner*. Denver, CO: DeLeon.

Smalley, R. (2003). Transcript of speech at the MIT Enterprise Forum, Houston, Texas, January 22, 2003. Retrieved from: http://www.americanenergyindependence.com/energychallenge.html

Spearman, C. (1904). "General intelligence" objectively determined and measured. *American Journal of Psychology, 15*, 201–293.

Stanovich, K. (2009). *What intelligence tests miss: The psychology of rational thought*, New Haven, CT: Yale University Press.

Stein, D. (2008, Nov. 19). Plasticity. Personal interview. Alyssa Walz. 19 Nov.

Steinberg, D. (2001, April). Money from nothing. *Smart Business for the New Economy*, 68–74.

Sternberg, R. J. (1990). *Metaphors of mind: Conceptions of the nature of intelligence*. Cambridge, UK: Cambridge University Press.

Steuer, J. (1992). Defining virtual reality: dimensions of telepresence. *Journal of Communication, 42(4)*, 73–93.

Sweetland, J., Reina, J., & Tatti, A. (2006). Wisc-III verbal/performance discrepancies among a sample of gifted children. *Gifted Child Quarterly, 50(1)*, 7–10.

Talberth, J., Cobb, D., & Slattery, N., (2007). The Genuine Progress Indicator 2006: A tool for sustainable development. Oakland, CA: Redefining Progress. Retrieved from http://www.rprogress.org/publications/2007/GPI%202006.pdf

Tammet, D. (2009, April/May/June). Think better: Tips from a savant, *Scientific American Mind*, 60–63.

Thatcher, M. (1995). *The path to power.* New York: HarperCollins.

Trotter, A. (1991). Are today's kids having too much fun in your classrooms? *Executive Educator, 13(6),* 20–24.

Tufte, E. R. (1990). *Envisioning information.* Cheshire, UK: CNL Graphics Press.

U.S. Census Bureau (2006). Annual estimates of the population by five-year age groups and sex for the United States: April 1 2000 to July 1, 2006 (NC-EST2006-01) and annual estimates of the population by selected age groups and sex for the united states: April 1, 2000 to July 1, 2006 (NC-EST2006-02).

US Department of Labor (1996, May). Presenting effective presentations with visual aids. OSHA, Office of Training and Education. Washington DC: Government Printing Office.

US Department of Labor (1970). Manual for the USES General Aptitude Test Battery. Section III: Development. Washington, DC: Government Printing Office.

University of Hawaii (2008). Measuring our progress. Council of Chief Academic Officers and Office of Academic Planning and Policy, University of Hawaii. Retrieved from http://www.hawaii.edu/ovppp/mop/mop08.pdf

Vaill, P. B. (1990). *Managing as a performing art.* San Francisco, CA: Jossey-Bass.

Vygotsky, L. (1978) *Mind in society: The development of higher psychological processes.* In M. Cole, S. Scribner, V. John-Steiner, & E. Souderman (Eds.). Cambridge, MA: Harvard University Press.

Vygotsky, L. (1986). *Thought and Language.* (A. Kozulin, Trans.). Cambridge, MA: MIT Press. (Original work published 1934).

Wai, J., Lubinski, D., & Benbow, C. (2009). Spatial ability for STEM domains: Aligning over 50 years of cumulative psychological knowledge solidifies its importance. *Journal of Educational Psychology, 101(4)*, 817–835.

Ward, T. B., Finke, R. A., & Smith, S. M. *Creativity and the mind: Discovering the genius within.* New York, NY: Perseus Publishing, 2002.

Webb, R., Lubinski, D., & Benbow, C. (2007). Spatial ability: a neglected dimension in talent searches for intellectually precocious youth. *Journal of Educational Psychology, 99(2)*, 397–420.

Wheeler, J. V. & Hall, R. (2003). Understand emotional intelligence: A conversation with Richard Boyatzis. *Organization Development Journal, 21(4)*, 65–72.

Wiley, S. (1990). An hierarchy of visual learning. *Engineering Design Graphics Journal, 54(3)*, 30–35.

Winn, W. D. & Bricken, W. (1992). Designing virtual worlds for use in mathematics education: the example of experiential algebra. *Educational Technology, 32(12)*, 12–19.

Winner, E. (2000). The origins and ends of giftedness. *American Psychologist, 55*, 159–169.

Winograd, T. & Flores, F. (1986). *Understanding computers and cognition: A new foundation for design.* Norwood, NY: Ablex.

Witelson, S., Kigar, D., & Harvey, T. (1999) The exceptional brain of Albert Einstein. *The Lancet, 353*, 2149–2153.

Witkin, H. A. & Goodenough, D. R. (1977). Field dependence and interpersonal behavior. *Psychological Bulletin, 84*, 661–689.

Zimler, J. & Keenan, J. M. (1983). Imagery in the congenitally blind: How visual are visual images? *Journal of Experimental Psychology, 9(2)*, 269–282.

Zohar, D., & Marshall, I. (2004). *Spiritual capital: Wealth we can live by*. San Francisco, CA: Berrett-Koehler Publishing.

Morris A. Graham, PhD and Kevin Baize, OD

APPENDIX

POWERS of EXECUTIVE THINKING CAPACITY
Brief Bright1+2+3+4+CC Assessment

Verbal Height Processing (B1)

    1. Exercises strong reading and writing, listening and speaking capabilities.

    2. Organizes information and knowledge in a linear, sequential, step-by-step order/fashion.

LOW 1. ____ 2. ____ 3. ____ 4. ____ 5. ____ 6. ____ 7. ____ 8. ____ 9. ____ 10. ____ HIGH

Quantitative Width Processing (B2)

    3. Uses symbolic/quantitative/numeric information and reasoning to tackle, solve problems, and make informed decisions.

    4. Analyzes possibilities by means of symbols/numbers, that come to mind through quantitative investigation/analysis.

LOW 1. ____ 2. ____ 3. ____ 4. ____ 5. ____ 6. ____ 7. ____ 8. ____ 9. ____ 10. ____ HIGH

Spatial Depth Processing (B3)

    5. Visualizes multiple perspectives/initiatives holistically, not just in words and numbers, but with pictures and visualization.

    6. Synthesizes several conflicting ideas/options simultaneously and creates a whole new integrated idea/option/invention.

LOW 1. ____ 2. ____ 3. ____ 4. ____ 5. ____ 6. ____ 7. ____ 8. ____
9. ____ 10. ____ HIGH

Global Decisiveness: Insight, Direction and Speed (B4)

7. Evaluates quickly, acts decisively with confidence on challenging opportunities to innovate, change and improve.

8. Conceives sound, rapid directives in an atmosphere of increasing time pressures, uncertainty, conflicting advice, and crisis.

9. Formulates intuitive, novel, inspiring solutions/directions and insightfully moves the team/organization to a higher place, function, and direction.

LOW 1. ____ 2. ____ 3. ____ 4. ____ 5. ____ 6. ____ 7. ____ 8. ____
9. ____ 10. ____ HIGH

Character Capacity: Integrity and Authenticity (CC)

10. Personifies goodness through humility, example, authenticity, integrity, and wisdom.

11. Sustains the self-confidence, dignity, self-esteem, and positive growth in others.

12. Navigates with a moral compass that inspires and sets a direction that others can trust and follow. ****

LOW 1. ____ 2. ____ 3. ____ 4. ____ 5. ____ 6. ____ 7. ____ 8. ____
9. ____ 10. ____ HIGH

POSTSCRIPT

Developing Bright to the Fourth Power:
The High-Tech, Educational Pathway to Brilliance

In 1958, Professor Jerome Bruner of Harvard University challenged fifth-grade students to think spatially for themselves, using a paper outline map and a pencil. Today, students can be challenged to think spatially for themselves, using a database, a virtual map, and a mouse. In both cases, the responses from students are based on a spatial reasoning process that involves critical observation, exploration, posing questions, developing hypotheses, and generating answers. Both sets of tools offer the power to learn. Dr. Jerome Bruner's work is clear: the contrast between receiving passive knowledge and learning actively; the focus on describing and understanding spatial patterns; the search for multiple explanations; the process of collaborative learning; and above all, the excitement of success. The differences are equally clear: the richness of the data sources and the number of maps; the scale of the project; the low-tech support system versus the high-tech support system. Yet the intent remains the same in both cases: fostering the creative power of spatial thinking in young students. There can be a support system at work: material support, instructional support, and curriculum support combine to offer the opportunity to practice and develop spatial thinking skills. There is a creative juxtaposition between students and teachers, between tools and questions, and between learning and achievement.

In 2008, 1,546,020 high school students participated in Advanced Placement (AP) exams with 150,724 (9.7%) participating in AP Biology, 96,458 (6.2%) participating in AP Chemistry, and 94,176 (6.1%) participating in AP Physics. We have discovered a method that dramatically raises the scientific aptitude of students. We have incorporated this breakthrough into a five-tiered solution that will enable all high school students (100%) to be certified by the College Board as qualified in AP Biology, AP Chemistry, and AP Physics. Tier one: Potential AP Calculus Superstars and science. Tier two: Potential AP English Superstars and science. Tier three: Students who love science but perform inadequately on AP science exams. Tier four: Science education for those students who are not presently on a college track. Tier five: A second chance to become a STEM (Science, Technology, Engineering, and Math) Superstar.

Physical Science & Engineering are Strongly Correlated with Economic Growth

Since World War II, America has evaluated economic progress from the limited viewpoint of gross domestic product (GDP). GDP considers only one side of the economic ledger: products and services bought and sold. An alternative to GDP is the Genuine Progress Indicator (GPI) that includes a comprehensive tally of economic benefits and economic costs. John Talberth, Clifford Cobb, and Noah Slattery have calculated GPI per capita rates for the US from 1950 through 2004. They found that **GPI per capita rates peaked in the mid-1960s** and then progressively declined throughout the rest of the twentieth century (Talberth, Cobb, & Slattery, 2007, p.23). Remarkably, the **US baccalaureate graduation rates in physical science also peaked in the mid-1960s** and then progressively declined throughout the rest of the twentieth century (National Science Foundation, 2007, p.9).

The biggest problem facing us in the twenty-first century is the Energy-Climate Challenge. In 1950, the world's population was 2.6 billion; by 2044 it will reach 9 billion. The world needs new sources of cheap, clean, abundant, renewable energy that will not cause climate change (Smalley, 2003). **To solve this problem, America is going to need technology that currently does not exist—we need more scientists capable of creating new technology. We will** suggest why we think America's best and brightest are not going into science, and what can be done to fix this problem.

The National Science Foundation reported in 2004 that only 1.3% of all bachelor's degrees awarded in the United States were in physics, chemistry, geosciences, or environmental science (National Science Foundation, 2007). That same year only 4.6% of all bachelors' degrees were awarded in engineering. This means that 94% of all degrees awarded in America are in subjects that may never be able to directly solve the twenty-first century's energy challenge.

We think the primary reason so few American students are going into the physical sciences and engineering is because they lack the prerequisite intellectual development to deal with the abstractions of these sciences and therefore are unable to compete on the same level as those who have developed these abilities. **In the same way that you need prerequisite courses (such as calculus before attempting physics for scientists and engineers), these students also need the prerequisite aptitudes to ensure their success in classes that are dependent on not only math aptitude and verbal aptitude but also spatial aptitude.** We think the ability to reason in three dimensions (i.e., spatial aptitude, not only with words and numbers but with pictures and visualization) is vitally important.

John Marburger III, Director, Office of Science and Technology Policy Executive Office of the President, in a speech to the United States Senate on March 29, 2006 said, **"Certain areas of physical science and engineering are strongly correlated with innovation and economic growth ... A broad consensus exists that these are the most important areas for generating additional breakthroughs that drive the economy"** (Marburger, 2006, p. 5).

The Search for Scientific Talent in the Twentieth Century

The Verbal Breakthrough (1905–Present)

In 1905 French psychologist Alfred Binet developed the first intelligence test. By 1916, Lewis Terman, professor at Stanford, published his adaptation of the Binet Intelligence Test (i.e., The

Stanford-Binet Intelligence Test). Researchers in the United States now had an American instrument to identify intellectually talented youth. In 1921, Dr. Lewis Terman began his famous longitudinal study of gifted children using the highly verbal Stanford-Binet (Feldhusen, 1994). By 1928, Terman had tracked 1,528 children between the ages of 3 and 28 (his son Fred included in the study was then 28 years old). Initially, only those children who had verbal IQs in the top 1% of mental ability qualified for inclusion in his study. He later added the siblings of many participants, including his daughter Helen. The results are contained in Terman's work, *Genetic Studies of Genius*.

Terman believed that gifted children were gifted in all areas of academic achievement and that "the one-sidedness of precocious children is mythical" (Winner, 2000, p. 17). It is highly probable that Terman's experience in his own family led him to believe that all children with high aptitude were like his son Fred, who had an undergraduate degree in chemical engineering from Stanford and a doctorate in electrical engineering from Boston Tech (later renamed MIT).

Unfortunately for Lewis Terman, not all scientists were like his son Fred. **Terman rejected two Nobel Laureates in physical science, Luis Alvarez and William Shockley, from his study through the verbal selection process** (Webb, Lubinski, & Benbow, 2007). This is particularly noteworthy because William Shockley and Fred Terman are widely credited with being the fathers of Silicon Valley. A longitudinal follow-up of the Terman study revealed that no one selected for Terman's study ever received a Nobel Prize or a Pulitzer.

As a result of Dr. Terman's work, the intellectual movement in America was in high gear. By 1919, almost two million World War I inductees had been evaluated with the Army Alpha and Beta Tests of Intelligence. In 1923, Carl Brigham, who had worked on the Alpha and Beta Test during World War I, was commissioned by the College Board to develop an examination for entering college students (Benton, 1994). In 1926, Brigham introduced the first Scholastic

Aptitude Test (SAT). Eight thousand men took a three-hour test of verbal ability that was believed to indicate "global giftedness."

There have been many changes to the SAT Verbal section since 1926. In 2002, Ida Lawrence, Gretchen Rigol, Thomas Van Essen, and Carol Jackson published "A Historical Perspective on the SAT 1926–2001." In this article they state, "Changes were made in the interest of making the test more relevant to the process of reading: the test is still a verbal reasoning test, but the balance has shifted somewhat from *reasoning* to *verbal*" (p.3). In 2005, the SAT Verbal section was renamed the SAT Critical Reading section to better align itself with its competitor, ACT Reading. **This is important because the SAT Verbal section has evolved over time to become less of a reasoning test and more of a verbal test and ironically has chosen to abandon its historic name—SAT Verbal.**

The Math Breakthrough (1930–Present)

From the very beginning, the math section of the SAT has been a test in which the ability to answer questions quickly is necessary for a high score—800 being the maximum score. Failure to attempt every question within the time limit will result in a lower score. Timed tests are known as speed tests in contrast to untimed tests, which are known as power tests. Every question that is doable must be attempted for an individual to receive the highest score; if the buzzer sounds and you have only attempted half of the problems, even though you may have every problem correct, you will not receive a top score on a speeded test. Ida Lawrence, Gretchen W. Rigol, Thomas Van Esen, and Carol Jackson cite the 1934 test: "The directions from a 1934 math subtest stated: Write the answer to these questions as quickly as you can" (Lawrence, et al., 2002, p.6). The students had 80 minutes to solve 100 questions. From the beginning, math has been a speed test in which the prize goes not necessarily to the student who can solve the most complex mathematical problems but to the student who can solve basic problems very quickly. **Multivariable calculus is the foundation of physical science and engineering but it is not contained on the math section of the SAT or GRE.**

Who Gets Passed Over with a Math/Verbal SAT?

David F. Lohman and Katrina A. Korb of the University of Iowa have created statistical tables to demonstrate how gifted children can score gifted on one test but not gifted on another test (Lohman & Korb, 2006). If two tests were perfectly correlated we would expect a person who scores above the 90th percentile on one test to score above the 90th percentile on the second test. Unfortunately the correlation between Math and Verbal is approximately .70. This is precisely how talented children fall through the cracks of educational systems. When we base admissions on two tests that are moderately correlated, we end up picking only those fraction of students who are good on both of these tests to the exclusion of those who may not be as gifted on the second test or may be more gifted in a completely different subject area. For example, Shea, Lubinski, and Benbow report, **"It can be shown that selecting for the top 3% of verbal-mathematical ability will result in the loss of more than half of the students representing the top 1% of spatial ability"** (Shea, Lubinski, & Benbow, 2001, p. 612). Analysis of a sample of over 100,000 ninth graders by Webb, Lubinski, and Benbow found **"only 30% of the top 1% on spatial ability scored within the top 1% on either mathematical or verbal reasoning"** (Webb et al., 2007, p. 398).

The Spatial Breakthrough (1947–Present)

In 1947, the US Department of Labor released the General Aptitude Test Battery (GATB), which contained spatial testing. John E. Hunter, a psychologist who worked extensively on methodology, writes about the development of the GATB:

> During the years 1934–1942, the US Department of Labor developed aptitude tests to predict job performance for 100 specific occupations. During the years 1942–1945, the department invited a blue ribbon panel of the top experts in industrial psychology and measurement to help create a battery of employment tests to cover all of the 100 occupations and more. The subsequent battery became the General Aptitude Test Battery (GATB). The GATB was then and is now a state-of-the-

art broad spectrum test measuring all of the aptitudes most useful in predicting job performance." (Hunter, 1994, p. 467)

The GATB defined intelligence as general learning aptitude. The tests used to assess intelligence were verbal aptitude, numerical aptitude, and spatial aptitude. Spatial aptitude was defined as "the ability to think visually of geometric forms and to comprehend the two-dimensional representations of three-dimensional objects" (Hunter, 1983, p. 74). Spatial ability was now recognized as a fundamental aspect of intelligence.

Norms were developed using the GATB for specific occupations through specific research studies and minimum aptitude requirements were developed for over 100 occupations (US Department of Labor, 1970). **For example, in 1951 it was found that an engineer required a minimum general learning aptitude at the 95th percentile (125), a minimum numerical aptitude at the 84th percentile (115), and a minimum spatial aptitude at the 84th percentile (115). This is important because it allows a prospective engineer to understand the unique abilities that a typical engineer should have.** It is informative to contrast the unique abilities required for an engineer compared to other scientific career fields. For example, in 1948, it was found that a physician in general practice required a minimum general learning aptitude at the 95th percentile (125), a minimum numerical aptitude at the 75th percentile (110), and a minimum spatial aptitude at the 75th percentile (110). This is significant because it demonstrates that engineers and physicians require the same level of general learning aptitude but that engineers require even greater numerical and spatial aptitude.

John E. Hunter, who has done a meta-analysis of over 700 validation studies, states: "For the purpose of selecting employees who must be trained after hiring, the GATB predicts job performance far better than any known alternative except other directly congruent ability tests" (1994, p. 468).

In 1965, Henry Chauncey, then president of the Educational Testing Service, which administers the Scholastic Aptitude Test (SAT), published an article with Thomas L. Hilton in *Science* magazine entitled, "Are aptitude tests valid for the highly able?" In this paper the authors document their assistance in Anne Roe's 1952 study involving 64 eminent scientists. Mr. Chauncey and Dr. Hilton state, "The nominated scientists were individually given a high-level academic aptitude test, the Verbal-Spatial-Mathematical (VSM) test prepared by Educational Testing Service" (Chauncey & Hilton, 1965, p. 1298). **From Anne Roe's study we discovered that among the 64 eminent scientists, the physical scientists as a group scored significantly higher on the spatial test than the biologists or social scientists.** Why was this? We think it is because of their exposure to highly theoretical concepts that have required extensive practice in conceptualization and visualization to develop it.

The Second Spatial Breakthrough (1976–Present)

In 1971, Julian C. Stanley of John Hopkins University founded a longitudinal study, the Study of Mathematically Precocious Youth (SMPY), to identify intellectual talent in Science, Technology, Engineering and Mathematics (STEM). As of 2006, this study has tracked more than 5,000 intellectually talented individuals in five cohort ability groups. Entrance into the study by 12- to14-year-olds was by way of an SAT Verbal and Math score obtained three to five years earlier than the typical high school student.

A major breakthrough in the study was found with the children that were studied initially from 1976 to 1979 (Cohort 2). Three hundred and ninety-three boys and 170 girls, 13 years of age, were identified by scoring in the top 0.5% of general intelligence on the SAT. In addition to the SAT, these children were administered spatial tests. Spatial ability is the ability to think in three dimensions, not just with words and numbers, but with pictures and visualization. Spatial ability has long been associated with scientific creative thought. David Lohman states, "One way to appreciate the diversity of spatial abilities and their impact on individuals and society is to survey some of the abilities and occupations that require (and develop) spatial abilities. **High levels of spatial abilities are common among architects, engineers, draftspersons, and designers of all sorts,** cabinetmakers and mechanics, quilt makers, airplane pilots and air traffic controllers, to name a few occupations" (Lohman, 1994, p.1000).

The twenty-year follow-up study on Cohort 2, published by Daniel Shea, David Lubinski, and Camilla Benbow in 2001, is particularly revealing. Spatial ability was more predictive than verbal or math in STEM bachelor's degrees. They found, **"Spatial ability provided somewhat greater overall discriminative power than quantitative ability. This finding is in line with theories about human abilities that stress the importance of a verbal-spatial bipolar dimension" (2001, p.611). Those students in Cohort 2 that had obtained degrees in math, computer science, engineering, and physical science had spatial and math abilities above the average of this gifted group. The students who obtained degrees in humanities, social science, biology, and business had lower spatial and math scores compared to the average of this gifted group.** This study showed that physical scientists led the pack of gifted children in scientific (verbal-math-spatial) giftedness. The physical scientists were the only majors that scored above the average of this gifted group on verbal, math, and spatial aptitude.

The Third Spatial Breakthrough (1986–Present)

In 1960, the United States collected research for the Project Talent data bank. Test data were amassed on a random sample of 900 US high schools. The total sample size is approximately 400,000 students. Approximately 50,000 students of each gender were tested for each grade 9 through 12. During a one-week period, a number of aptitude and achievement tests, along with scales for attitude, interests, and personality traits, were collected. This data bank is particularly valuable because it also contains longitudinal follow-up data available at 1, 5, and 11 years after high school.

In 1986, 26 years after the original data had been collected; Humphreys, Davey, and Kashima discovered something unexpected. While researching on the subject of intellectual privilege/deprivation, they serendipitously discovered that tenth-grade males who went on to study physics and engineering had a higher mean value on their mechanical-spatial tests than they did on their intelligence composite. **"The conclusion is inescapable that engineers and physical scientists in Humphreys, et al. (1986) had been self-selected for mechanical-spatial abilities"** (Humphreys, Lubinski, & Yao, 1993, p. 252).

In 1993, Humphreys, Lubinski, and Yao published their study investigating the effects of using Spatial-Math testing to identify talent in physical science and engineering. From the 400,000 students in the Project Talent Data they grouped aptitude tests into a Verbal-Math composite (approximately equivalent to the SAT) and a Spatial-Math composite. They then examined the top 20% in each composite and evaluated their longitudinal outcomes. They found that those students who scored in the top 20% on the Spatial-Math composite were drawn to the physical science majors. When they compared students with high verbal ability to those with high spatial ability, they found that more than twice as many students who majored in the physical sciences were identified with the Spatial-Math composite compared to the Verbal-Math composite. They concluded that **"a measure of spatial visualization ... should provide useful, perhaps essential information on students being considered for admission to schools of engineering and several physical science disciplines...** spatially talented individuals not only have the ability to achieve career excellence in engineering and the physical sciences but they are more likely to remain committed to those disciplines" (1993, p. 258).

In 1985, Thomas L. Hilton of the Educational Testing Service published, "National Changes in Spatial-Visual Ability from 1960 to 1980." **Dr. Hilton reported the spatial ability of high school students, "declined appreciably from 1960–1980"** (1985, p.20). We feel that this decline in visual-spatial ability of high school students adversely effected the U.S baccalaureate graduation rate in physical science. In 1966, 3.0% of baccalaureate degrees in the United States were in physical science. By 1984, that number had fallen to 1.6% (National Science Foundation, 2007).

Global Competition for Scientific Talent

For most of the twentieth century, the United States reigned supreme as the world leader in scientific innovation. America's Apollo program propelled Neil Armstrong and Buzz Aldrin onto the moon in 1969. The lunar moon walk is still considered one of the greatest technological triumphs in the history of the world (NASA History Office, 2002). By the end of the twentieth century, worldwide competition began intensifying to develop intellectual talent. Asia, in particular, took on this challenge with a fierce competitiveness that focused on raising their production of STEM degrees which they considered to be the key to scientific innovation.

The Congressional Research Service reported that in 2002, Asia's production of STEM degrees was 1,073,369, while the United States produced only 219,175 (Kuenzi, 2008). Japan led the way in educational efficiency for STEM degrees with a remarkable 64 % (351,299 STEM degrees out of 548,897 total degrees). China was not far behind in educational efficiency for STEM degrees with 52.1% (484,704 STEM degrees out of 929,598 total degrees). The US educational efficiency was a meager 16.8% (219,175 STEM degrees out of 1,305,730 total degrees). Only Brazil had a lower educational efficiency than the United States at 15.5% (61,281 STEM degrees out of 395,988 total degrees).

America's educational efficiency for STEM degrees has been in decline for over 40 years. For example, in 1966, 6.8% of all undergraduate degrees conferred in America were in engineering. In 2002, only 4.6% of bachelor's degrees in America were in engineering. Males in particular have seen dramatic reductions in physical science graduation totals. **The National Science Foundation reported that in 1969, 15,962 American males received a baccalaureate degree in physical science. By 2002, that number had fallen by 49.7% to 8,034** (National Science Foundation, 2007). These numbers are even more alarming when you consider that 141,092 additional males graduated in 2002 compared to 1969.

Following are the highest national scores/rankings on the Graduate Record Examination (GRE) by major.

Ranking of Top 10 Majors by Average GRE Scores: 2004–2006

	Verbal Reasoning	*Quantitative Reasoning*	*Combined*
Physics	07	01	08
Mathematics	13	02	15
Philosophy	01	15	16
Engineer—Materials	15	03	18
Economics	12	10	22
Engineer other	17	07	24
Humanities	03	22	25
Chemical Engineering	22	05	27
Earth/Atmosphere/Marine	14	14	28
Religion	06	24	30

Physics is the front runner and clearly produces high-level thinking capabilities in both quantitative and verbal reasoning (three- and four-dimensional thinking), but is regretfully, like math and science, suffering from diminishing American student enrollments. The highest *quantitative reasoning* scores ranked separately and in order by major were: (1) Physics—Astronomy; (2) Mathematics; (3) Engineering—Materials; (4) Engineering—Electrical; (5) Engineering—Chemical; (6) Engineering—Mechanical; (7) Engineering—other; (8) Engineering—Industrial; (9) Business—Bank & Finance; (10) Economics; (11) Computer and Information Sciences; (12) Engineering—Civil; (13) Chemistry; (14)

Earth/Atmosphere/Marine Science; and (15) Philosophy. A most popular major, English, ranked 32 on quantitative reasoning and 16 on the combined and rankings.

Advanced Placement (AP) exams are the gold standard for evaluating America's high school preparation for college. These exams are scored on a 1 to 5 scale, with a score of 4 indicating well qualified and a score of 5 indicating extremely well qualified. In 2008, 2,736,445 AP exams were taken by 1,546,020 high school students (College Board, 2008). The top five AP exams students participated in were: US History (344,199), English Literature (314,051), English Language (301,862), Calculus AB and BC (281,871), and US Government and Politics (176,903). AP exams in "hard science" (physics and chemistry) didn't even crack the top 10.

AP Chemistry was taken by 96,458 high school students. Physics has been subdivided into three distinct exams. Physics B (with no calculus required) was taken by 55,227 high school students. Physics C: Mechanics (requiring calculus) was taken by 27,237 high school students. Physics C: Electricity and Magnetism (requiring calculus), a fundamental high-tech class for collegiate physical science and engineering majors, was taken by only 11,712 high school students (0.75% of test takers) with only 6,664 students receiving a score of 4 or 5. **This means that only 0.43 % of AP tests takers (6,664 out of 1,546,020) will enter college well qualified in calculus-based physics. What does 0.43% round to, when considering its practical significance? The answer is zero.**

Science Literacy

On October 4, 1957 the Russians launched Sputnik, a 184-pound communications satellite, into orbit. America was caught by surprise and realized that science literacy was a key component of education that needed improvement. In April 1958, Walter C. Michels wrote a paper for *Scientific American* entitled, "The Teaching of Elementary Physics." Over 50 years ago, Michels wrote, **"Many scientists and some of our best educators believe that ... our educational system is failing to give most of our population an adequate**

understanding of the nature of physical science and of its role in the economic, political, and cultural life of the twentieth century ... An understanding of science is as important to the businessman, to the lawyer, to the statesman or to any other citizen as an understanding of language or literature or of political and military history" (1958, p. 57).

In May 2004, the *New York Times* raised a front-page alarm that the United States was losing its dominance in the sciences. William J. Broad reported that the US share of its own patents and share of Nobel Prizes had significantly fallen over decades. American scientific papers are no longer in the majority in learned journals. And, at this writing, there are many voices who deplore a declining interest of young Americans in science careers and/or in acquiring hard science cores as part of their educational preparation.

Science is a rigorous subject that teaches students a disciplined way to access knowledge. Michaels points out:

> Physics courses contribute to the student's education many things that he cannot obtain from other studies ... he learns to observe phenomena with care, to extract from them the parts that are most important, and to use his observations to test a theory. Because the phenomena dealt with are simple and subject to measurement, he obtains practice in the analysis of their causes—practice which will stand him in good stead when he later faces the problem of analyzing more complicated happenings without allowing his prejudices to influence his interpretation of them. His interest and understanding of algebra and geometry are likely to be advanced as he sees that these subjects supply valuable tools for the description both of nature and of the products of modern technology. **He learns to read carefully, with the idea that every word in a well-written piece of exposition is there for a purpose; at the same time, he learns to communicate ideas in a clear, succinct and unambiguous manner, using graphic methods and mathematical descriptions as well as words.** (1958, p.58)

With only 16 % of college graduates, in 2006, receiving a degree in science and engineering, a case could be made for focusing on increasing the **quantity** of science and engineering graduates. A far more compelling issue is the **quality** of science literacy of every US college graduate. Michel comments on the misstep taken by some educators to teach descriptive physical sciences courses as part of a general education program:

> No doubt a descriptive course is better than no course at all. **But can it give a student the understanding of physical nature and of science that the times require?** The distinguishing characteristic of physics is that it involves a central theory, of very broad validity, in terms of which observed phenomena are interpreted and understood. **To omit large parts of that theory in order to avoid mathematical difficulty is to deny the able student the intellectual stimulation that is one of the prime rewards of education … we cannot afford such (descriptive) courses for the able students who promise to become the intellectual, political and cultural leaders of the future.** (1958, p.64)

We are proposing a five-tiered solution that will enable all Americans to be certified by the College Board as qualified (score of 3) in AP Biology, AP Chemistry, and AP Physics. We are defining a third-class science education to include AP certification in only one area (Biology or Chemistry or Physics). A second-class science education would include certification in two areas. A first-class science education would include certification by the College Board as qualified (a score of 3) in AP Biology, AP Chemistry, and AP Physics. A first-class science education results in scientifically literate citizens.

Tier One: Potential AP Calculus Superstars and Science

The gateway to STEM careers is the physical sciences. In 2004, only 1% of American students received a degree in physical science, also known as "hard science." The term "hard science" aptly describes the difficulty students encounter in mastering this subject area. Unlike any other course of study, physical science requires the simultaneous integration of high levels of verbal, mathematical, and spatial aptitude. As David Lubinski and Camilla Persson Benbow point out, **"Physical sciences appear to require appreciable amounts of all three abilities"** (2006, p.324). It should not be surprising to learn that the withdrawal rates from calculus-based physics at American colleges are as high as 50%.

High levels of verbal, mathematical, and spatial aptitude are commonly found in students who receive degrees in physical science, but are uncommonly found among degree holders in other fields of study (Lubinski & Benbow, 2006, p.325). This is consistent with Ellen Winner's work on giftedness: **"While globally gifted children certainly do exist, many other academically gifted children present a much less balanced picture; unevenness between verbal and mathematical abilities may be the rule, not the exception"** (Winner, 2000, p.16). Neil Dorans, in his paper, "Correspondences Between ACT and SAT I Scores," evaluated a sample of 103,525 students who took both the ACT and the SAT I. In this sample, SAT I Verbal had a correlation of .71 with SAT I Math (Dorans, 1999). Lloyd G. Humphreys, David Lubinski, and Grace Yao evaluated the results of 400,000 high school students who participated in verbal, math, and spatial testing. They reported that in their sample, Math had a .76 correlation with Verbal and a .61 correlation with Spatial (Humphreys, Lubinski, and Yao, 1993). This is important because it clearly shows that an individual's performance in verbal, math, and spatial testing is not perfectly correlated, and we would anticipate a variety of unique performances in each area of verbal-math-spatial testing. **This means that an AP Calculus Superstar may not perform as well in physical science that requires verbal-math-spatial aptitude as they would in a subject that required only math or math-verbal aptitude.**

AP historical data reveal that many Potential AP Calculus Superstars will not achieve in physical science at the same level they will achieve in Calculus. In 2008, 132,086 high school students out of 281,871 were certified by the College Board as being well qualified in Calculus AB or Calculus BC—this is a significant STEM achievement (College Board, 2008). **America's big problem is that too few of these 132,086 students have a comparable achievement in chemistry and physics—physical science is the collegiate gateway to a STEM degree.** For example, in 2008, only 33,772 students out the 96,458 students who sat for the AP Chemistry exam were certified by the College Board as being well qualified in AP Chemistry. Only 17,587 out of 55,227 students who sat for the AP Physics B exam were certified by the College Board as being well qualified. Finally, only 6,664 students out of 11,712 who sat for the AP Physics C: Electricity and Magnetism exam were certified by the College Board as being well qualified in calculus-based physics electricity and magnetism.

Physical science is the gateway to a STEM career. Math is one of the important skills that must be highly developed to do well in physical science. In addition, physical science requires highly developed verbal and spatial aptitude. Many Potential AP Calculus Superstars need more physical science aptitude (verbal-math-spatial) and more physical science coursework to ensure their success in collegiate STEM programs. **The key high school STEM class for Potential AP Calculus Superstars is AP Chemistry, taken predominantly by 11th graders. Although 281,871 high school students will take Calculus AB (215,086) and BC (66,785), only 96,458 will take AP Chemistry, with only 50,460 taking AP Chemistry as 11th graders.** Potential AP Calculus Superstars are either not being programmed appropriately for AP Chemistry or self-selecting to avoid AP Chemistry because it is known to be very hard and might jeopardize a student's grade-point average.

In 2008, 37.3% (18,843/50,460) of 11th graders were certified by the College Board as being well qualified in AP Chemistry. For many of the 62.7% (31,617/50460) who failed to be certified as well qualified in AP Chemistry, this class is the end of the line in physical science. If for any reason they received a grade of B or lower in chemistry, then the probability that they will take physics as a senior is very small. For this reason, high schools should allow these students to take these "hard science" courses pass/fail to encourage/enable students with very high grade-point averages to take the classes without jeopardizing their GPAs or valedictorian status by taking these difficult subjects. From an aptitude standpoint, many of these potential AP Calculus Superstars need more spatial aptitude that is commensurate with their mathematical skills. **The transition from paper and pencil mathematics to laboratory chemistry and physics requires spatial aptitude.**

Tier Two: Potential AP English Superstars and Science

John Sweetland, Jacqueline Reina, and Anne Tatti studied gifted children in upper-middle class Long Island, New York, and found that **"gifted children demonstrate[d] much higher verbal scores than performance (spatial) scores. Apparently, it is common for very bright children to attain unusually high scores in only some aspects of cognitive functioning"** (Sweetland, Reina, & Tatti, 2006, p.7). We agree and add that it is our frequent clinical observation that verbally gifted children have a relative weakness in spatial aptitude when compared to their relative strength in verbal aptitude. Linda Silverman, who directs the Institute for the Study of Advanced Development and the Gifted Development Center in Denver, Colorado said, **"Of all the disabilities, visual weaknesses appear to be the easiest ones to correct.** When visual processing issues are apparent in either children or adults, we recommend an evaluation by a behavioral optometrist and six to nine months of vision therapy. **We've seen enormous improvement in visual perception"** (Silverman, 2002, p. 182).

AP historical data reveal that many Potential AP English Superstars will not achieve in physical science at the same level they will achieve in English. In 2008, 80,843 high school students out of 301,862 were certified by the College Board as being well qualified in English Language—this is a significant achievement (College Board, 2008). **America's big problem is that too few of these 80,843 students have a comparable achievement in chemistry and physics—physical science is the collegiate gateway to a STEM degree.**

Potential AP English Superstars are at risk for a STEM career. In America, the language of education is primarily English. Those students that have mastered English are at a distinct advantage in all things verbal. Potential AP English Superstars should be identified as an underserved talent pool that could contribute significantly to physical science, because physical scientists as a group require very high verbal aptitude (Lubinsky & Benbow, 2006, p.325). America's AP English Superstars are also the group most at risk to abandon a career in STEM because of frustration with the verbal-math-spatial aptitude requirement of physical science. Students with high verbal aptitude are ideal candidates for proven training programs that raise math and spatial aptitude.

The Breakthrough

In 1905, Albert Einstein explained the photoelectric effect and in doing so established the dual capacity of light. It took 16 years for him to receive the Nobel Prize for that discovery. Einstein's transformational theory seemed too radical for the time. To think that light simultaneously could have two completely distinct capacities (wave and particle) took time to gain acceptance. In 2005, Dr. Baize, Dr. Graham, and Amanda Baize discovered that academic (verbal-math) aptitude and physical science (verbal-math-spatial) aptitude are two completely distinct thinking capacities that propel students into completely different academic trajectories—into the arts or into STEM. Our discovery makes it possible to transform academic thinkers into physical science thinkers. The door to that pathway is spatial aptitude. Math may be one of the languages of physical science, but spatial aptitude is the magnet that attracts America's brightest and best into "hard science laboratories" and keeps them there.

In 2002, Amanda was a sophomore in high school and on track to become a valedictorian with an eye on a future career in law. Amanda was motivated, and she had a strong work ethic. Her only complaint was that she "hated math." Closer examination revealed that although Amanda's verbal aptitude was above the 91st percentile (Amanda's ACT reading score was better than 91 out of every 100 students who took the test), her ACT math score was at the 73rd percentile. Previous spatial testing using objective (pencil-and-paper) instruments had identified that Amanda's spatial aptitude was at the 50th percentile. By using normal curve equivalents, we determined that Amanda's initial verbal-math-spatial (physical science) aptitude was at approximately the 74th percentile. From our testing, it was obvious that what Amanda lacked was experience in a visual-spatial laboratory, training in visual memory and visual decision speed, and practice in visualizing math and science problems. In short, Amanda, like most gifted high school students, had grown up in an environment loaded with opportunities for verbal enrichment and relatively deprived of science enrichment.

Amanda faithfully attended our visual-spatial laboratory class for one year. At the end of her program Amanda's confidence soared as she improved to the 95th percentile in SAT Critical Reading, 84th percentile in SAT Math, and the 98th percentile in spatial aptitude. Between 2002 and 2004, Amanda's verbal-math-spatial (physical science), aptitude as calculated with academic instruments (pencil-and-paper) improved from the 74th percentile to the 94th percentile (calculated by using normal curve equivalents).

In addition to academic tracking, Amanda was also tracked with an assessment tool we call the VMS (Verbal-Math-Spatial). On this instrument, Amanda scored in the 82nd percentile in July 2003. After graduating from high school (as a valedictorian) and before starting college at Northwestern University in Evanston, Illinois, Amanda was re-evaluated with the VMS. Amanda's scientific aptitude on the VMS had improved from the 82nd percentile in July 2003 to the 99.74th percentile in July 2005. This represents an increase of 1.9 standard deviations and is an extraordinary scientific breakthrough. As this paper has pointed out, verbal-math-spatial aptitude is synonymous with physical science aptitude. With a VMS score at the 82nd percentile, it is doubtful that Amanda would have even considered pursuing a degree in physical science. She would most likely have avoided physical science because "it's just too hard." With a VMS score at the 99.74th percentile, Amanda was looking for an academic environment that involved multidimensional thinking. Amanda ultimately self-selected to double major in Chemistry and Human Communication Science at Northwestern University and will graduate with honors. Amanda's case study is an excellent example of how to tap into Potential AP English Superstars to meet the scientific/economic challenges of the twenty-first century.

We have developed an Applied Vision Science (verbal-math-spatial) laboratory class for potential AP English superstars. This two-semester class can be taken in high school prior to or concurrently with AP Chemistry. **This novel class, implemented on a national scale, has the capability of enabling 301,862 high school students in the AP English talent pool with the confidence and aptitude to self-select to enroll in AP Chemistry as 11th graders and then AP Physics as seniors. These students have the potential to provide America's high schools, colleges, and research institutions with a bumper crop of turbocharged brain power to grow the economy and solve the Energy-Climate Challenge.**

Tier Three: Students who Love Science but Perform Inadequately on AP Science Exams

There are many enthusiastic high school students who love science laboratories and sign up for AP Calculus, AP Chemistry, AP Biology, and AP Physics, but are unable to perform adequately on these exams. In 2008, 149,785 students were unable to receive certification by the College Board as being well qualified in AP Calculus—these students are at risk in freshman college calculus classes. AP Biology had 99,951 students who were unable to receive certification by the College Board as being well qualified in freshman biology. **In addition, 62,686 students with an interest in STEM were unable to receive certification by the College Board as being well qualified in Chemistry—these students are at risk in college chemistry classes.** Finally, 37,640 Physics B and 5,048 Physics C Electricity and Magnetism were unable to be certified by the College Board as being well qualified in physics (College Board, 2008). **Many enthusiastic high school students who love science need more**

physical science (verbal-math-spatial) aptitude and more math and physical science coursework.

In Hawaii, only 12 out of every 100 ninth graders will graduate from high school and then go on to graduate with a baccalaureate in six years (University of Hawaii, 2008). Every transition point in Hawaii's Educational System is laden with student casualties. The STEM pathway is no exception. **Less than 2% of ninth graders in Hawaii went on to receive a STEM degree from the University of Hawaii in six years. In the 2006–2007 academic year, Hawaii had 43,500 undergraduate students attending the University of Hawaii System, but only 374 undergraduate STEM degrees were awarded at the University of Hawaii at Manoa, despite spending $1.15 billion on collegiate education** (Hammes, 2007). If we consider the mathematically rigorous STEM subjects, excluding biological/life sciences, a mere 221 students would have completed degrees in the physical science and engineering related STEM subjects—the areas previously identified by Dr. Marburger as being strongly correlated with innovation and economic growth. We are thus losing our scientific foundation.

The Organization for Economic Cooperation and Development reported that in 2005, the United States spent $24,370 per student in tertiary education (collegiate education) while Japan spent only $12,326 per student (OECD, 2008). Compare the University of Hawaii's STEM totals (13.2%) with Japan's STEM totals (64.0%).

We have developed an Applied Vision Science (verbal-math-spatial) laboratory class for students who love science but perform inadequately on AP Science exams. This two-semester class can be taken in high school prior to or concurrently with AP Chemistry. This program could produce a bumper crop of future Thomas Edison– and Henry Ford–like scientific entrepreneurs who are committed to science and have the prerequisite scientific background and aptitude to start their own companies and provide needed job opportunities for the people of America—sooner rather than later.

Tier Four: Science Education for those Students not presently on a College Track

The U.S. Census Bureau estimates that in the year 2006, the age group from 15 to 19 had 21,324,186 people (U.S. Census Bureau, 2006). This results in an average of 4,264,837 people of each age. The College Board reports that in the academic year 2007–2008, 7,930,042 students were enrolled in 11th and 12th grade. In 2007, 1,464,254 students participated in AP exams. In 2008, 1,580,821 students participated in AP exams (College Board, 2008). As you can see, we have a large number of students who are not participating in any AP exams. In addition, some students never make it to the 11th grade. **How could science education help these students who are not presently on a college track?** Many of these students who do poorly in school are relatively verbally disadvantaged and often spatially advantaged. Science education could be an alternative lifeline for these students in much the same way that sports is often a major lifeline for children who do poorly scholastically. The verbal-math-spatial aptitudes required in science allow these students the opportunity for a measure of success not available in verbal or math subjects that have no spatial content. Science has the potential to unveil an entire group of talented students much like sports often unveils athletic talent that many children may have been unaware that they had. We are advocating for these students to receive a high school education that is primarily centered on math and science and minimizes classes that are exclusively verbally loaded.

We have developed an Applied Vision Science (verbal-math-spatial) laboratory class for students who are not currently on a college track. This two-semester class can be taken in junior high school. This course will help these students to understand their relative strengths and weaknesses. This program will motivate many of these students to go into science and technical education. **We feel that all of these students are capable of certifying with The College Board as qualified in AP Biology, AP Chemistry, and AP Physics B.** For these students, we recommend that these classes be taught over four semesters rather than two. In addition, it is imperative that students with mathematical shortcomings in science receive math training from their science teacher. After-school study halls are essential. Perfect practice makes perfect and these students need to practice under the supervision of a science coach.

Tier Five: A Second Chance to be a STEM Superstar: the STEM2 Program

We are proposing that every university in America rid its campus of descriptive science courses. All students need science literacy that descriptive classes are unable to provide. All students need the opportunity to learn the disciplined methodology of how to solve problems with words, with numbers, and with three-dimensional analysis and synthesis.

Despite the best efforts of teachers and students, some children will slip through the cracks of high school STEM programs and be unprepared for college science classes. Many students in science are late bloomers whose interest in science may have been developed very late—as late as their senior year in high school or even after high school. Many of these students may have lacked appropriate motivation when taking high school science classes and will need additional help in science before entering a four-year university. The transition to a STEM career can be very difficult for students deficient in math and physical science prerequisite classes (science illiterate). Many students are simply not qualified with aptitude or coursework to enroll in freshman college chemistry and still will enroll, to learn painfully that college STEM classes require science literacy.

For those students who were unable to be certified as well qualified in calculus, chemistry, and physics while in high school, a second chance to become a STEM Superstar, **the STEM2 Program, could be made available. The STEM2 Program would enable every American to pursue a first-class science education at any point in their lives.** For almost a century, the US Navy has provided a second-chance opportunity for future naval officers who have potential but were unable to receive an adequate scientific background in high school. In 1914, the United States Congress established by law a scientific preparatory school for the US Navy known as Naval Academy Preparatory School—this program is essentially a grade 13 program in physical science.

In Hawaii, 12% of ninth graders will graduate from the University of Hawaii within six years. At the Naval Academy Preparatory School, 59% of those who attend will graduate from the Naval Academy (General Accounting Office, 2003). **Every graduate of the Naval Academy is fundamentally a STEM graduate.** The Naval Academy requires every student to complete four semesters of mathematics (including three semesters of calculus), two semesters of chemistry, two semesters of calculus-based physics, and six semesters of engineering courses regardless of major. The Naval Academy's high STEM requirements demand that every candidate be handpicked and nurtured through their STEM experience. **The Naval Academy Preparatory School reports that in 2002, they spent $9,395,421 to operate their school for 315 students. This cost included: free tuition, free room and board, free medical and dental care, and a stipend paid to students for attending** (General Accounting Office, 2003).

As good as the Naval Academy Preparatory School is, it could be made even better by adding Applied Vision Science to the curriculum. Vision Science is an academic subject that is currently only being taught at US Schools and Colleges of Optometry as part of the professional optometric program (Berkeley Optometry, 2008). We are advocating for Doctors of Optometry (who have received specialized training in Applied Vision Science from Dr. Graham and Dr. Baize) to teach those students in the **STEM2 Program** a ten-month course in Applied Vision Science, focusing on individual development of visual perception and spatial perception. **We propose that every student in the STEM2 Program would learn the requisite verbal knowledge (literature, history, etc.), mathematical knowledge (trigonometry, calculus, etc.), and spatial/conceptual knowledge (physics, chemistry, etc.) that forms a factual base for the physical scientist to draw from. In addition, every student would have the opportunity to develop verbal aptitude** (Socratic thinking, word power, etc.), mathematical aptitude (numerical computation, numerical application, etc.), and spatial aptitude (visual perception, space perception, etc.) that increases the capacity of the physical scientist to solve the novel unexpected problems encountered in the laboratory and in life.** A Physical Science Preparatory School that includes Applied Vision Science would raise the visual-spatial capacity of its students. Capacity building would enable these students to stand on the shoulders of the scientific giants of the past and visualize solutions that were previously unimaginable. A ten-month course in Applied Vision Science has the potential to raise the baccalaureate graduation rate of Naval Academy Preparatory School students from 59% to 90% at the Naval Academy.

We are proposing that every state in the Union should offer its students a second chance to be a STEM Superstar: the **STEM2 Program.** Imagine if every state's **STEM2 Program** could graduate a minimum of 350 students who go on to study STEM at the university level. In 2006, the federal government spent $943 million on STEM undergraduate educational programs and $574 million on STEM K–12 (Kuenzi, 2008). If the federal government redirected some of that 1.52 billion to assist individual states with their **STEM2 Program**, then a major drain in the STEM supply system could be alleviated—those students who are motivated and show promise, but need to be nurtured with additional aptitude experiences and coursework experiences before beginning a collegiate STEM degree.

Concluding STEM Perspectives

With 94% of all college degrees being awarded in subjects other than "hard science" and engineering, it is obvious that America has a multitude of students who could be nurtured to a much greater extent to seek a scientific career. **The application of the principles discussed here has the potential to produce a bumper crop of undergraduate degrees in STEM conferred by United States institutions of higher learning.** The spillover effects that would result from this great pursuit would rain scientific talent on all graduate fields of study and throughout the US economy.

The National Science Foundation stated in its 2003 report, "Ensuring Manufacturing Strength through Bold Vision": **"Civilization is on the brink of a new industrial world order. The big winners in the increasingly fierce global competition for supremacy will not be those who simply make commodities faster and cheaper than the competition. They will be those who develop talent, techniques, and tools so advanced *there is no competition*"** (Bordogna, et al., 2003, p. 4).

If we do not restore science literacy to high school and college education, then the United States will be unable to compete adequately in the world platform in creatively solving the current and future world problems—Economic Growth and the Energy-Climate Challenge. Spatial capacity is a critical resource for the development of civilization. As the global economy transforms and small countries combine with larger blocks, assessing, developing, and even enhancing spatial capacity talent may well become the neuroscience challenge this new century.

About the Authors

Morris Graham heads a Honolulu-based, international organization development consulting firm. He received a PhD in cognitive-developmental psychology from the University of Arizona and a Post-Doctorate in Organization Psychology from Edinburgh University, Scotland. Dr. Graham is internationally recognized for his expertise in executive capacity building and is the author of *Horizontal Revolution*. He and his wife, family, and ocean kayak reside in Hawaii. morrisgraham@hotmail.com

Kevin Baize is a graduate of Brigham Young University and the Michigan College of Optometry. Dr. Baize is a scientist and expert practitioner in Visual Information Processing Technologies (VIPT). He is highly qualified to develop apprentices in VIPT and has over 17 years of experience in the field. He presently heads the Hawaii Arts and Science Academy for developing visual-spatial giftedness.

www.ingramcontent.com/pod-product-compliance
Lightning Source LLC
LaVergne TN
LVHW012246070526
838201LV00090B/135